Springer Series in Cognitive Development

Series Editor
Charles J. Brainerd

Springer Series in Cognitive Development

Series Editor: Charles J. Brainerd

Learning in Children
Progress in Cognitive Development Research

Edited by
Jeffrey Bisanz
Gay L. Bisanz
Robert Kail

Springer-Verlag
New York Berlin Heidelberg Tokyo

Jeffrey Bisanz
Department of Psychology
University of Alberta
Edmonton, Alberta
Canada T6G 2E9

Gay L. Bisanz
Centre for the Study of
Mental Retardation
University of Alberta
Edmonton, Alberta
Canada T6G 2E9

Robert Kail
Department of Psychological
Sciences
Purdue University
West Lafayette, Indiana
47907, U.S.A.

Series Editor
Charles J. Brainerd
Department of Psychology
University of Western Ontario
London, Ontario

With 5 Figures

Library of Congress Cataloging in Publication Data
Main entry under title:
Learning in children.
    (Springer series in cognitive development) *39,250*
    Bibliography: p.
    Includes index.
    Contents; Structural invariance in the developmental analysis of learning/
by C.J. Brainerd—The learning paradigm as a technique for investigating
cognitive development/by Bruce A. Linder and Linda S. Siegel—A learning
analysis of spatial concept development in infancy/by C. Donald Heth and
Edward H. Cornell—[etc.]
    1. Learning, Psychology of—Addresses, essays, lectures. 2. Cognition in
children—Addresses, essays, lectures. I. Bisanz, Jeffrey. II. Bisanz, Gay L.
III. Kail, Robert V. IV. Series. [DNLM: 1. Learning—In infancy and
childhood. 2. Cognition—In infancy and childhood. WS 105.5.D2 L438]
BF318.L387   1983   155.4'13   82-19475

Typeset by Ms Associates, Champaign, Illinois.
Printed and bound by R.R. Donnelley & Sons Company, Harrisonburg, Virginia.
Printed in the United States of America.
9 8 7 6 5 4 3 2 1

ISBN 0-387-90802-1   Springer-Verlag   New York   Berlin   Heidelberg   Tokyo
ISBN 3-540-90802-1   Springer-Verlag   Berlin   Heidelberg   New York   Tokyo

Series Preface

For some time now, the study of cognitive development has been far and away the most active discipline within developmental psychology. Although there would be much disagreement as to the exact proportion of papers published in developmental journals that could be considered cognitive, 50% seems like a conservative estimate. Hence, a series of scholarly books devoted to work in cognitive development is especially appropriate at this time.

The *Springer Series in Cognitive Development* contains two basic types of books, namely, edited collections of original chapters by several authors, and original volumes written by one author or a small group of authors. The flagship for the Springer Series is a serial publication of the "advances" type, carrying the subtitle *Progress in Cognitive Development Research*. Each volume in the *Progress* sequence is strongly thematic, in that it is limited to some well-defined domain of cognitive-developmental research (e.g., logical and mathematical development, development of learning). All *Progress* volumes will be edited collections. Editors of such collections, upon consultation with the Series Editor, may elect to have their books published either as contributions to the *Progress* sequence or as separate volumes. All books written by one author or a small group of authors are being published as separate volumes within the series.

A fairly broad definition of cognitive development is being used in the selection of books for this series. The classic topics of concept development, children's thinking and reasoning, the development of learning, language development, and memory development will, of course, be included. So, however, will newer areas such as social-cognitive development, educational applications, formal modeling, and philosophical implications of cognitive-developmental theory. Although it is anticipated that most books in the series will be empirical in orientation, theoretical and philosophical works are also welcome. With books of the latter sort, heterogeneity of theoretical perspective is encouraged, and no attempt will be made to foster some specific theoretical perspective at the expense of others (e.g., Piagetian versus behavioral or behavioral versus information processing).

C. J. Brainerd

Preface

Learning is the focus of this fourth volume in the *Springer Series in Cognitive Development Research*. The choice of this topic reflects renewed interest in what traditionally has been a key issue for child and developmental psychologists. We see evidence for four phases of North American research on learning in children. The first phase began during the second decade of this century, when experimental research on children, although infrequent, began to gain some recognition. Investigators adopted precise behavioral definitions of learning and studied it in a variety of contexts, including memory, problem-solving, and sensorimotor tasks. In retrospect, these researchers made little effort to accommodate potential differences between children and other experimental subjects; research on children's learning tended to be interpreted as confirming the similarities in learning phenomena across animals, children, and adults. The presumed generality of the laws of learning made it possible for some psychologists to make direct and often facile extrapolations from highly circumscribed research on animals, human adults, and the occasional child to such broad and complex topics as child rearing and education.

What research on children's learning lacked during the first phase was vitality: The number of related publications was small, and the general topic was not widely viewed as central for understanding the important and pervasive questions of psychology. These characteristics were reversed during the second phase, which began during the late 1940s and early 1950s. For example, the study of mediation in children helped to combine issues of learning and development with the productive concepts and methods of S-R psychology, and the result was a proliferation of research that began in the 1950s and lasted almost two decades. Investigations of this period were characterized by well-controlled but very constrained laboratory experiments. These studies included new angles on such traditional concerns as reinforcement, transfer, and motivation, as well as the development or rediscovery of such topics as observational learning and perceptual learning. During this second phase, learning was clearly one of the most important concerns of developmental psychology.

The transition from the second to the third phase was marked by an influx of new ideas about cognition and its development during the 1960s and, subsequently, by a sharp decline in research on learning in children during the early 1970s. The seminal work of Jean Piaget began to receive wide recognition and a controversy soon developed: The issue was whether learning, as defined and studied during the second phase, was even relevant for understanding the qualitative changes described in Piaget's theory of cognitive development. This controversy was never resolved satisfactorily, but for a variety of reasons a new wave of research on cognitive development soon replaced studies of learning in the developmental literature. Concepts and paradigms also emerged from cognitive psychology that enabled developmental psychologists to identify a host of "new" phenomena, and theoretical tools became available to represent different states of cognitive competence. As a result of these influences, the acquisition and modification of relatively simple behaviors became less important on the agenda for investigation. Instead, many developmental psychologists adopted novel ideas and methods that allowed them to gain a more comprehensive understanding of the organization and functions of human knowledge.

Our understanding of cognition in children and adults has expanded enormously over the past 15 years, but rarely in these years did investigators consider how knowledge was acquired and modified. We believe the transition has already begun to a fourth phase, in which the powerful methods and theories that evolved during the third phase are brought together in an intensive analysis of knowledge acquisition. To facilitate the development of this fourth phase, several researchers agreed to share, in this volume, their ideas and suggestions for research on learning in children.

The chapters in this volume illustrate some of the broad themes that are likely to constitute a new agenda for research on learning in children. One theme is the goal of integrating social, motivational, and cognitive aspects of learning. During the third phase, motivation and the social contexts of learning were often ignored or treated as topics separate from that of cognitive development. Paris and Cross react to this state of affairs by proposing a general framework for integrating motivational factors and cognitive development. Bransford and Heldmeyer outline motivational and cognitive factors that may enhance learning in preschool children. Perry and Perry review research on the development of moral behavior and describe how disciplinary practices and social-cognitive factors may account for the increasingly "internalized" standards adopted by children. The thrust of these chapters is that it is no longer necessary or even useful for investigators to maintain the pervasive and previously convenient fiction that social, motivational, and cognitive factors are best studied separately.

A second theme is a concern for identifying the competencies of very young children. This goal was revived in the mid-1970s after years during which young children were viewed primarily in terms of their deficiencies relative to older children and adults. Linder and Siegel show how these cognitive competencies can be easily underestimated with traditional methods, Heth and Cornell seek to identify concepts acquired in the first 2 years of life, Brainerd finds evidence for developmental invariance in some aspects of learning, Perry and Perry bring the social learning and attribution perspectives together by examining the development of moral behavior in young children, and Bransford and Heldmeyer speculate about the apparent ease with which young children learn. The obvious implication is that learning in young children has emerged as a key topic for inquiry in its own right, rather than simply providing a basis for evaluating learning in older children and adults.

A third theme involves the generality and application of research on children's learning. The relationship between descriptive research and practical application is rarely straightforward; direct extrapolations from descriptive studies are no substitute for *prescriptive* research that is designed to apply scientific knowledge for the purpose of achieving socially determined goals. Attempts to bridge the gap between purely descriptive research and prescription often have mutually beneficial effects: from descriptive research we gain psychological principles that might be useful in practical applications; from prescriptive research we learn about the boundary conditions of those principles and thus gain opportunities to improve our theories. Because the lessons learned during the third phase have made possible descriptive research on a wide range of activities that children learn in their daily environment, questions about how to optimize children's learning are once again coming to the fore. The chapters by Kail, Perry and Perry, Bransford and Heldmeyer, and Paris and Cross all reflect this growing concern with possible relationships between scientific research on children's learning and application of the resulting knowledge to education and/or child rearing. It is unlikely that all research on learning in children could be translated readily into practice, and perhaps it would be undesirable. However, the vitality and longevity of research in the area may well depend on the degree to which some of this research is relevant to important socially determined goals.

A fourth and final theme involves a heightened concern for sophisticated methodological tools to allow more perceptive insights into children's behavior. Brainerd, for example, shows how mathematical formalisms can be used to identify critical characteristics of how children learn, and similar techniques are used by Heth and Cornell to discover how and what infants and toddlers learn about spatial concepts. Kail discusses several aspects of design and analysis that must be considered if future research on learning is to have greater generality and explanatory power than that in previous phases. We expect that the fourth phase of research on children's learning will be characterized by increasing application of diverse mathematical, statistical, and computer simulative techniques that will enhance the design of studies, the analysis of data, and the development of theories.

Given the reliance of our species on learning as a means of adapting to the environment, the study of children's learning must be considered as one of the most important challenges facing developmental psychologists. It is our hope, and no doubt the hope of our contributors, that this volume will help stimulate the kind of thinking and research that will lead to an exciting and productive fourth phase in the study of learning in children.

Preparation of this volume was facilitated by research grants from the Natural Sciences and Engineering Research Council of Canada. We are especially grateful to Cindy Scott and Cecile Woodcock for their expert assistance.

Jeffrey Bisanz
Gay L. Bisanz
Robert Kail

Contents

Contributors

C. J. Brainerd Department of Psychology, University of Western Ontario, London, Ontario, Canada N6A 5C2

John D. Bransford Department of Psychology, Vanderbilt University, Nashville, Tennessee 37240, U.S.A.

Edward H. Cornell Department of Psychology, University of Alberta, Edmonton, Alberta, Canada T6G 2E9

David R. Cross Combined Program in Education and Psychology, 3210 School of Education, University of Michigan, Ann Arbor, Michigan 48109, U.S.A.

Karen Heldmeyer Department of Psychology, Vanderbilt University, Nashville, Tennessee 37240, U.S.A.

C. Donald Heth Department of Psychology, University of Alberta, Edmonton, Alberta, Canada T6G 2E9

Robert Kail Department of Psychological Sciences, Purdue University, West Lafayette, Indiana 47907, U.S.A.

Bruce A. Linder Department of Psychology, McMaster University, Hamilton, Ontario, Canada L8S 4K1

Scott G. Paris Combined Program in Education and Psychology, 3210 School of Education, University of Michigan, Ann Arbor, Michigan 48109, U.S.A.

David G. Perry Department of Psychology, Florida Atlantic University, Boca Raton, Florida 33431, U.S.A.

Louise C. Perry Department of Psychology, Florida Atlantic University, Boca Raton, Florida 33431, U.S.A.

Linda S. Siegel Department of Psychiatry, McMaster University, Hamilton, Ontario, Canada L8N 3Z5

1. Structural Invariance in the Developmental Analysis of Learning

C. J. Brainerd

Generality is a prized commodity in any science. The laws that we prefer are those with the widest possible scope of application, the ones that hold across as many situational perturbations as possible. As S. S. Stevens (1951) once remarked, Newton's rule that force is the first derivative of time with respect to momentum "would not be worth very much if it worked only in Europe or only at sea level or only for circular motions or only for objects larger than elephants" (p. 20). In fact, one widely accepted definition of the task of a science is to describe the phenomena that it studies in terminology that remains unchanged whenever the frame of reference is altered. A law (or principle or relationship) that holds within a given domain of study, regardless of the frame of reference, is usually called an *invariant*.

The importance of invariants lies chiefly in their powers of simplification. In general, application of an invariant reduces uncertainty by reducing degrees of freedom. Specifically, an invariant constrains us in such a way that we are not allowed to make statements (or devise theories) that violate the invariance rule. In

Preparation of this chapter and most of the experiments reported herein were supported by Grant No. A0668 from the Natural Sciences and Engineering Research Council. Computer funds for the optimization analyses were provided by a grant from the Faculty of Social Science, University of Western Ontario. The experiments were conducted between 1975 and 1981 in various elementary schools, preschools, and day-care centers in Edmonton, Alberta, and in London, Ontario. I should like to thank Mary Ann Fisher for some helpful comments on an earlier draft of this chapter. I am deeply indebted to the pupils, staff, and parents for their cooperation. I am also indebted to the following students, who assisted in aspects of the data collection: Joyce Boyd, Norman Greenberg, Brian Heisel, Mark Howe, Diane Love, and Carol Wagg.

the familiar language of measurement theory, invariance rules define the class of permissible transformations within some domain. Once this class of transformations is known for some field of study, the task of the theorist is greatly simplified because the range of potentially acceptable theoretical assumptions is sharply delimited.

Each of us is acquainted with prominent examples of invariants from the physical and biological sciences. The conservation laws of physics (conservation of energy, conservation of mass, conservation of momentum, etc.) are surely the best known illustrations. Certain fields within psychology have enjoyed some success in identifying invariants. Examples from animal conditioning include the familiar law of stimulus generalization and the matching law (e.g., Herrnstein, 1974). But the power-function law of psychophysics, which assumes that all sensations are controlled by power transformations and that each sensory continuum has its own characteristic numerical constant, is probably psychology's best example of a true invariance principle.

The science of behavioral development has been conspicuously less successful than some other branches of psychology when it comes to identifying invariants. Indeed, the question of what things or relationships remain constant during ontogenesis is almost never asked (but for a recent exception, cf. Keil, 1981), and hence the developmental literature is largely devoid of candidates for invariance rules. Of course, there are certain theories, notably Piaget's, that include so-called functional invariants, guiding principles of developmental change that are the same for all age levels. But these principles are vague metaphorical abstractions. As such, they are not open to empirical test; they are articles of faith. What we are seeking when we speak of developmental invariants are solid descriptive generalizations, ultimately in the form of mathematical relationships, accruing from some broad data base.

The lack of success in isolating developmental invariants can perhaps be explained on the ground that our task is conceptually more difficult than in most other disciplines of psychology. In other fields, research proceeds under an implicit assumption that we might refer to as "the hypothesis of the ideal subject." It is assumed, usually implicitly, that the subjects in an experiment (e.g., rats in a conditioning study or undergraduates in a memory study) can be treated as ideal organisms whose psychological processes are frozen, or at least frozen for whatever period of time is required to complete the experiment. Thus, the search for invariance is one in which the organism is assumed to remain constant while the situation is systematically varied. But in the study of behavioral development we obviously cannot assume that psychological processes remain untransformed. If there is a truism in developmental research, it is that, given any task, infants will perform differently than preschoolers, preschoolers will perform differently than elementary schoolers, and elementary schoolers will perform differently than adolescents. These changes are normally so massive that, historically, theories in which it is assumed that psychological development consists of qualitative changes in process have tended to dominate the thinking of developmental investigators.

Despite the intrinsic difficulty of discovering developmental invariants, I believe that we can begin to make progress if we realize that a shift in perspective may be helpful. Whereas the search for invariants in other areas of psychology involves holding the structure of the organism constant while varying the structure of the experimental context, we build in organismic variation in developmental research because we are interested in age-related changes in behavior. Consequently, if we seek developmental invariants, the structure of the experiment must be held constant. Hence, developmental invariants become synonymous with *empirical regularities in performance on given tasks that hold regardless of subjects' developmental status.* As in other disciplines, the ultimate statement of such a regularity would be a mathematical relationship of some sort.

When the search for developmental invariants is conceptualized in this manner, the research areas that provide the most fertile ground for the discovery of developmental invariants are those that satisfy three criteria. First and most important, a well-defined set of experimental paradigms must be used with subjects of various developmental levels. It is self-evident that we shall not be able to "hold the structure of the experiment constant" unless a consensus has formed around certain tasks. Second, a broad and stable data base should be available showing that these tasks produce interesting age variation. Obviously, it does not make much sense to look for developmental invariants with tasks that do not produce much age variation. Third, if we hope to represent developmental invariants as mathematical relationships, it would be helpful if mathematical technologies were available for the target paradigms. Although we can always work out mathematical machinery as research proceeds, progress would be much more rapid if these tools were already in hand.

At least one important field of developmental research meets all three criteria, namely, the developmental analysis of learning. To begin with, there is a well-defined and extensive set of human learning paradigms (e.g., concept learning, discrimination learning, recognition memory, free recall, paired-associate learning) that accounts for nearly all work in the area. Second, the data base on age changes in performance on these paradigms is vast (e.g., see Stevenson, 1970, 1972). Finally, a refined mathematical technology, in the form of finite Markov chains, exists for these paradigms (cf. Greeno, 1974).

My concern in this chapter is to outline a general perspective on the invariance question in the developmental analysis of learning and to illustrate its potential with data from several experiments with preschoolers and elementary schoolers. In the first section below, the basic concept of structural invariance is introduced and a structural-invariance conjecture about the development of learning is considered. According to this conjecture, the structure of the data generated by given paradigms (e.g., discrimination learning) is normally age invariant. Here, "structure of the data" refers to the mathematical model that gives the best statistical approximation to the data. At the end of the first section, the standard human learning paradigms are partitioned into two classes—tasks wherein subjects respond by choosing among the members of a small set of alternatives (e.g., recognition memory, discrimination learning) and tasks wherein subjects respond by acquiring a novel behavior of some sort (e.g., recall memorizing, concept learning, Pavlovian conditioning). Evidence bearing on the structural invariance of data from tasks of the former sort is reported in the second section of this chapter. Evidence bearing on the structural invariance of data from tasks of the latter sort is reported in the third section.

Background

The Concept of Structural Invariance

The search for invariance rules operates under two general constraints. First, we seek principles of sufficient power that the phenomena we study are unified and simplified in important respects. In other words, we desire principles that are non-trivial in their impact on what we already know about our phenomena. In the developmental analysis of learning, for example, the statement "Younger children will learn anything more slowly than older children" is certainly an invariance rule because it proposes a relationship that may hold for all tasks and age ranges. But it is completely trivial, both because it does not contain any information that we do not already know, and because we cannot use it to reduce the range of potentially acceptable developmental theories in any significant way.

Second, we seek principles that allow us to account for the widest possible amount of variation in our phenomena. That is, although we aim for strong, non-trivial statements of invariance, we desire that these statements be able to explain or account for the inevitable *lack* of invariance in certain aspects of our data. As regards the developmental analysis of learning, the statement "Children always learn discrimination shifts along the same conceptual dimension more rapidly than discrimination shifts along different conceptual dimensions" is a fairly powerful rule because it can be used to eliminate any developmental theory that assumes that intradimensional transfer might sometimes be harder than interdimensional transfer. But this rule is unsatisfactory when it comes to explaining the fact that the size of the intra- versus interdimensional transfer effect normally increases with age.

Since Newton's time, the strategy that scientists have favored for identifying invariants relies on mathematical models. Briefly, relationships are sought that always hold in data from some target domain. Because these relationships must be true regardless of the particular measurements that make up specific sets of data, the type of invariance delivered by a mathematical model is *structural invariance*— that is, an invariance in underlying patterns of results, not an invariance in the numerical values of individual data points. Whenever the word *structure* is uttered nowadays, psychologists, especially developmentalists, are apt to think of certain psychological constructs (e.g., the cognitive structures posited in Piaget's theory). It is worth emphasizing, therefore, that this is not the sort of structure with which I shall be concerned in the present chapter. Instead, the "structure" in "structural invariance" is *in the data, not in the organism.* It turns out that this type of structure has a signal advantage over the usual psychological concept: Data structures can be measured directly; psychological structures can only be inferred.

In addition to imposing nontrivial amounts of simplification and unification on our phenomena, a good mathematical model permits the systematic and routine treatment of variability. This is achieved by building in a variance mechanism in the form of free parameters. The numerical values of free parameters can change from one situation to another, thereby allowing for variations in the data from one subject to another and from one experiment to another. But the mathematical *relationships* among these parameters remain constant, thereby preserving the basic integrity of the structural invariances posited in the model.

To illustrate these points, let us consider the power law of psychophysics, which assumes that the physical intensity of a stimulus is related to the subjective perception of its intensity by the transformation

$$R = aS^b, \qquad (1\text{-}1)$$

where S is some measure of physical intensity (e.g., decibels), R is some measure of perceived intensity (e.g., numerical judgments), and a and b are constants estimated from data by some standard parameter-estimation procedure (e.g., the method of least squares). The power law entails certain invariant relationships in all psychophysical data. One of them, for example, is that increments in S produce larger increments in R when one starts from a small value of S than one starts from a large value of S. This will be true, according to Equation 1-1, regardless of the sense modality involved or the response measure. On the other hand, there are many other aspects of psychophysical comparison data that may vary as a function of the sense modality and/or the nature of the response measure (e.g., the average rate of increase in R as a function of S will be greater for some modalities than for others). Such differences are accommodated by estimating the constants a and b separately for different sets of comparisons.

Because the structural-invariance conjecture deals with the invariance of models, some further remarks are in order about what it means to say that a mathematical model is invariant. We have just seen that a model is invariant under transformations of the numerical values of its free parameters. Thus, $R = 1.45(S)^{.67}$, $R = .92(S)^{1.53}$, and $R = 2.76(S)^{1.11}$ are all examples of the power law. Another permissible transformation that leaves the basic model invariant is the addition of parameters. Generally speaking, when we add free parameters to a model (usually, to improve fit), the model is invariant as long as we do not alter the relationships between the original parameters. With the power law, for example, it is often possible to improve the fit of Equation 1-1 to data by expanding it to

$$R = aS^b + c. \qquad (1\text{-}2)$$

Equation 1-2 is still a power function because the original relationship between a and b is preserved. But if Equation 1-1 were changed to

$$R = \log a + bS + c, \qquad (1\text{-}3)$$

it would be an exponential function rather than a power function.

The Structural-Invariance Conjecture

My thesis about invariance in the developmental analysis of learning is quite simple, but it requires some space to develop and to illustrate. Suppose that some standard learning task T (e.g., paired-associate learning, discrimination learning) is used to study age-related changes in learning within some reasonably broad age range. I assume that it will normally be possible to find a model M that holds for the data of all ages within the range. This is the structural-invariance conjecture.

The main claims of the conjecture are that (a) there are certain patterns in the learning data for T that are the same for all ages and that (b) changes observed in these data between age levels are confined to age changes in the numerical values of M's free parameters. The conjecture simplifies the task of devising valid theories of age-related changes in T data by eliminating whole classes of theories that otherwise would be potentially viable. Explicitly, it restricts theorizing to proposals about developmental transformations in psychological processes that imply transformations in the numerical values of a model's free parameters *but do not imply a transformation of the model itself.* In the language of measurement theory, theories of the development of learning are valid up to and excluding hypotheses that imply transformations in mathematical models.

Although this constraint seems rather ethereal at first, it has a substantial payoff in most developmental research on learning because several theories, including some of the most influential ones, tend to be ruled out. To jump ahead a bit, it will be suggested in the sequel that one-stage Markov processes are developmentally invariant models for discrimination learning between the early preschool years and adulthood. Hence, theories whose assumptions entail that discrimination learning data will have multistage properties at some age levels cannot be valid. Interestingly, two of the most prominent theories in the area, Kendler and Kendler's (1962) nonmediational-mediational theory and Tighe and Tighe's (1972) object-concept theory, imply that discrimination learning data should be multistage in young children and one stage in older children, adolescents, and adults. Another prominent theory, Zeaman and House's (1963) attentional theory, implies multistage data in both children and adults.

Mathematical Models of Learning

One of the oldest topics in mathematical psychology deals with the study of the shape of learning curves. To be precise, we do not study learning curves per se because learning is a theoretical notion, a hypothetical construct, that cannot be directly measured. Instead, we study the shape of curves in which the dependent variable is some measurable aspect of performance that we assume is monotonically related to learning. Although many such variables might be possible, the only ones that are used in practice are errors-successes and response latencies, with the former being the more commonly used.

Curves in which errors-successes or latencies are plotted as the dependent variable and learning trials are plotted as the independent variable have negatively accelerated shapes that resemble exponential decay functions. In other words, (a) the rate of decline in errors or latencies is greater on initial learning trials than subsequently, and (b) the relationship between the logarithm of the performance measure and trial number appears to be roughly linear. Investigators have, therefore, most often expressed the shape of such curves with general exponential rules. Examples of historically influential theories in which exponential models of performance curves appear include those of Hull (1943), Estes (1950), and Bush and Mosteller (1955). This emphasis notwithstanding, it is also known that hyperbolic models of the form

$$Y = X \div (a + bX) \tag{1-4}$$

fit performance curves as well as or better than exponential functions in many situations (Mazur & Hastie, 1978).

In view of this long-standing emphasis on the learning curve, it might be thought that mathematical models of learning would be synonymous with models of the learning curve. Although this was true in Hull's time, the situation has changed during the past 25 years. The nominal starting point for these developments was the appearance of Bush and Mosteller's (1955) book, *Stochastic Models for Learning*. Bush and Mosteller proposed a model of the exponential type which they called the linear-operator model. The basic expression for the model was

$$P_{j+1} = \theta P_j + P_1, \tag{1-5}$$

where P_1 is the probability of a correct response on Trial 1, P_j is the probability of a correct response on any arbitrary subsequent trial j, P_{j+1} is the probability of a correct response on the trial immediately following Trial j, and θ is a learning-rate parameter. This model has two free parameters, θ and P_1, which are estimated from data. The model can be used to predict the shape of the learning curve, with the specific expression being

$$P_{j+1} = P_\infty - (P_\infty - P_1)(1 - \theta)^j, \tag{1-6}$$

where P_∞ is the probability of a correct response at the asymptote of learning and the other variables are defined as in Equation 1-5.

The objective of Bush and Mosteller's (1955) book was to show that linear-operator models were capable of bringing order to the data of many animal and human learning situations that had hitherto been islands unto themselves; but for our purposes, a technical feature of their demonstrations is of primary interest. Given any particular performance measure, we can describe the data of a learning experiment in numerous ways other than the learning curve. With errors-successes, for example, the learning curve is simply a plot of the probability of a correct response (or an error) against trial number. Alternative statistics for the same performance measure include mean total errors, variance of total errors, mean trial of last error, variance of the trial of last error, mean errors before first success, variance of errors before first success, and many others. A model that accurately describes the learning curve for several paradigms is an important achievement, but it would not necessarily give a good account of any of these other measures.

Ideally, we would like to have a model that, first, gives an appropriate mathematical expression for any conceivable statistic of learning data (e.g., mean total errors, variance of the trial of last error) and, second, gives a statistically acceptable forecast of all aspects of observed data. That is, we should be able to make numerical predictions about any conceivable learning statistic, and these predictions should be confirmed in data.

Bush and Mosteller (1955) proved that in addition to the learning curve, it is possible to derive expressions from the linear-operator model for other common learning statistics such as those just mentioned. For example, the linear-operator expression for expected total errors is

$$E(T) = (1 - P_1) \div \theta, \qquad (1\text{-}7)$$

and its expression for the variance of total errors is

$$\text{var}(T) = E(T) - [(1 - P_1)^2 \div \{1 - [1 - (1 - \theta)^2]\}], \qquad (1\text{-}8)$$

where T is a random variable that counts the total number of errors in a protocol and maps it with its appropriate sampling probability. To determine whether or not the linear-operator model gives an acceptable account of such fine-grain learning statistics, we merely estimate the two free parameters, calculate the predicted value of the relevant statistic, and compare the predicted and observed values by using a standard goodness-of-fit test.

Bush and Mosteller (1955) found that the linear-operator model gave a statistically acceptable approximation to the observed values of most common learning statistics across several experiments. A few years later it was discovered that another class of models, finite Markov chains, did an even better job than linear-operator models, especially with human data (e.g., Bower, 1961; Estes, 1960). But the key point is that since Bush and Mosteller's book, it has not been considered satisfactory for a potential learning model merely to provide an acceptable fit to learning-curve data. Unless a candidate model delivers expressions for just about any performance statistic that an investigator can think of, it is not usually considered to be of sufficient generality to warrant putting it to experimental test. Therefore, references to mathematical models of learning in this chapter are always made with the explicit understanding that we are concerned with models that, at least in principle, are capable of expressing any conceivable learning statistic in terms of their parameters.

Types of Learning Models

During the 1960s and early 1970s, models that could forecast minute aspects of learning data underwent vigorous development. By the mid-1970s, it had become apparent that the two simplest types of Markov chains, the so-called one-stage all-or-none model (e.g., Polson, 1970) and the so-called two-stage all-or-none model (e.g., Greeno, 1968), were in close agreement with the fine-grain details of many types of learning data. Although some work on Markov models of response latency was done during this period (e.g., Millward, 1964), the one-stage and two-stage models are concerned with error-success data. Before examining the manner in which these models represent learning, I consider the sorts of paradigms to which they are relevant.

The tasks that account for most learning research with infants and children come from three categories: (a) the basic conditioning paradigms (Pavlovian and instrumental); (b) the many variants of discrimination learning; and (c) the standard verbal learning paradigms. Pavlovian and instrumental conditioning are typically used to study the development of learning in early infancy (for some recent reviews, see Fitzgerald & Brackbill, 1976; Sameroff & Cavanaugh, 1979), although they are sometimes used with older individuals as well. Under Category b, we usually think of the multidimensional concept identification tasks from the large literature on children's discrimination transfer. But some other less familiar tasks, such as the solution of simple mazes by toddlers (e.g., Heth & Cornell, 1980), also belong in the discrimination learning category. Category c includes such familiar rote memorization tasks as recognition, paired-associate learning, free recall, and serial learning. Normally, these paradigms are subdivided in terms of whether individuals respond by making a choice among alternatives ("recognition") or by production ("recall").

Learning tasks have traditionally been classified in terms of their physical attributes, as I have just done. But when the performance measure is errors-successes, it turns out that another classification procedure is more meaningful from the standpoint of mathematical models. Learning paradigms can be divided into two categories that reflect structural properties of subjects' protocols. These categories will be referred to as choice tasks and production tasks in order to avoid confusion with other classification schemes.

In some learning experiments, a naive subject can respond correctly *before the first learning trial.* Because a naive subject can only guess before the first learning trial, this simply means that there is a nonzero guessing probability in such experiments. These are choice paradigms. For example, consider an experiment in which the subjects' task is to learn to recognize the members of a list of words. The experiment consists of alternating study and test cycles. On each study cycle, the words on the target list are shown one at a time. On each test cycle, pairs of words are shown, one belonging to the list and one a distractor. People respond by indicating which word belongs to the list. In this experiment, and in nearly any other experiment in which responses involve selection from a small set of alternatives, individuals would be able to respond correctly some of the time if the first test cycle were administered before the first study cycle.

Generally speaking, all the paradigms in Category b and all the paradigms in Category c that do not involve recall are choice tasks. The only important exceptions to this rule are tasks that involve some sort of reversal transfer, such as reversal shifts in discrimination learning and AB-ABr transfer in paired-associate learning. Insofar as modeling is concerned, the crucial property of choice tasks is that protocols typically consist of *two stages,* namely, an initial sequence of alternating errors and successes followed by a terminal criterion sequence of successes. (Of course, this statement assumes that subjects are being run to strict acquisition criteria.)

In other learning experiments, the structure of the task makes it impossible for a naive subject to respond correctly before the first learning trial, which is simply to say that the guessing probability is zero. These are production paradigms, and any task that requires subjects to generate rather than to select responses falls into this category. Pavlovian and instrumental conditioning are obviously both production tasks: A naive subject cannot make a conditioned response before the conditioned stimulus and the unconditioned stimulus have been paired at least once. If this statement is not true for some given experiment, then we have violated the maxim that a conditioned stimulus shall always be a "previously neutral" stimulus in simple conditioning. Similarly, all verbal learning paradigms in which the response measure is recall are necessarily production tasks: People cannot produce the words on a target list unless they have first seen the list. Finally, on some tasks subjects cannot respond correctly before the first learning trial even though the response measure involves choice. On a reversal shift problem, for example, the subject will always choose the wrong stimulus on the first trial after the shift occurs, assuming that there has been no forewarning.

Whereas choice protocols normally consist of two stages, the key feature of production protocols is that they involve three stages, namely, an initial sequence of errors, an intermediate sequence of alternating successes and errors, and a terminal criterion run of successes. (Again, I am assuming that subjects must meet strict acquisition criteria.)

Protocols from choice tasks are often well fit by a model that assumes that learning consists of a single all-or-none transition. The statistical machinery that is brought to bear when this model is applied to data is given in a review article by Polson (1970). I shall describe the model in qualitative language here. To begin with, all the stochastic information in the model can be summarized in an elementary matrix equation consisting of a row vector, a square matrix, and a column vector:

$$P[L(1), U_E(1), U_C(1)] = [m, (1-m)n, (1-m)(1-n)];$$

	$L(n+1)$	$U_E(n+1)$	$U_C(n+1)$		P(correct)	
$L(n)$	1	0	0		1	
$U_E(n)$	d	$(1-d)(1-p)$	$(1-d)p$	;	0	
$U_C(n)$	c	$(1-c)(1-s)$	$(1-c)s$		1	(1-9)

The row vector contains the probabilities of being in the various states of the model on Trial 1, the matrix contains the probabilities of making transitions between the various states after Trial 1, and the column vector contains the probability of a correct response in each state.

In the one-stage model, learning is described as follows. To begin with, the subject may be in either of two states at any point during learning, an initial "unlearned" state U and a terminal "learned" state L. At the onset of an experiment, a subject may be in either State L, with probability m, or State U, with probability $1 - m$. Subjects who are in State L respond correctly on Trial 1 and on all subsequent trials (i.e., their protocols are errorless). Subjects who begin in State U either err (Substate U_E) on Trial 1, with probability n; or they respond correctly (Substate U_C) on Trial 1, with probability $1 - n$. Since the row vector in Equation 1-9 contains these particular probabilities, it is usually called a starting vector.

According to the model, only subjects who start in State U must learn something. Subjects who are in Substate U_E on Trial 1 either make an all-or-none jump to State L after Trial 1, with probability d, or they remain in State U, with probability $1 - d$. In the latter event, they either remain in Substate U_E (and make another error), with probability $1 - p$, or they jump to Substate U_C (and respond correctly), with probability p. Subjects who are in Substate U_C on Trial 1 either make an all-or-none transition to State L after Trial 1, with probability c, or they remain in State U, with probability $1 - c$. In the latter event, they either remain in Substate U_C (and make another correct response), with probability s, or they jump to Substate U_E (and err), with probability $1 - s$. Thus, a subject who started in Substate U_E will be in L, U_E, or U_C at the end of Trial 1 with probability d, $(1 - d)(1 - p)$, or $(1 - d)p$, respectively; and a subject who started in Substate U_C will be in L, U_E, or U_C at the end of Trial 1 with probability c, $(1 - c)(1 - s)$, or $(1 - c)s$, respectively. Since it is the matrix of Equation 1-9 that gives these probabilities, it is usually called a transition matrix. Finally, in the one-stage model these same interstate transition probabilities are assumed to apply on all trials after Trial 1.

For production protocols, these data are often well fit by a model that involves two all-or-none transitions, not one. A review of the various procedures that are used to apply this model to data appears in a paper by Brainerd, Howe, and Desrochers (1982). The matrix equation for this second model is

$$P[L\,(1),\, P_E\,(1),\, P_C\,(1),\, U(1)] = [a'b',\, a'(1 - b')r,\, a'(1 - b')(1 - r),\, 1 - a'];$$

	$L(n+1)$	$P_E(n+1)$	$P_C(n+1)$	$U(n+1)$	$P(\text{correct})$
$L(n)$	1	0	0	0	1
$P_E(n)$	d	$(1-d)(1-g)$	$(1-d)g$	0	0
$P_C(n)$	c	$(1-c)(1-h)$	$(1-c)h$	0	1
$U(n)$	ab	$a(1-b)e$	$a(1-b)(1-e)$	$1-a$	0

$$(1\text{-}10)$$

As was the case with the one-stage model, the row vector contains the probabilities of being in the various states of the process on Trial 1, the matrix contains the probabilities of transitions between the various states after Trial 1, and the column vector contains the probability of a correct response in each state.

In the two-stage model, learning involves three stages—an initial "unlearned" state U in which errors occur with probability 1; an intermediate "partially learned" state P in which successes (Substate P_C) and errors (Substate P_E) occur with average probabilities of p and $1 - p$, respectively; and a terminal "learned" state L in which successes occur with probability 1. The subject may be in any one of these states on any trial. On Trial 1, the subject is in State L, with probability $a'b'$, or is in State U, with probability $1 - a'$, or is in State P, with probability $a'(1 - b')$. Thus, a' is the probability of escaping from U at the first learning opportunity, and b' is the probability of going directly from U to L after such an escape. If the subject is either in State L or in State U on Trial 1, then a correct response (State L) or an error (State U) occurs with probability 1. If the subject is in State P on Trial 1, then a correct response (Substate P_C) occurs with probability $1 - r$ or an error (Substate P_E) occurs with probability r.

Suppose that the subject starts in State L. No learning is required. The subject makes a correct response on Trial 1 and remains in State L, continuing to make correct responses, on all subsequent trials.

For subjects who start in State U, after making an error on Trial 1, these subjects may either escape State U, with probability a, or they may remain there, with probability $1 - a$. In the latter event, another error occurs on Trial 2. In the former event, subjects may either go directly to State L, with probability b, or they may enter the intermediate state, with probability $1 - b$. Subjects who go directly to L respond correctly on Trial 2 and on all subsequent trials. Subjects who enter State P either respond correctly (Substate P_C) on Trial 2, with probability $1 - e$, or they make an error (Substate P_E) on Trial 2, with probability e. This description of the learning events on Trial 1 is also assumed to apply to all subsequent trials on which the process in Equation 1-10 was in State U at the beginning of the trial.

Consider now that subset of subjects who started in State U on Trial 1 and who entered the intermediate state after the trial on which they left State U. As just mentioned, successes and errors occur with probabilities $1 - e$ and e, respectively, on the first trial on which the process occupies State P. Assuming that the first response in State P is a success, the subject either jumps from P to L at the end of the trial, with probability c, or the subject remains in State P, with probability $1 - c$. If a P-to-L transition occurs, the subject responds correctly on all the remaining trials. If the process remains in State P, either an error is made on the next trial, with probability $1 - h$, or another correct response is made, with probability h. Suppose, however, that the first response in State P is an error. At the end of this trial, the subject either jumps from P to L, with probability d, or remains in State P, with probability $1 - d$. In the event of a P-to-L transition, correct responses occur on all subsequent trials. If the process remains in State P, either another error is made on the next trial, with probability $1 - g$, or a correct response is made, with probability g. The description of learning on all later trials in State P is the same as on the first Trial in State P.

Last, consider those subjects who start in State P on Trial 1. According to the model, the course of learning for these subjects is identical to the course of State P learning in subjects who (a) started in State U on Trial 1 and (b) made U-to-P jumps on their trials of escape from U. In other words, the description of learning for subjects who were in P on Trial 1 is identical to that in the preceding paragraph.

Reformulation of the Structural-Invariance Conjecture

The one- and two-stage models have been extensively applied to choice and production data in two types of subjects, namely, adult humans (undergraduates) and nonprimate infrahumans. In human experimentation, the one-stage model has been used with tasks such as various forms of discrimination learning (e.g., Bower & Trabasso, 1964; Restle, 1962; Trabasso, 1961), paired-associate learning situations where the task is to map a relatively large number of stimulus items with a small number of responses (e.g., Bower, 1961; Greeno, 1967; Greeno & Scandura, 1966; Millward, 1964), and recognition memorization (e.g., Kintsch, 1966; Kintsch & Morris, 1965). Also in human learning, the two-stage model has been used with certain forms of transfer (e.g., Greeno, James, & DaPolito, 1971; Pagel, 1973; Theios & Hakes, Note 1), cued recall (e.g., Brainerd, Howe, & Desrochers, 1980; Humphreys & Greeno, 1970; Greeno, James, DaPolito, & Polson, 1978; Kintsch, 1963), and free recall (e.g., Kintsch & Morris, 1965; Waugh & Smith, 1962). With infrahumans, Theios and his associates have reported an impressive series of experiments on both Pavlovian and instrumental conditioning of rats and rabbits (Theios, 1963; Theios & Brelsford, 1966a, 1966b; Theios, Note 2).

There are certain instances in which the two-stage model provides a better description of choice data than the one-stage model, and there are other situations in which the one-stage model provides a better description of production data than the two-stage model. Reversal-shift data are examples of the former anomaly, whereas relearning data in cued recall are an example of the latter anomaly (Brainerd, Desrochers, & Howe, 1981). It is generally conceded, however, that the best statistical accounts of choice and production data are given by one-stage and two-stage models, respectively. Naturally, whenever one says that a certain model gives the best fit to a certain type of data, this statement is relative to whatever other models it has been compared to. As Theios, Leonard, and Brelsford (1977) have pointed out, there is always a trade-off between parsimony and adequacy in modeling. On the one hand, we seek the simplest possible model for the phenomena under study, with the ultimate goal being a model with no free parameters. On the other hand, we seek a model that will cover as much data as possible. Thus, when I say that the one-stage model is regarded as providing the best fit to choice data, I mean only that, of the models that have been studied with such data, the one-stage model seems to deliver the best combination of parsimony and adequacy. The statement that the two-stage model provides the best fit to production data has the same meaning.

The important thing about these statements is that they allow us to translate the structural-invariance conjecture into some simple predictions about developmental research with choice and production paradigms. Since we already know the models that give the best fit to such data for adults, the same models might work at younger age levels. Unfortunately, such predictions cannot be evaluated with extant data on age-related changes in learning. Despite the long history of application of these models in the animal and adult literatures, they have almost never been studied with infants and children. With children, the only exceptions to this rule are early applications of the one-stage model to concept learning (Suppes & Ginsburg, 1962a, 1962b, 1963) and to verbal learning (Atkinson & Crothers, 1964), plus some recent applications of both models to verbal learning (Bisanz, Vesonder, & Voss, 1978; Brainerd & Howe, 1980, 1982) and concept learning (Brainerd & Howe, 1979). With infants, the only exceptions appear to be Heth and Cornell's (1980) application of the one-stage model to maze learning and Heth and Cornell's (Chapter 3, this volume) application of the two-stage model to rule learning. Because rather extensive amounts of data are required to draw any conclusions as to the validity of the structural-invariance conjecture, the balance of this chapter is given over to reporting several choice and production experiments with pre-schoolers and elementary schoolers.

One-Stage Learning

In this section, I summarize the results of 15 experiments with preschool and elementary school children in which the one-stage model was fitted to choice data. Because the general objective is to produce presumptive evidence for or against the structural-invariance conjecture, a question arises as to what type of experiments would be the appropriate place to begin. On this point, I have adopted a strategy suggested by Brainerd and Howe (1980), namely, to concentrate on the youngest age level at which normal children can learn most of the target tasks. The rationale for this strategy is elementary. If the best fitting model is already known for the upper age bound (adults), then data showing that the same model fits the lower age bound provide strong preliminary evidence in favor of structural invariance, because we would otherwise have to assume that the learning of individuals who are separated by larger age differences is more similar than the learning of individuals who are separated by smaller age differences. Although the latter is a logical possi-bility, it has almost never been observed in the developmental analysis of learning.

With the choice tasks, the lower age bound is usually the preschool years. Hence, most of the experiments were concerned with preschool children, though some data on younger elementary schoolers will also be reported. Two choice paradigms were studied, discrimination learning and paired-associate learning with choice responses. The discrimination learning studies were further subdivided into experiments in which subjects learned a magnitude discrimination of some sort (size, number) and experiments in which subjects learned categorical discriminations (shape, color). I summarize the details of the three classes of experiments under separate headings.

Discrimination Learning: Magnitude

Experiment 1. Seventy preschoolers (mean age 4 years, 2 months) learned two tasks, an intermediate-size discrimination followed by an intermediate-size trans-position. The stimuli on Task 1 were three squares measuring 2 cm, 4 cm, and 6 cm, respectively. The stimuli on Task 2 were three squares measuring 8 cm, 10 cm, and

12 cm, respectively. At the start of each task, the children were told that a sticker (clown face) was on the back of one of the stimuli and that the object was to learn which stimulus it was. Training proceeded via a standard correction routine. That is, the stimuli were arranged in front of the subject at the beginning of each trial, the child made a response, and the experimenter then showed the child whether the response was correct or incorrect. Training continued on both tasks until a criterion of five consecutive correct responses had been met.

Experiment 2. One hundred first graders (mean age 6 years, 8 months) learned the same two tasks as in Experiment 1 under identical conditions.

Experiment 3. One hundred first graders (mean age 6 years, 5 months) learned two tasks like those in the first two experiments, except for the following changes. On Task 1, the stimuli were index cards on which there were two, three, or four randomly positioned black dots. On Task 2, the stimuli were index cards on which there were three, four, or five randomly positioned black dots. The three-dot stimulus was the winner on the first task, and the four-dot stimulus was the winner on the second task.

Experiment 4. Eighty preschoolers (mean age 4 years, 11 months) learned a single small-number discrimination. The stimuli on each trial were two index cards on which two, three, or four randomly positioned black dots appeared. Half the children were presented with three types of pairs (two vs. three, two vs. four, three vs. four) and learned to select the stimulus with more dots; the other half were presented with two types of pairs (two vs. three and three vs. four) and learned to select the stimulus with three dots. The learning criterion was seven consecutive correct responses.

Experiment 5. Sixty-four preschoolers (mean age 4 years, 5 months) learned the same task as the first half of the children in Experiment 4, except that (a) the stimuli also varied on color (red, yellow, white) and (b) one of the colors (yellow) was redundant with the winning number.

Experiment 6. Fifty-eight preschoolers (mean age 4 years, 5 months) learned the same task as the second half of the children in Experiment 4, except that (a) the stimuli also varied on color (red, yellow, white) and (b) one of the colors (yellow) was redundant with threeness.

Experiment 7. Forty kindergartners (mean age 5 years, 9 months) learned a small-number discrimination. The stimuli were pairs of rectangles that varied on three dimensions: length (9 cm or 14 cm); height (7 cm or 12 cm); and number of columns (five or eight). The winning member of each pair was the stimulus with eight columns, and the learning criterion was seven consecutive correct responses. The procedure for this experiment is the same as that in a study reported by Brainerd and Howe (1979).

Experiment 8. Eighty-nine preschoolers (mean age 4 years, 6 months) learned a small-number discrimination. The stimuli were quartets of rows of black dots that varied on four dimensions simultaneously: row length, row density, size of dots in a row, and number of dots in a row. The winning member of each quartet was the stimulus containing the same number of dots as a fifth, sample stimulus presented by the experimenter (i.e., this was a match-to-sample discrimination). The learning criterion was five consecutive correct responses. This experiment is described in detail in Greenberg (1981, Experiment 1).

Experiment 9. One hundred and eighty-four preschoolers (mean age 4 years, 5 months) learned the same small-number discrimination as the children in Experiment 8. The difference between the two studies was that the children in this experiment were divided into four groups that received pretraining experiences that were designed to improve the learning of this discrimination. The pretraining task for Group 1 was designed to reduce the salience of nonnumerical cues (size, length, density), the pretraining task for Group 2 was designed to increase the salience of numerical cues, and the pretraining task for Group 3 was a generalized attentional treatment that was not specific to particular cues. Group 4 was a control condition in which the children received no pretraining. This experiment is described in detail in Greenberg (1981, Experiment 2).

Discrimination Learning: Categories

Experiment 10. Ninety-six preschoolers (mean age 4 years, 9 months) learned a color-shape discrimination. The stimuli were presented in pairs that varied along two dimensions: shape (star or circle) and color (red or black). Shape and color were redundant (i.e., the star was always red and the circle was always black, or conversely). The winning member of each pair was the stimulus with a particular color-shape combination (e.g., red star). The learning criterion was seven consecutive correct responses.

Experiment 11. One hundred and ten preschoolers (mean age 4 years, 3 months) learned a shape discrimination. The stimuli varied simultaneously along two dimensions: shape (circle, square, triangle) and the position of a black dot (top, center, bottom) on the stimulus. The children were divided into two groups. Stimuli were presented in pairs to children in Group 1 and in triads to children in Group 2. For both groups, however, the winning stimulus on each trial was the one with a particular value of the shape dimension (e.g., triangle). The learning criterion was eight consecutive correct responses for Group 1 and five consecutive correct responses for Group 2.

Experiment 12. Sixty-four preschoolers (mean age 4 years, 5 months) learned a color discrimination. The stimuli were presented in pairs, and they varied simultaneously along two dimensions: color (red, blue, yellow) and shape (circle, square, triangle). The winning member of each pair was the one with a particular value of the color dimension (e.g., blue). The learning criterion was seven consecutive correct responses.

Verbal Learning

Experiment 13. Twenty-two preschoolers (mean age 4 years, 4 months) memorized a paired-associate list consisting of four stimuli (the letters A, E, G, and L) and two responses (the numerals 2 and 4). Learning was via the anticipation method, and training continued for each child until he or she made two consecutive errorless passes through the list.

Experiment 14. Twenty-three preschoolers (mean age 4 years, 3 months) memorized a paired-associate list consisting of four consonant letters as stimuli and two color names as responses. Apart from the list, the procedure was the same as in Experiment 13.

Experiment 15. Twenty-five preschoolers (mean age 4 years, 5 months) memorized a paired-associate list consisting of line drawings of four familiar animals (cow, fish, tiger, bird) as stimuli and two color names as responses. Apart from the list, the procedure was the same as in Experiments 13 and 14.

Results and Discussion

The number of data sets for which the structural-invariance conjecture can be evaluated is larger than the number of experiments: Six of them, Experiments 1–4, 9, and 11 had more than one condition, resulting in 23 data sets in all. The numerical estimates of the one-stage model's parameters appear in Table 1-1 for these data sets.

Evaluating structural invariance for these experiments comes down to an evaluation of goodness of fit. If choice data are normally one stage, regardless of age level, it follows that the satisfactory degree of fit that obtains in such data when the subjects are adults (cf. Bower & Trabasso, 1964; Greeno, 1974) will also be obtained with children. As noted earlier, goodness of fit is assessed by determining how well a model accounts for different aspects of the data. In particular, a model must predict the empirical distributions of fine-grain statistics of learning data, such as the total number of errors in a protocol, the number of the trial on which the last error occurs, and so forth. Four such statistics were used in the present goodness-of-fit analysis: total errors per protocol (T), trial number of the last error in a protocol (TLE), the length of consecutive runs of errors in a protocol (LE), and the length of consecutive runs of successes before the last error in a protocol (LC).

The results of the observed-predicted comparisons for these four learning statistics appear by data set in Table 1-2. For each statistic, the mean and the variance are reported. The corresponding values predicted from the one-stage model are also shown for the various data sets. These predicted values are calculated by substituting the parameter estimates (Table 1-1) in algebraic expressions for the sampling distributions of the statistics. The appropriate expressions for the sampling distributions appear in Brainerd and Howe (1980, Appendix).

Table 1-1 Parameter Estimates (One-Stage Model)
for Experiments 1–15

Experiment	Parameter					
	m	d	c	n	p	s
Experiment 1						
Task 1	.04	.15	0	.16	.33	.33
Task 2	.20	.12	0	.28	.31	.33
Experiment 2						
Task 1	.37	.17	0	.42	.44	.33
Task 2	.23	.31	0	.18	.44	.33
Experiment 3						
Task 1	.26	.09	0	.13	.28	.33
Task 2	.34	.11	0	.27	.31	.33
Experiment 4						
More	.05	.08	0	.42	.50	.45
Threeness	0	.05	0	.42	.44	.50
Experiment 5	.26	.31	0	.51	.50	.50
Experiment 6	.26	.26	0	.48	.47	.50
Experiment 7	0	.07	0	.65	.50	.56
Experiment 8	.15	.12	0	.46	.39	.50
Experiment 9						
Group 1	.26	.23	0	.29	.60	.50
Group 2	.28	.16	0	.64	.48	.33
Group 3	.22	.18	0	.14	.48	.33
Group 4	.15	.12	0	.54	.39	.50
Experiment 10	.14	.54	0	.46	.50	.23
Experiment 11						
Pairs	0	.24	0	.39	.34	.50
Triads	.13	.15	0	.35	.33	.27
Experiment 12	.29	.22	0	.38	.44	.50
Experiment 13	.25	.30	0	.64	.53	.50
Experiment 14	.21	.35	0	.38	.65	.50
Experiment 15	.31	.33	0	.70	.60	.50

Note. m is the probability of starting in the learned state on Trial 1; n is the probability of an error on Trial 1 if the process is in the unlearned state; d is the probability of jumping to the learned state following any error in the unlearned state; c is the probability of jumping to the learned state following any success in the unlearned state; p is the probability that any error in the unlearned state is followed by a success if the process does not jump to the learned state; s is the probability that any success in the unlearned state is followed by another success if the process does not jump to the learned state.

Table 1-2 Point Predictions for the One-Stage Experiments

Experiment	T μ	T σ²	TLE μ	TLE σ²	LE μ	LE σ²	LC μ	LC σ²
Experiment 1								
Task 1								
Observed	6.30	45.87	8.89	91.73	2.33	6.78	1.49	.59
Predicted	6.60	40.89	9.61	77.64	2.35	2.35	3.14	.73
Task 2								
Observed	6.28	68.96	9.03	142.14	2.50	3.91	1.48	.57
Predicted	6.48	55.96	9.35	104.59	2.13	5.72	1.48	.71
Experiment 2								
Task 1								
Observed	3.63	31.34	6.13	85.45	1.86	2.02	1.36	.49
Predicted	3.66	17.49	6.51	73.75	1.86	1.62	1.35	.49
Task 2								
Observed	2.56	17.18	3.93	36.00	1.61	2.57	1.63	.97
Predicted	2.44	6.92	3.84	19.27	1.63	1.02	1.54	.82
Experiment 3								
Task 1								
Observed	8.44	90.31	11.29	159.41	2.93	4.23	1.49	.77
Predicted	8.22	106.93	11.27	188.22	2.90	5.51	1.54	.82
Task 2								
Observed	5.90	81.96	8.24	141.69	2.46	4.58	1.53	.85
Predicted	6.00	67.09	8.66	128.40	2.59	4.13	1.49	.74
Experiment 4								
More								
Observed	12.89	230.32	25.54	764.80	2.04	2.47	1.80	1.07
Predicted	12.50	160.20	24.81	619.40	1.86	1.60	1.81	1.48

Table 1-2 (continued)

Experiment	T μ	T σ^2	TLE μ	TLE σ^2	LE μ	LE σ^2	LC μ	LC σ^2
Threeness								
Observed	19.76	377.25	34.70	1091.17	2.46	7.31	1.78	.94
Predicted	20.83	413.33	36.98	1260.53	2.14	2.59	1.82	1.48
Experiment 5								
Observed	2.35	8.27	4.65	29.06	1.51	.84	1.53	.79
Predicted	2.40	7.34	4.83	26.03	1.53	.79	1.97	1.87
Experiment 6								
Observed	2.70	9.44	5.14	27.05	1.67	1.04	1.93	1.41
Predicted	2.84	10.85	5.34	33.77	1.65	1.07	2.06	2.20
Experiment 7								
Observed	15.48	89.42	32.79	269.37	1.87	1.46	2.26	2.41
Predicted	15.15	214.46	31.20	784.98	1.88	1.65	2.27	2.48
Experiment 8								
Observed	6.94	65.34	11.52	164.99	2.34	2.66	2.09	1.77
Predicted	6.89	57.75	11.47	143.72	2.13	2.44	1.86	1.56
Experiment 9								
Group 1								
Observed	3.15	10.04	6.00	41.96	1.44	.52	1.70	.87
Predicted	3.17	14.01	7.33	81.17	1.45	.63	1.70	1.19
Group 2								
Observed	4.61	47.59	8.29	111.98	1.80	2.49	1.53	.77
Predicted	4.60	33.17	10.97	180.75	1.56	.85	1.54	.82
Group 3								
Observed	4.42	21.98	6.96	60.65	1.76	1.66	1.47	.81
Predicted	4.30	24.48	7.71	79.62	1.75	1.31	1.49	.72

Group 4								
Observed	6.98	43.72	12.11	98.36	2.16	3.27	1.84	1.19
Predicted	6.89	57.74	11.48	144.42	2.13	2.41	1.86	1.59
Experiment 10								
Observed	1.55	1.40	2.64	5.14	1.26	.29	1.30	2.77
Predicted	1.61	1.81	3.48	7.59	1.27	.34	1.31	2.60
Experiment 11								
Pairs								
Observed	4.12	17.99	7.09	44.75	1.99	2.37	2.06	1.76
Predicted	4.12	12.78	6.32	22.45	2.00	1.99	2.11	2.31
Triads								
Observed	5.78	32.36	8.37	69.90	2.33	3.80	1.34	.61
Predicted	5.94	40.13	8.87	77.61	2.34	3.15	1.36	.50
Experiment 12								
Observed	3.13	15.19	5.65	47.90	1.77	1.49	1.84	1.35
Predicted	3.19	15.36	5.66	44.19	1.76	1.34	1.79	1.39
Experiment 13								
Observed	2.67	5.55	3.03	10.57	1.50	.87	1.76	1.50
Predicted	2.12	5.24	2.83	9.06	1.48	.65	1.72	1.02
Experiment 14								
Observed	2.65	5.48	3.75	8.96	1.72	1.32	1.79	1.39
Predicted	2.20	4.69	2.85	8.02	1.46	.61	1.92	1.61
Experiment 15								
Observed	1.66	3.95	2.70	9.23	1.39	.54	2.11	3.06
Predicted	1.93	5.05	2.57	8.88	1.39	.52	2.09	2.03

Note. T is the total number of errors per subject, TLE is the trial on which the last error was committed, LE is the length of each consecutive run of errors, and LC is the length of each consecutive run of successes before the last error.

Inspection of Table 1-2 reveals that the one-stage model does a remarkably good job of predicting the statistical details of these experiments. For total errors and trial of last error, the average difference between the observed and predicted values of the means was only .22 and .69, respectively. The results were even better for length of consecutive runs of errors and length of consecutive runs of successes before the last error. The average difference between observed and predicted means was only .08 in the former case and .06 in the latter case. With these last two statistics, the numbers of cases (out of 23) in which the predicted-observed difference exceeded ±.1 were only six and four, respectively. There were 92 possible observed-predicted comparisons between the means of these statistics (23 data sets × 4 learning statistics). When tests of statistical significance were computed, the observed-predicted discrepancy was significant in only two cases (trial of last error in Experiment 7 and in the threeness condition of Experiment 4). But with 92 comparisons in all, we would expect four to five .05 null hypothesis rejections by chance.

Thus, the one-stage model predicts the quantitative details of these experiments quite well, and many predictions are virtually exact in the case of the means. I conclude that there is strong presumptive evidence that one-stage properties of the error-success data generated by choice learning paradigms are developmentally invariant.

Two-Stage Learning

Recall that the paradigms that tend to produce two-stage data when the subjects are adults or infrahumans are tasks that, broadly speaking, involve the acquisition of a novel response of some sort. Pavlovian conditioning, instrumental conditioning, most forms of reversal transfer, and certain types of concept learning are the principal examples of such paradigms.

I now report 14 more sets of data, distributed across five experiments, which were concerned with the potential developmental invariance of two-stage learning. All of these data sets are from recall memorization experiments with children in the kindergarten to sixth-grade range. All the data sets involved either cued recall or free recall. I briefly summarize the main methodological points before taking up the results.

Cued Recall Experiments

Experiment 16. Fifty kindergarten children (mean age 5 years, 8 months) were randomly assigned to one of two list conditions. In Condition 1, 25 children memorized an eight-item paired-associate list in which the stimulus and response members of each pair were familiar nouns (A or AA on the Thorndike-Lorge count). All nouns were names of concrete objects (e.g., pipe, table) and were obtained from a pool used by Brainerd et al. (1981). In Condition 2, 25 children memorized an eight-item paired-associate list in which the stimulus and response members of each pair were line drawings of the objects denoted by the nouns in Condition 1. In both conditions, learning was by the anticipation method under standard cued recall instructions. For each child, training continued until a criterion of two consecutive errorless passes through the list was met. The procedures for both conditions are reported more fully in Brainerd and Howe (1982, Experiment 2).

Experiment 17. One hundred second-grade children (mean age 7 years, 6 months) were randomly assigned to one of four list conditions. Conditions 1 and 2 were identical to Conditions 1 and 2, respectively, in Experiment 16. In Condition 3, 25 children memorized an eight-item list in which the stimulus members of each pair were the pictorial stimuli used in Condition 2 and the response members were the word responses used in Condition 1. In Condition 4, 25 children memorized an eight-item list in which the stimulus members of each pair were the word stimuli used in Condition 1 and the response members were the pictorial responses used in Condition 2. Learning in all conditions was by the anticipation method to a criterion of two consecutive errorless passes.

Experiment 18. One hundred sixth-grade children (mean age 11 years, 9 months) were tested under the same conditions as in Experiment 17.

Free Recall Experiments

Experiment 19. Forty second-grade children (mean age 7 years, 5 months) were randomly assigned to one of two list conditions. In Condition 1, 20 children memorized a 10-item list of familiar nouns (A or AA on the Thorndike-Lorge count). All were abstract nouns (e.g., mind, advice) drawn for the Paivio, Yuille, and Madigan (1968) pool. Memorization was via a standard study-test procedure. On each study trial, the words were presented individually at a 5-second rate, and the child pronounced each word. To eliminate short-term memory effects, the child circled pairs of numerals on a sheet of numerals provided by the experimenter for 30 seconds after the last word was presented. Following this buffer activity, the child was asked to recall as many words as possible in any order. Words were presented in the same order on all study trials. In Condition 2, 20 subjects memorized the same 10-item list. However, the presentation order was random rather than fixed. The learning criterion was two consecutive errorless passes through the list.

Experiment 20. Forty second-grade children (mean age 7 years, 10 months) were randomly assigned to one of two list conditions. Condition 1 was the same as the first condition in Experiment 19, except for the words. Here, the words were familiar concrete nouns (e.g., letter, string) drawn from the Paivio et al. (1968) pool. Condition 2 was the same as the second condition in Experiment 19, except that the words were the same concrete nouns memorized by the subjects in Condition 1. The learning criterion was again two consecutive errorless passes.

Results and Discussion

The goodness-of-fit analyses for the two-stage model are somewhat more complicated than for the one-stage model in that two steps are involved (see Brainerd et
al., 1982, pp. 648–652). The first step is to show that the two-stage model is
necessary in order to account for the data. Since the one-stage model is logically
simpler than the two-stage model, the first step consists of showing that the one-
stage model fails to give an acceptable account of the data. For these experiments,
the various statistics in Table 1-2 were computed and then the corresponding values
predicted by the one-stage model were calculated. In contrast with the results in
Table 1-2, the null hypothesis of no difference between predicted and observed
values was rejected in most cases. Hence, the data of these production experiments
are more complex than the one-stage model anticipates. The second step is to show
that the two-stage model is *sufficient* to account for the data.

Numerical estimates of the two-stage model's parameters are given for each of
the data sets in Table 1-3. As before, we are primarily concerned with the model's
ability to predict molecular aspects of the data. I have again chosen to illustrate the
model's predictive power by resorting to four different statistics of the data: the
total number of errors per item; the number of errors per item before the first correct response; the length of each run of consecutive errors for an item after the first
correct response has occurred; and the length of each run of consecutive correct
responses for an item before the last error has occurred. The relevant observed-
predicted comparisons for the mean and the variance of each of these statistics
appear by experiment in Table 1-4. Predicted means and variances were obtained
by substituting parameter estimates from Table 1-3 in the expressions for the
sampling distributions of the statistics given in Brainerd (1979, Appendix).

From a detailed inspection of Table 1-4, it appears that the two-stage model's
ability to account for these data is as good as the one-stage model's ability to
account for the data of the earlier experiments. For total errors per item and number of errors per item before the first correct response, the average discrepancies
between observed and predicted means were .52 and .21, respectively. Of the 14
observed-predicted comparisons for each of these two statistics, none was statistically reliable, though one or two .05 rejections could have occurred by chance.
Turning to the other two statistics, we find that the average discrepancy between
observed and predicted means was .15 for runs of consecutive errors after first
success and .06 for runs of consecutive successes before last error. Again, none of
the 14 observed-predicted comparisons for either statistic was reliable.

Finally, the discrepancies between the observed and predicted values of the
variances of the four statistics were, as usual, larger than the corresponding discrepancies for the means. But out of 56 possible comparisons for the variances,
only one comparison was significant (the random presentation condition in Experiment 19). Therefore, I conclude that for recall memorization at least, there is a
strong case for the view that the error-success data generated by children are as
likely to be two stage as the error-success data generated by adults.

Table 1-3 Parameter Estimates (Two-Stage Model) for Experiments 16–20

Experiment	Stage 1			Stage 2						
	a'	a	b'	b	d	c	$1-r$	$1-e$	g	h
Experiment 16										
Pictures	.64	.35	.69	.07	.42	0	.20	.20	.20	.40
Words	.38	.27	.58	.61	.27	0	.29	.29	.29	.41
Experiment 17										
Pictures	.67	.34	.57	.19	.34	0	.15	.15	.15	.26
Words	.50	.23	.32	.02	.16	0	.22	.22	.22	.45
Picture-word	.55	.35	.51	0	.28	0	.21	.21	.21	.35
Word-picture	.63	.26	.35	0	.22	0	.23	.23	.23	.36
Experiment 18										
Pictures	.64	.39	.61	1.00	.50	0	.33	.33	.33	.33
Words	.68	.39	.53	0	.31	0	.30	.30	.30	.47
Picture-word	.82	.46	.46	0	.37	0	.20	.20	.20	.37
Word-picture	.66	.35	.63	1.00	.25	0	.38	.38	.38	.45
Experiment 19										
Serial	.73	.44	.40	1.00	.61	0	.29	.29	.29	.41
Random	.58	.47	.33	.45	.29	0	.40	.40	.40	.48
Experiment 20										
Serial	.85	.56	.30	1.00	.70	0	.28	.28	.28	.37
Random	.85	.59	.33	1.00	.59	0	.29	.29	.29	.38

Note. See Equation 1-10 for definitions of parameters.

Table 1-4 Point Predictions for the Two-Stage Experiments

Experiment	T		FC		LE		LC	
	μ	σ^2	μ	σ^2	μ	σ^2	μ	σ^2
Experiment 16								
Pictures								
Observed	2.30	11.67	1.78	8.11	1.77	2.04	1.67	1.39
Predicted	2.27	8.71	1.82	12.59	1.87	1.85	1.67	1.11
Words								
Observed	3.58	16.86	2.84	11.56	1.94	2.40	1.67	2.92
Predicted	2.87	10.27	2.89	10.83	2.08	2.04	1.69	1.19
Experiment 17								
Pictures								
Observed	2.43	10.87	1.85	6.62	2.42	3.11	1.37	.50
Predicted	1.82	5.59	1.80	5.98	2.27	1.35	1.35	.48
Words								
Observed	6.02	28.51	4.06	23.72	2.45	4.77	1.82	1.48
Predicted	7.38	48.29	4.19	20.80	2.90	2.90	1.82	1.48
Picture-word								
Observed	3.00	13.39	2.11	8.15	2.17	4.00	1.54	.76
Predicted	3.45	14.35	2.43	8.24	2.32	2.32	1.54	.83
Word-picture								
Observed	4.56	22.07	3.00	14.26	2.23	3.49	1.46	1.11
Predicted	5.09	27.12	3.10	13.47	2.50	2.52	1.56	.89
Experiment 18								
Pictures								
Observed	1.48	1.61	.97	1.70	1.61	1.53	1.14	1.00
Predicted	1.25	.75	.73	.89	1.50	1.52	1.49	.74

Words								
Observed	2.80	14.86	1.78	8.84	1.84	3.24	1.77	1.64
Predicted	3.03	12.29	1.96	9.45	1.93	1.95	1.87	1.67
Picture-word								
Observed	1.92	8.26	1.20	3.77	1.90	1.83	1.61	1.10
Predicted	2.14	7.19	1.74	5.37	2.02	2.00	1.60	.92
Word-picture								
Observed	2.19	4.66	1.24	3.48	1.74	1.48	1.76	1.50
Predicted	1.65	4.95	.93	1.78	1.88	1.86	1.86	1.58
Experiment 19								
Serial								
Observed	1.73	2.49	1.18	2.04	1.43	1.77	1.67	.85
Predicted	1.91	3.25	.96	1.18	1.34	1.43	1.70	1.26
Random								
Observed	2.40	4.43	1.32	2.73	1.49	1.59	1.94	1.62
Predicted	3.22	10.42	1.74	1.24	1.74	1.75	1.92	1.78
Experiment 20								
Serial								
Observed	2.20	2.05	.88	1.22	1.26	.37	1.57	.83
Predicted	1.42	2.01	.67	.63	1.28	1.27	1.59	.93
Random								
Observed	1.46	1.59	.84	1.14	1.44	1.11	1.61	.82
Predicted	1.17	1.43	.71	1.27	1.41	1.41	1.61	.99

Note. T is the total number of errors per item, FC is the total number of errors before the first success, LE is the length of consecutive error runs after the first success, and LC is the length of consecutive success runs before the last error.

Theory and Metatheory in the Development of Learning

The original motivation of this chapter was to explore the possibility that progress can be made toward the detection of developmental invariants in learning by focusing attention on the *structure* of learning data. According to the structural-invariance notion, there exist underlying patterns in learning data, the grammar of the data so to speak, that are often age invariant. These patterns can be conveniently represented in mathematical models.

In most learning paradigms, subjects either respond by selecting from a small set of alternatives (choice tasks) or by acquiring novel behaviors (production tasks). When the target data are errors-successes, as opposed to latencies, and the subjects are adults, we have known for some years that choice protocols are normally one-stage Markovian and production protocols are normally two-stage Markovian. (There are, of course, some exceptions to this rule, with reversal transfer and re-learning in cued recall being prominent examples for choice and production, respectively.) This provides us with a straightforward method of gaining leverage on structural invariance: Administer choice and production tasks to children of various ages, fit the respective models to the data, and determine whether or not the degree of fit varies systematically with age. In the experiments that I have reported, the one-stage model and the two-stage model gave about as good an account of the data of very young children as they typically give of corresponding adult data.

Since the preliminary evidence favors structural invariance, it now becomes relevant to ask how the one- and two-stage models can be exploited in the developmental analysis of learning. Here, the key point to bear in mind is that the role either model plays with respect to any target paradigm is that of a metatheory (see Brainerd et al., 1982). In other words, each model provides an abstract description of the structure of learning, and this description, owing to its abstractness, will accommodate multiple theoretical interpretations. Thus, it becomes the business of research to decide which theoretical interpretations of a model's parameters are actually valid, where "theoretical interpretations" refers to hypotheses about psychological processes.

Given that these models are understood to be metatheories, the extant literature suggests three more explicit metatheoretical uses for these models in the developmental analysis of learning: (a) elimination of theories; (b) testing theoretical interpretations of particular learning stages; and (c) testing theoretical interpretations of particular learning parameters. I briefly discuss these metatheoretical functions of the one- and two-stage models to conclude this chapter.

Elimination of Theories

A general problem in any well-mined area of developmental research is that the ratio of theoretical hypotheses to stable findings is considerably greater than 1; for every solid developmental trend there are several theories professing to explain it. In such situations, it may be possible to rule out certain theories on the ground that their assumptions about development are prima facie inconsistent with the structural-invariance principle. The specific rule of thumb is this: Given some task to which the one-stage model or the two-stage model is known to apply across age levels, any theory whose assumptions imply developmental transformations in the model is automatically suspect.

Discrimination learning provides an illustration of how large tracts of theoretical literature can be rendered irrelevant if due attention is paid to structural invariance. During the 1960s, discrimination learning and discrimination transfer were perhaps the most extensively studied phenomena in cognitive development, and they remain important today. Leaving minor theories aside, three explanations of age-related changes in children's discrimination learning emerged, namely, Kendler and Kendler's (1962) mediational theory, Tighe and Tighe's (1972) differentiation theory, and Zeaman and House's (1963) attentional theory. Although the claims of these theories have been examined in many experiments, it turns out that they all violate the simple principle that the one-stage model is developmentally invariant for discrimination data.

To see why, let us consider how each theory explains age-related changes in children's performance on a very simple task. Suppose that the task is a two-dimensional discrimination problem involving two values of shape (circle and triangle) and two values of brightness (black and white). Thus, there are four distinct stimuli: black circle (BC), black triangle (BT), white circle (WC), and white triangle (WT). Assume that learning is via the method of simultaneous discrimination. That is, there are two types of trials: black circle versus white triangle (BC/WT) and black triangle versus white circle (BT/WC). Last, suppose that BC and BT are the positive stimuli—that is, the solution is "Black is the winner."

In Tighe and Tighe's (1972) differentiation theory, the fact that younger children solve this problem more slowly than older children is explained by postulating a developmental change in *object learning* versus *concept learning*. Preschooler's and younger elementary schoolers are said to rely primarily on object learning, which consists of learning the correct response on the BC/WT trials and the correct response on the BT/WC trials as independent "subproblems." If children are run to a strict acquisition criterion, the performance of those who engage in object learning must consist of three distinct states: (a) an initial state at the start of training when neither subproblem has yet been solved and the probability of a correct response is chance; (b) an intermediate state sometime later when one of the two subproblems has been solved and the probability of a correct response is somewhere between chance and 1; and (c) a terminal state during the criterion run when both subproblems have been solved and the probability of a correct response is 1. On the other hand, older children and adults are said to rely on concept learning, which involves acquiring the actual classification rule ("Black is the winner" in this case) rather than correct responses to distinct stimulus arrangements. For individuals who engage in concept learning, performance must consist of two states: (a) an initial state at the start of training when the classification rule is unknown and the probability of a correct response is chance, and (b) a terminal state during the criterion run when the classification rule has been isolated and the probability of a correct response is 1. Because only one stage is involved in concept learning, whereas two are involved in object learning, concept learning should be faster than object learning—hence, speed of discrimination learning increases with age.

In Kendler and Kendler's (1962) theory, age changes in discrimination learning are explained by invoking age changes in *mediational* versus *nonmediational* learning. Individuals who learn nonmediationally (preschoolers and young elementary schoolers) simply memorize the instrumental response (winner-loser) that goes with each stimulus, but individuals who learn mediationally acquire a semantic concept such as "white" or "triangle." Tighe and Tighe (1972) have observed that the implications of the mediational-nonmediational distinction for the solution of problems such as the one in our illustration are essentially the same as the implications of the differentiation theory. When learning is nonmediational, there will be an initial state in which none of the instrumental responses is known and the probability of a correct response is chance; there will be an intermediate state in which some of the instrumental responses are known and the probability of a correct response is greater than chance but less than one; and there will be a terminal state in which all the instrumental responses are known and the probability of a correct response is 1. But when learning is mediational, there will be only an initial state in which the concept has not yet been identified and a terminal state in which it has been identified.

In Zeaman and House's (1963) theory, the discrimination learning of subjects of all ages is assumed to involve an initial *attentional stage* followed by an *instrumental-response learning stage.* During the attentional stage, the indivdual learns which of the dimensions of stimulus variation is correlated with reinforcement (brightness in our sample problem). The probability of a correct response is chance until the relevant dimension has been identified. Once the attentional stage has been completed, the next task is to learn the specific values of the relevant dimension that are winners and losers. The probability of a correct response is greater than chance but less than 1 during the second stage. When the second stage is completed, the probability of a correct response is 1. Developmental changes in the rate of discrimination learning are explained in terms of developmental changes in the attentional stage. With sophisticated subjects, such as adults or older children, the attentional stage is said to be completed very rapidly, usually requiring only a single trial with problems as simple as the one in our illustration. With infrahumans and young children, however, several trials are usually required to identify the relevant dimension.

It is not difficult to see that all three of these theories imply age-related changes in the underlying structure of discrimination learning data, albeit for somewhat different reasons. In particular, each theory entails that the complexity of such data, where complexity refers to the number of distinct performance levels, should be greater for younger subjects. Insofar as Tighe and Tighe's (1972) differentiation theory and Kendler and Kendler's (1962) mediational-nonmediational theory are concerned, we would anticipate, first, that the fit of the one-stage model will be systematically poorer for younger subjects and that, second, at the preschool level, where multistage learning predominates, the two-stage model should give a better account of the data than the one-stage model. The same two predictions hold for Zeaman and House's (1963) attentional theory. Although learning is always two stage in this theory, the stages are more distinct in younger children because more trials are required to identify the relevant dimension.

Obviously, these predictions are inconsistent with the results of Experiments 1–12. It was found in these studies that when young children learn two-choice and three-choice discrimination problems, the correspondence between fine-grain aspects of the data and the predictions of the one-stage model is very precise. Hence, the differentiation, mediational-nonmediational, and attentional theories cannot be correct, at least in their standard forms. This leaves us with two basic theoretical options. First, we can seek to modify one or more of the theories in such a way that their psychological assumptions remain essentially intact but one-stage learning is predicted for all age levels. After attempting various modifications, I have concluded that the chances of bringing the differentiation and the mediational-nonmediational theories into conformity with the data are not promising. Such modifications seem to do damage to the theories' fundamental assumptions, and specifically, they seem to preclude ideas such as independent sub-problem learning and the learning of separate instrumental responses for different discriminanda. However, two simple adjustments, either of which will produce the desired results, are available for attentional theory. It is only necessary to assume either (a) that instrumental-response learning is a one-trial event and it occurs on the *same trial* on which the relevant dimension is identified or (b) that completion of the attentional stage does not increase the probability of a correct response (i.e., the probability of a correct response is chance during both the attentional stage and the instrumental stage).

The other option is to consider theoretical explanations of discrimination learning that do not require modification in order to deliver one-stage data. One possibility is hypothesis theory. In this theory, the cues in a discrimination learning problem (black, white, circle, and triangle in our example) are represented in working memory as hypotheses. To solve problems, subjects sample hypotheses and test them against feedback, usually by employing a win-stay/lose-shift rule. Age-related changes in discrimination learning are explained in terms of age-related changes in the efficiency of hypothesis-testing mechanisms (e.g., Phillips & Levine, 1975).

Testing Interpretations of Learning Stages

A second metatheoretical function of the one- and two-stage models is to pit different theoretical interpretations of learning stages against each other. As previously noted, the abstract nature of these models means that they will accommodate more than one theoretical interpretation of how learning develops. But these interpretations will usually imply different patterns of age-related change in a model's parameters, and consequently, developmental comparisons of patterns of parameter behavior can be used to evaluate different theories.

As yet, research of this sort is rare in developmental journals. However, Howe and I have reported a series of experiments that serve to illustrate this metatheoretical use of the models (Brainerd & Howe, 1980). We noted that theories of one-stage paired-associate learning in adults fall into two categories, namely, conditioning theories, which assume that study trials "stamp in" the connection between stimulus and response words; and cognitive theories, which assume that pairs are memorized by sampling from a pool of memorization strategies using a win-stay/lose-shift principle. Although both types of theories can be shown to imply one-stage data, they make different predictions about certain parameters of the one-stage model. Conditioning theories imply that subjects are equally likely to learn on study trials following errors and following successes (i.e., $c = d$ in Equation 1-9), whereas cognitive theories imply that subjects only learn on study trials following errors (e.g., $c = 0$ or is very close to 0). Howe and I examined the possibility that age-related changes in speed of paired-associate learning may be due to age-related changes in subjects' degree of reliance on conditioning-based versus strategy-based learning, with the specific prediction being that young children's learning would tend to be more in line with conditioning interpretations than adults' learning. This hypothesis leads one to expect that between early childhood and adulthood, the value of c in Equation 1-9 should decrease steadily relative to the value of d. This result was obtained.

Testing Interpretations of Parameters

The last and most precise metatheoretical use of the models is to pit theoretical interpretations of specific parameters against each other. Research of this type grows out of research of the type discussed in the preceding paragraph. When converging evidence is available on some general theoretical interpretation of the learning stages for a target paradigm (e.g., the cognitive interpretation of one-stage paired-associate learning), the relevant model can then be used to sort out competing hypotheses about specific components of theory.

Since the one- and two-stage models have rarely been put to the second metatheoretical use in developmental research, as yet there are no extensive developmental literatures with which to illustrate this third metatheoretical function. However, such illustrations can be found in the literature on cued recall in adults. When adults memorize a list of AB pairs and the performance measure is recall, we already know that error-success data will be two-stage Markovian to a close approximation. Greeno and his associates have reported several experiments concerned with a theory in which it is assumed that learning consists of storing a unitary trace of the AB pair followed by learning how to retrieve that trace. This theory seems to give a better explanation of how the parameters of the two-stage model react to various manipulations than do competing theories (see Greeno et al., 1978).

Even if we accept this general theoretical framework, several questions still remain about the component processes that are involved in storing and retrieving a unitary trace. For example, two different interpretations of retrieval have been proposed. Greeno and his associates have argued that retrieval is primarily a matter of stimulus discrimination; the main task in learning to retrieve is to learn how to find the trace when A is presented as a retrieval cue. Thus, learning to retrieve is synonymous with acquiring a search algorithm. Brainerd et al. (1981) have proposed that retrieval is a matter of both stimulus discrimination and response discrimination; learning to retrieve is a joint task of learning how to find the trace when A is presented as a retrieval cue *and* of learning how to decode B features from the trace once it is found. In this second theory, one must acquire both a search algorithm and a decoding algorithm before one can retrieve reliably.

These two interpretations are tested by comparing how the second-stage learning parameters of the two-stage model (i.e., b', b, c, and d in Equation 1-10) react to AB difficulty manipulations. In the storage-retrieval framework, the first stage of the two-stage model is mapped with the process of storing a unitary trace and the second stage is mapped with the process of learning to retrieve the trace. Hence, theories of retrieval are concerned with second-stage parameters. If the stimulus-discrimination interpretation is correct, then we would expect that these parameters will be chiefly affected by the difficulty of the stimulus word in an AB pair because this word is the search cue on test trials. But if the search-and-decode interpretation is correct, these parameters should be affected by the difficulty of both the stimulus and response words in an AB pair. Thus, the two theories can be compared by conducting experiments in which various difficulty factors (meaningfulness, familiarity, etc.) are manipulated factorially over both members of AB pairs and the effects on second-stage parameters are noted.

Concluding Remarks

The apparent developmental invariance of the one- and two-stage models for choice and production data, respectively, confers some advantages when it comes to theorizing about the development of learning. In particular, it permits us to restrict the domain of viable theories considerably, it permits systematic tests of different interpretations of learning stages to be conducted, and it permits systematic tests of different interpretations of particular learning parameters to be conducted. Unfortunately, that these models are not in general use in the literature means that these advantages have yet to be exploited.

Reference Notes

1. Theios, J., & Hakes, D. T. Paired-associate response shifts in two-stage all-or-none learning. Paper presented at the meeting of the Midwestern Psychological Association, Chicago, May 1962.
2. Theios, J. *A three-state Markov model for learning* (Tech. Rep. 40). Stanford, CA: Stanford University, Institute for Mathematical Studies in the Social Sciences, 1961.

References

Atkinson, R. C., & Crothers, E. J. A comparison of paired-associate learning models having different learning and retention axioms. *Journal of Mathematical Psychology*, 1964, *1*, 285–315.

Bisanz, G. L., Vesonder, G. T., & Voss, J. F. Knowledge of one's own responding and the relation of such knowledge to learning. *Journal of Experimental Child Psychology*, 1978, *25*, 116–128.

Bower, G. H. Application of a model to paired-associate learning. *Psychometrika*, 1961, *26*, 255–280.

Bower, G. H., & Trabasso, T. Concept identification. In R. C. Atkinson (Ed.), *Studies in mathematical psychology*. Stanford, CA: Stanford University Press, 1964.

Brainerd, C. J. Markovian interpretations of conservation learning. *Psychological Review*, 1979, *86*, 181–213.

Brainerd, C. J., Desrochers, A., & Howe, M. L. Stages-of-learning analysis of picture-word effects in associative memory. *Journal of Experimental Psychology: Human Learning and Memory*, 1981, *7*, 1–14.

Brainerd, C. J., & Howe, M. L. An attentional analysis of small cardinal number concepts in five-year-olds. *Canadian Journal of Behavioural Science*, 1979, *11*, 112–123.

Brainerd, C. J., & Howe, M. L. Developmental invariance in a mathematical model of associative learning. *Child Development*, 1980, *51*, 349–363.

Brainerd, C. J., & Howe, M. L. Stages-of-learning analysis of developmental interactions in memory, with applications to developmental interactions in picture-word effects. *Developmental Review*, 1982, *2*, 251–273.

Brainerd, C. J., Howe, M. L., & Desrochers, A. Interpreting associative-learning stages. *Journal of Experimental Psychology: Human Learning and Memory*, 1980, *6*, 754–765.

Brainerd, C. J., Howe, M. L., & Desrochers, A. The general theory of two-stage learning: A mathematical review with applications to memory development. *Psychological Bulletin*, 1982, *91*, 634–665.

Bush, R. R., & Mosteller, F. *Stochastic models for learning*. New York: Wiley, 1955.

Estes, W. K. Toward a statistical theory of learning. *Psychological Review*, 1950, *57*, 94–107.

Estes, W. K. Learning theory and the new "mental chemistry." *Psychological Review*, 1960, *67*, 207–223.

Fitzgerald, H. E., & Brackbill, Y. Classical conditioning in infancy: Development and constraints. *Psychological Bulletin*, 1976, *83*, 353–376.

Greenberg, N. A. *Young children's perceptual judgments of nonredundant cardinal number equivalence*. Unpublished doctoral dissertation, University of Western Ontario, 1981.

Greeno, J. G. Paired-associate learning with short term retention: Mathematical analysis and data regarding identification of parameters. *Journal of Mathematical Psychology*, 1967, *4*, 430–427.

Greeno, J. G. Identifiability and statistical properties of two-stage learning with no successes in the initial stage. *Psychometrika*, 1968, *33*, 173–215.

Greeno, J. G. Representation of learning as discrete transition in a finite state space. In D. H. Krantz, R. C. Atkinson, R. D. Luce, & P. Suppes (Eds.), *Contemporary developments in mathematical psychology.* San Francisco: Freeman, 1974.

Greeno, J. G., James, C. T., & DaPolito, F. J. A cognitive interpretation of negative transfer and forgetting of paired associates. *Journal of Verbal Learning and Verbal Behavior,* 1971, *10,* 331–345.

Greeno, J. G., James, C. T., DaPolito, F. J., & Polson, P. G. *Associative learning: A cognitive analysis.* Englewood Cliffs, NJ: Prentice-Hall, 1978.

Greeno, J. G., & Scandura, J. M. All-or-none transfer based on verbally mediated concepts. *Journal of Mathematical Psychology,* 1966, *3,* 388–411.

Herrnstein, R. J. Formal properties of the matching law. *Journal of the Experimental Analysis of Behavior,* 1974, *21,* 159–164.

Heth, C. D., & Cornell, E. H. Three experiences affecting spatial discrimination learning in ambulatory children. *Journal of Experimental Child Psychology,* 1980, *30,* 246–264.

Hull, C. L. *Principles of behavior.* New York: Appleton-Century-Crofts, 1943.

Humphreys, M. S., & Greeno, J. G. Interpretations of the two-stage analysis of paired-associate memorizing. *Journal of Mathematical Psychology,* 1970, *7,* 275–292.

Keil, F. C. Constraints on knowledge and cognitive development. *Psychological Review,* 1981, *88,* 197–227.

Kendler, H. H., & Kendler, T. S. Vertical and horizontal processes in problem solving. *Psychological Review,* 1962, *69,* 1–16.

Kintsch, W. All-or-none learning and the role of repetition in paired-associate learning. *Science,* 1963, *140,* 310–312.

Kintsch, W. Recognition learning as a function of the length of the retention interval and changes in the retention interval. *Journal of Mathematical Psychology,* 1966, *2,* 412–433.

Kintsch, W., & Morris, C. J. Application of a Markov model to free recall and recognition. *Journal of Experimental Psychology,* 1965, *69,* 200–206.

Mazur, J. E., & Hastie, R. Learning as accumulation: A reexamination of the learning curve. *Psychological Bulletin,* 1978, *85,* 1256–1274.

Millward, R. B. Latency in a modified paired-associate learning experiment. *Journal of Verbal Learning and Verbal Behavior,* 1964, *3,* 309–316.

Pagel, J. C. A Markov analysis of transfer in paired-associate learning with high intralist similarity. *Journal of Verbal Learning and Verbal Behavior,* 1973, *12,* 456–470.

Paivio, A., Yuille, J. C., & Madigan, S. Concreteness, imagery, and meaningfulness values for 925 nouns. *Journal of Experimental Psychology,* 1968, *76* (1, Part 2).

Phillips, S., & Levine, M. Probing for hypotheses with adults and children. *Journal of Experimental Psychology: General,* 1975, *104,* 327–354.

Polson, P. G. Statistical methods for a general theory of all-or-none learning. *Psychometrika,* 1970, *35,* 51–72.

Restle, F. The selection of strategies in cue learning. *Psychological Review,* 1962, *69,* 329–343.

Sameroff, A. J., & Cavanaugh, P. J. Learning in infancy: A developmental perspective. In J. D. Osofsky (Ed.), *Handbook of infant development.* New York: Wiley, 1979.

Stevens, S. S. Mathematics, measurement, and psychophysics. In S. S. Stevens (Ed.), *Handbook of experimental psychology*. New York: Wiley, 1951.

Stevenson, H. W. Learning in children. In P. H. Mussen (Ed.), *Carmichael's manual of child psychology* (Vol. 1). New York: Wiley, 1970.

Stevenson, H. W. *Children's learning*. New York: Appleton-Century-Crofts, 1972.

Suppes, P., & Ginsburg, R. Application of a stimulus sampling model to children's concept formation with and without overt correct responses. *Journal of Experimental Psychology*, 1962, *63*, 330–336. (a)

Suppes, P., & Ginsburg, R. Experimental studies of mathematical concept formation in young children. *Science Education*, 1962, *46*, 230–240. (b)

Suppes, P., & Ginsburg, R. A fundamental property of all-or-none models, binomial distribution of responses prior to conditioning, with applications to concept formation in children. *Psychological Review*, 1963, *70*, 139–161.

Theios, J. Simple conditioning as two-stage all-or-none learning. *Psychological Review*, 1963, *70*, 403–417.

Theios, J., & Brelsford, J. W., Jr. A Markov model for classical conditioning: Application to eye-blink conditioning in rabbits. *Psychological Review*, 1966, *73*, 393–408. (a)

Theios, J., & Brelsford, J. W., Jr. Theoretical interpretations of a Markov model for avoidance conditioning. *Journal of Mathematical Psychology*, 1966, *3*, 140–162. (b)

Theios, J., Leonard, D. W., & Brelsford, J. W., Jr. Hierarchies of learning models that permit likelihood ratio comparisons. *Journal of Experimental Psychology: General*, 1977, *106*, 213–225.

Tighe, T. J., & Tighe, L. S. Stimulus control in children's learning. In A. D. Pick (Ed.), *Minnesota symposia on child psychology* (Vol. 6). Minneapolis, MN: University of Minnesota Press, 1972.

Trabasso, T. *The effect of stimulus emphasis on the learning and transfer of concepts*. Unpublished doctoral dissertation, Michigan State University, 1961.

Waugh, N. C., & Smith, J. E. A stochastic model for free recall. *Psychometrika*, 1962, *27*, 141–154.

Zeaman, D., & House, B. J. The role of attention in retardate discrimination learning. In N. R. Ellis (Ed.), *Handbook of mental deficiency*. New York: McGraw-Hill, 1963.

2. The Learning Paradigm as a Technique for Investigating Cognitive Development

Bruce A. Linder and Linda S. Siegel

For decades researchers studying cognitive development have used paradigms that are based on the procedures described by Piaget and others. The basic design of these assessments is that children are presented with a set of materials (e.g., rows of objects) and asked questions based on these materials (e.g., "Which one has more or do they both have the same number?"). Children's responses to the questions are taken as an index of their cognitive processes. The aim of these procedures is to find out what children know when they enter the session. This approach is a *structural* one, intended to find out what children do and do not understand about the situation.

In this chapter we will explore alternatives to these types of assessments. Specifically, we are interested in what children are capable of learning and what they can understand with instruction and feedback. We are not interested in the static state of a concept at a certain point in time. Our approach is a *dynamic* one. We are interested in asking questions about how concepts change with learning and in measuring thought processes with techniques that are sensitive to short-term change and growth within an individual child.

In this chapter we will discuss the use of techniques of learning to investigate cognitive development in children. First, some definitions are in order. What do we mean by learning? The definition is an operational one. In this context we are concerned with an experimental situation in which children are presented with a particular set of stimuli and, after responding, receive feedback about the correctness

Both authors shared equally in the preparation of this chapter.

of this response. Feedback is the key to learning. A task cannot properly be called a learning task without this feedback. The second major dimension in which learning tasks differ from traditional cognitive developmental tasks is that a child is not necessarily expected to understand the task at the beginning of the interaction with the experimenter. Instead we investigate how a child learns or acquires a concept in the course of performing the task. In addition, in the learning task a child must be presented with a situation more than once and usually many times so that more than his or her initial responses are measured.

An assumption underlying our view of assessment is that thinking abilities and cognitive operations can exist independent of factors such as language comprehension and production, memory, and attention. In relation to the measurement of logical thinking abilities, these other factors can be viewed as contaminants or confounds in the assessment technique if that technique measures performance that depends heavily on these factors. Evidence for the independence of language and thought in young children has been reviewed elsewhere (Siegel, 1978), where a variety of studies showed that children could pass a nonverbal concept attainment task without being able to pass an equivalent task that requires a verbal expression of concept knowledge. Although data concerning the independence of thought and other assessment contaminants do not exist, our working assumption is that rational analysis of assessment task demands suggests that the independence view is at least plausible.

In this chapter, we will consider (a) historical precedents for using learning techniques as an alternative assessment strategy and (b) methological problems with traditional assessment techniques. Following this, studies of children's learning of quantitative concepts, dimensional concepts, and seriation will be reviewed to show that learning techniques often reveal cognitive capabilities in young children that are not revealed by traditional assessment techniques. Interpretive problems with learning assessment techniques will then be discussed, and studies of children's discrimination learning and concept utilization will be reviewed in order to show how these interpretive problems might be avoided. Finally, we will describe future directions for research on the use of learning techniques to assess cognitive development.

Historical Precedents

There are some historical precedents for regarding learning as important to assessment; the roots are evident in early discussions of the nature of intelligence. As Thorndike said (Estes, 1974):

Intellect is the ability to learn, and our estimates of it are or should be estimates of ability to learn. To be able to learn harder things or be able to learn the same things more quickly, would then be the single basis of evaluation. . . . We have learned to think of intellect as the ability to succeed with intellectual tasks, and to measure it by making inventory of a fair sampling from these tests, arranging these in levels of intellectual difficulty, and observing how many the intellect in question succeeds with at each level. . . . Such a definition in terms of tasks accomplishable, and such a measurement in terms of the contents of a graded inventory is sound and useful, but is not entirely satisfying. (pp. 740-741)

Thorndike outlined the position that we need more than static measures of intellect; we need measures of learning and of ability to change. Estes (1974) proposed application of the principles of learning to standardized intelligence tests. He noted that we should try to see how a child, adult, or mentally deficient person may be taught a strategy and thus to improve performance by training. According to Estes, we have a need for "understanding what brings about specific kinds of competence and incompetence in intellectual activity." Intelligence should be characterized in terms of a learning process, not as a static, fixed characteristic.

Although coming from a completely different tradition than Estes and Thorndike, Vygotsky (1978) also opposed the static approach to studying cognition. Vygotsky outlined three theoretical positions on the interaction between learning and development: (a) development is independent of learning; (b) development is learning; and (c) learning and development are mutually interactive.

The assumption of the first position, that the process of child development is independent of learning, is a key postulate of the Piagetian system. Learning does not modify the course of development. The real issue of concern for a theory such as that of Piaget and his colleagues is specifying the underlying processes involved in the development of the child. Learning is not relevant to this theory. Piaget and his colleagues believe that you do not teach children until their capacity has matured. Maturation or development is the basis of learning, but is not significantly modified by it.

The assumption of the second position is that development is a manifestation of learning. The Skinnerian position would be an example of this approach. Cognitive behaviors are a result of learning.

The third position is that development is based on two processes that mutually influence each other. One of these processes is maturation, which depends on the development of the nervous system; the other is learning. Learning and maturation are mutually dependent and interactive. Maturation makes learning possible. Learning stimulates maturation.

Vygotsky was not completely satisfied with any of these positions, particularly as regards issues involving the assessment of cognitive development; therefore, he developed his own position as an outgrowth of the third one. His description of assessment procedures, although written in 1930, is an accurate picture of the state of the art today. According to Vygotsky, children are typically given a battery of tests, and judgments about their mental development are made on the basis of these tests. As he says, "If we offer leading questions to show how the problem is to be solved, and the child then solves it, or if the teacher initiates the solution, and if the child completes it or solves it in collaboration with other children—in short, if the child daily misses an independent solution of the problem—the solution is not regarded as indicative of his mental development" (p. 85).

According to Vygotsky, we need to investigate what a child is capable of learning. (For a detailed discussion of these ideas see Brown & French, 1979.) Following Vygotsky, we think it is more fruitful to investigate how much children can learn when we give them a chance to learn. According to Vygotsky, the difference between what a child's test scores are and what he or she is capable of understanding with help is the *zone of proximal development,* "the distance between the actual developmental level as determined by independent problem solving and the level of potential development as determined through problem solving under adult guidance or collaboration with more capable peers" (p. 86). What is in this zone is a function of the processes that have not matured; what we assess with conventional approaches are the products of development. The actual developmental level is a retrospective picture of development. We know only the end product, not how a child reached this point. In the zone of proximal development we can see where development is going. In this zone, processes are beginning to mature and develop. By examining what is in this zone, we can begin to understand the course of development. The mental age that emerges from a psychometric assessment and the "stage" that emerges from the traditional Piagetian assessment are completed development, achieved at that point in time.

For Vygotsky and for us and others, the study of learning is an important part of the study of developmental change. We will examine this concept in this chapter.

Methodological Difficulties with Traditional Assessment

We have previously discussed some of the difficulties that arise when cognitive development is assessed with paradigms that do not involve learning (Siegel, 1978, 1982; Siegel & Hodkin, 1982). Language, memory, attention, and social factors may interfere with these assessments. Let us examine these briefly in one situation. Siegel and Goldstein (1969) tested conservation of number by showing children two rows of six pennies and then spreading out one row; children were asked in each case whether the number of pennies in each row was the same or if one row had more. Depending on their responses, children were classified as conservers or nonconservers. This is a traditional conservation of number paradigm. However, suppose the child did not understand what the words *same number* meant. Failure may have been a language problem, not a conceptual problem. Evidence for the child's linguistic confusion came from the fact that many children, especially the younger ones, used a recency strategy in that they always selected the last alternative in the series, whether or not it was the correct one. When an adult asks a question and then minutes later asks the identical question, the child may assume that his or her answer to the first question must have been wrong; the normal rules of conversation are such that the repetition of a question implies that your first response was incorrect. Thus, it may appear that children are inconsistent or wrong in a typical conservation experiment when in fact they are following normal rules about the expectations of behavior in social situations or perhaps conversational situations.

Simplification of tasks may be useful in the study of cognitive development. (See Surber, 1979, for a discussion of these related issues.) A learning task may allow us to break the task down into components and to remove some of the difficulties associated with traditional assessment tasks. Directing a child's attention to relevant dimensions may result in improved performance.

We have developed a series of nonverbal concepts that are a test of a variety of cognitive concepts, many based on Piagetian concepts. These tasks, although different in superficial characteristics from the traditional Piagetian tasks, appear to us to be identical in the deep structure; that is, the same logical abilities are involved in performance. We are studying learning; we are not assessing the child's level of knowledge when he or she enters into the situation. We are asking whether or not the child can learn, with very simple manipulations, the particular concept in question.

Miller (1976) and Larsen (1977) have argued against nonverbal and alternate definitions of Piagetian tasks because these alternate tasks are different in surface features from the traditional ones. We think that they have missed the crucial point. What they have failed to understand is that an operational definition of a concept is completely arbitrary. The critical test of its validity is whether or not a particular operational definition has a coherent and consistent logical basis. For example, conservation is defined by Piagetians as the ability to recognize invariance in a particular dimension, in spite of change in other irrelevant features, so that the child must recognize that transforming length does not influence number. Our conservation task, in which a child must match two sets that are heterogeneous or spatially nonequivalent, seems to preserve the essence of conservation (e.g., Siegel, 1978). However, the two tasks are very different in superficial aspects. These two approaches, the traditional Piagetian one and the learning one, use a different definition of the concept, but we think that these tasks share the same underlying logic. It seems to us that the children must use the same logical process or rule in order to succeed in both the Piagetian and nonverbal alternatives. In other words, the tasks share the same deep structure.

The contention that these nonverbal learning tasks do not tap the same logical abilities is not justified because the proponents of this viewpoint have not been successful in specifying how the tasks are different other than in their surface features. Are the learning tasks that we have proposed measuring the same concepts as the structures identified by Piaget? We think that the same rules are being tested by the nonverbal tasks, but doubts still remain (e.g., Greco & Bideau, 1980). Because of the difficulties with Piagetian tasks we need alternative ways to measure performance. We need to understand the process or operation by which a response is made, not just the response itself (Glaser, 1981).

In the tasks outlined in Siegel (1978) we assessed the extent to which children can learn a rule. We do not know whether or not they understand the rule when they start the task. We are able to determine whether or not they can acquire the rule within the context of this experimental situation.

Training as a Technique to Assess Cognitive Processes

Piagetian psychologists assert that, in general, specific training does not help children to acquire basic logical operations, although it may speed the transition between stages. Non-Piagetian researchers, however, have pursued the question of the training of logical and other cognitive operations. This is not simply a result of the North American proclivity to make everything bigger and better, including children's minds. We have previously discussed various aspects of the arguments for training (Siegel, 1978, 1982; Siegel & Hodkin, 1982). By training a concept, we can examine the specific experiences that might be relevant and the specific nonlogical factors that may impede children in demonstrating understanding of the concept. For example, Siegel, McCabe, Brand and Matthews (1978) gave children an increasingly difficult series of class inclusion problems. Simple training based on feedback was successful for both 3- and 4-year-olds. The training was very brief, and we believe that this improvement reflects what Vygotsky referred to as the zone of proximal development. These children were in the process of acquiring the class inclusion concept or were almost ready to acquire it and therefore were able to learn.

Similar results were obtained by Judd and Mervis (1979), who trained 5-year-old children to be aware of the contradiction between their counting and their answers to class inclusion questions. Children first were asked to count out the superordinate class (e.g., toys: "Count all the toys"). Next they were asked to count the larger subordinate class (e.g., balls) and then the smaller subordinate class (e.g., teddy bears). Finally, they were asked the typical class inclusion questions. If children were incorrect, the procedure was repeated until they were able to get a correct answer. These children, in contrast to children who did not receive the training, were able to solve new class inclusion problems on immediate and delayed posttest. The counting contradiction procedure is a good example of a learning procedure.

An example of the efficacy of training in a totally different area is the work of Saltzman and Townsend (1980), who have used learning techniques to train children's communication skills. While the generalization has persisted that young children are egocentric—that is, they cannot understand others' viewpoints and perspectives and do not adjust their language appropriately—there is increasing evidence that this supposition is at least partially incorrect. (For reviews see Borke, 1978; Siegel & Hodkin, 1982.) Saltzman and Townsend used learning to try to determine how the young child's apparent egocentrism in communication might be modified by learning. The communication task involved children being shown pairs of words (e.g., cow-horse), one of which was underlined. The children were told that an imaginary person, Mr. Nobody, could not see which word was underlined, and they were then instructed as follows: "You have to think of a clue that would help Mr. Nobody guess which word is underlined. The clue has to be one word, and it can't rhyme with cow." Some of the children were poor communicators, and half of these poor communicators were trained to provide a good clue. The other half were not. The training was successful, producing significantly better communication in the trained children. This type of study is an example of how learning can be used to assess cognitive development. Without the training the children would have been called egocentric, but a more accurate estimate of their cognitive abilities was obtained through training. Such an approach has been especially useful in the study of quantitative, dimensional, and seriation concepts.

Quantitative Concepts

From a number of studies like these in which learning techniques have been used, our understanding of the young child's concepts of quantity has been enlarged considerably. Investigators conducting such studies provide us with an understanding of the child's concepts that involves minimal language skill. Using some nonverbal tasks, Siegel (1971a, 1971b) has shown that 3- and 4-year-olds were capable of learning a complex relative magnitude concept where they were reinforced for choosing the larger (or smaller, for counterbalancing) set size. Similarly, Bullock and Gelman (1977) taught young children ($2\frac{1}{2}$-5 years old) the distinction between 1 and 2. The sets consisted of toy animals, and the child had to guess which one was the "winner." Children learned this discrimination quite easily. In a transfer phase children chose between 3 and 4. The correct relational response would be set size 4. Most of the 3- and 4-year-olds responded relationally but 2-year-olds did so only when it was made clear to them that it was a new task. In other words, children could learn the concept of larger than (or smaller than) with the small-number sets. Here is an example of a learning and transfer paradigm appropriate to the interests of young children that allows us to understand something about their numerical concepts.

Recently McLaughlin (1981) has challenged these claims that "preoperational" children can understand relative numerosity. She argues that Siegel has not actually tested for relative numerosity concepts, since in her materials relative size and density were confounded with number. Unfortunately, the fundamental premise of her argument is incorrect. One of us (Siegel, 1971a, 1971b, 1972a, 1972b, 1973, 1974a, 1974b, 1982) has stated that these concepts involve a judgment not of number per se but of *relative* magnitude or size. In most cases length and/or density is correlated with set size. However, the child must use the rule "larger than" (or "smaller than") to solve the problem; because the absolute values change on every trial, it is truly a relational response. One task that Siegel used is an exception to the fact that other dimensions are correlated with set size. In a task called nonlinear magnitude (Siegel, 1972b) the child had to select the longer or smaller of two set sizes (absolute value of the number in a set ranged from 2 to 9) when the dots were arranged in a nonlinear spatially irregular array. Although this task was very difficult for the 3-year-olds, many 4-year-olds could solve the problem. This task represents a test of the concept of numerical magnitude.

Dimensional Concepts

An interpretation of Piagetian theory is that in some situations young children cannot attend to two dimensions simultaneously; that is, they can process only one dimension at a time. This limited capacity is postulated as at least part of the reason why they fail the traditional conservation of number task. For example, when a row of objects is made shorter and young children are asked about number, they attend to the length rather than the number dimension and respond that the longer row has more. However, Watson and Danielson (1969) have shown that 2-year-olds can sort objects on the basis of two dimensions. Here is a case of simplifying the task and using feedback to demonstrate cognitive competence. Watson, Hayes, and Vietze (1979) examined the hypothesis that preschool children could learn a bidimensional sorting task with feedback for correct responding when the response requirements or the stimuli are made less complex. Most of the 3- and 4-year-olds learned this bidimensional sorting task. Significantly fewer, but still almost half, of the 2-year-olds were able to reach criterion on the bidimensional task. Children who erred were continuing to sort on a single dimension—either form or color. Therefore, many of these young children were capable of attending to two dimensions simultaneously in this very simplified situation. The significance of this task is that here a very simplified learning situation has been used to enable us to examine the dimensional concepts of young children. According to the authors, even this task was probably not appropriate for the youngest children because they did not appear to understand the task requirements.

Let us consider one specific case in which a learning paradigm might be useful for an analysis of cognitive development. In an innovative series of studies Smith (Note 1) attempted to determine whether 2-, 3-, and 4-year-old children could understand the concept of a dimension. She used a nonverbal follow-the-leader task in which children were instructed to do as the experimenter did. An experimenter chose two red objects of different sizes from an array (e.g., a red 3-inch house and a red 5-inch house). The second experimenter chose two yellow objects of different sizes (e.g., a yellow 1-inch house and a yellow 5-inch house). The child had a choice of a blue 1-inch, a blue 3-inch, and a yellow 3-inch house. A choice of the two blue houses on the part of the child would indicate an understanding of a dimensional concept. Many 3- and 4-year-olds appeared to understand this concept. Two-year-olds had difficulty with the concept of the dimension. This methodology is an important step forward in studying children's concept development. An addition to this approach would be examining whether 2-year-olds could, in fact, learn to make the correct choices. Would they be able to learn the concept of dimension? The application of learning to this situation would be useful.

Seriation

Siegel (1972a) found that children as young as 3 years of age are able to understand some rudimentary seriation concepts. Children were shown a series of lines of different sizes in random order and were able to select the end one (largest or smallest) of the series. However, when 3-year-olds were required to find the next to the smallest of the sets, many failed to reach criteria. Even 6-year-olds had a high rate of failure on this task. Marshark (1977) introduced an important procedural variation, in which children were reinforced for selecting the next to the biggest instead of the next to the littlest in a series of sticks. Marshark found that the children were able to do this. They understand the "biggest, next biggest" relationship before the "littlest, next littlest." While this is an illustration that task parameters influence learning, it is also an illustration that young children can learn elementary seriation concepts.

Gollin, Moody, and Schadler (1974) introduced a perceptual motor component by having children point to the end member of a height series before being required to find the nonterminal member (littlest and next to the littlest). This procedure facilitated the development of learning the concept. Griep and Gollin (1978) used this strategy to investigate whether learning to solve a problem in one dimension will transfer to another dimension. They used the dimensions of height and brightness. Children participated in three different conditions: (a) point to the end member first, with feedback; (b) feedback about the correctness of their answer but also correction; and (c) no training. Children were trained on the dimension of brightness or height. Subjects then received the task, either height or brightness, that they had not received in training. All subjects were able to transfer to the other dimension, with the subjects who had received corrective feedback gaining the most. Training in one dimension transferred to another dimension.

Factors in Discrimination Learning

(Although a variety of learning paradigms have been adapted in order to assess or train cognitive competencies in children, basic to most of them is learning discriminations.)It will be the purpose of the following discussion to look carefully at the problems associated with interpreting demonstrated discrimination failures. We will focus, in particular, on the so-called concept utilization task or, as it is also known, the multidimensional discrimination learning procedure.

A central feature of structural descriptions of cognitive development is that children will show behavorial abilities is some cognitive domain at a particular age, and will not show those abilities at earlier ages. Often when stage descriptions are made, theoretical statements follow that assert that competence in the cognitive domain is not present until a critical developmental age is reached. However, because task performance may be determined by many variables, cognitive incompetence is difficult to establish. We have reviewed these variables elsewhere (Siegel, 1978, 1982; Siegel & Hodkin, 1982). The possibility always exists that the reason for behavioral incompetence lies in limitations imposed by a variety of variables, and that if those variables were appropriately manipulated, behavioral competence would be shown.

Discrimination procedures are useful for assessment because the experimenter need not use words to communicate the nature of the problem to the child, and the child need not use words to respond. This eliminates one confounding variable in the analysis of cognitive competence. However, evidence has been produced recently that under some conditions, young children will not show concept learning even with nonverbal discrimination learning procedures similar to the one described above (McLaughlin, 1981). As with the traditional assessment techniques, this negative finding raises again the issue of whether cognitive incompetence can be inferred from failure in a discrimination learning situation. The question becomes one of whether important confounding variables may be responsible for this behavioral incompetence as well. We suggest that this confounding is indeed possible, especially in light of accumulating developmental evidence from the literature of traditional discrimination learning in children. In this section of the chapter we discuss factors that may influence nonverbal discrimination learning of Piagetian and other more complex concepts. Prior to doing this, however, we consider learning of relative number as a good example of discrimination learning procedures used to assess Piagetian cognitive concepts.

In a typical task involving the discrimination learning of relative number (e.g., McLaughlin, 1981), the stimuli contain many stimulus dimensions. Each choice has a given number of dots, a given constant distance between dots (density or interdot distance), and a given length of dots (display length). The number of dots is the relevant stimulus dimension for the problem, whereas the dot density and display length are irrelevant dimensions. The dot displays are constructed such that across trials the correlation between dot density or display length and dot number is zero. Therefore, criterion performance can only be achieved if choice is consistently based on the relevant dimension. Discrimination learning problems like these have been termed multidimensional discrimination learning tasks (MDL) in the traditional learning literature. They are also called simple concept learning or concept utilization tasks.

In the standard MDL task, children are confronted with a series of trials with a choice between two stimuli, one of which is correct. The stimuli are constructed of two or more dimensions with, for example, two values on each dimension (e.g., large or small, red or green, triangle or circle as values along the dimensions size, color, and form, respectively). Typically, the choice stimuli presented on any trial are different along all dimensions, and because only two values can exist for each dimension, all possible values exist in the two choice stimuli for each trial. A trial might contain a choice between a small red triangle and a large green circle. The correct stimulus may be defined as the red stimulus, and in this case, color would be a relevant dimension and size and shape would be irrelevant. It would not matter if the red one was a circle or triangle, or large or small. Multidimensional discrimination problems are concept formation tasks in which the concept is defined along one dimension, such as color. For example, all choice stimuli that contain a red stimulus value are positive instances of the concept "red" and all others are negative instances.

One conspicuous difference between standard MDL procedures and the relative number discrimination task is that the former involves absolute cue learning, whereas the latter involves relational cue learning. That is, in standard MDL the child confronts a series of trials in which the correct choice alternative always contains the same cue across trials. In the relative number discrimination task, the correct choice alternative is defined with respect to a relation between trial choice alternatives; thus, the correct number on one trial may be incorrect on another trial. For example, if a child is reinforced for "more than," 4 is correct on the trial when the choice is between 2 and 4; however, 4 is incorrect when the choice is between 7 and 4. Because of the difference, findings derived from absolute MDL may not generalize to relational MDL and Piagetian concept learning. However, absolute MDL findings may implicate some important factors that can be explicitly tested in the relational MDL situation.

What follows is a review of some children's studies of absolute MDL in which we emphasize what they reveal about the cognitive processes that influence such learning. The perspective taken here is that these processes may be important in relational MDL, and therefore in the nonverbal assessment of cognitive competence using the discrimination learning paradigm.

Developmental Findings

Simple S-R discrimination theory (Spence, 1936) has been applied to MDL. However, adults display systematic trial-to-trial choice behavior that suggests the use of rules for responding and of hypothesis-testing strategies to arrive at the correct rule (Levine, 1966). Accordingly, complex MDL tasks have been the focus of considerable research aimed at elucidating the varied hypothesis-testing strategies employed by adults (cf. Levine, 1975) and children (Eimas, 1969, 1970; Gholson, Levine, & Phillips, 1972; Phillips & Levine, 1975). Because hypothesis testing is an important process in MDL, variables that affect hypothesis testing are relevant to our assessment issue. Failure to use appropriate hypothesis-testing strategies may lead to failure to show concept learning in absolute and relational MDL. Thus, age differences in learning a relative number task may reflect differences in hypothesis-testing strategies rather than differences in knowledge about the number concept.

Hypothesis-testing behavior changes systematically with age. Gholson et al. (1972) observed that kindergarten children evidence no hypothesis-testing behavior; the dominant strategy is position alternation. That is, the children's choices will randomly change across trials from one spatial location to another. Others have observed different response strategies by kindergarten children under different testing conditions (Cantor & Spiker, 1977; Kemler, 1978). For example, children at this age will also base their choices on some specific preferred stimulus dimension (e.g., color) across trials, ignoring the other less preferred dimensions, such as shape (Cantor & Spiker, 1977).

In contrast to kindergartners, second graders use hypothesis-testing strategies, but their strategies are not optimal. Their modal strategy is to test each constituent dimension one at a time, rejecting a dimension only when negative feedback is obtained (Phillips & Levine, 1975). This has been called "dimension checking" and is judged to occur if the following kind of trial-to-trial choice behavior is observed. Consider three trials on a concept formation task in which color is the relevant dimension (red is correct) and size and shape are irrelevant. On the first trial, the child selects a large red triangle and is correct, although the choice is based on size, not color. On the next trial, the child chooses a large blue triangle, again on the basis of large size, but is given negative feedback because red is correct. The dimension-checking strategy dictates a subsequent choice based on a new dimension (e.g., shape). Therefore, on the third trial, the child might choose a small red circle on the basis of the circular shape. This choice would not be logically inconsistent with the second-trial data, since the correct choice on that trial was a small red circle; but it would be inconsistent with information from Trial 1, where the small blue circle alternative was not correct. Thus, the dimension-checking strategy involves choosing dimensions one at a time, even though some of these choices are not optimal given past trial information.

Adolescents and adults tend to display "focusing," the optimal learning strategy in these problems, to reject as many hypotheses as possible (Phillips & Levine, 1975). In the example described earlier, focusing would be said to occur if after being nonreinforced for a choice of small red triangle, all of these dimensional values are rejected from future consideration as bases of choice, and only large blue square attributes were selected as correct unless specific negative feedback was received on subsequent trials.

The picture concerning kindergartners' inability to employ hypothesis-testing strategies has recently been complicated by Kemler (1978), who showed that under specific conditions kindergartners will generate a hypothesis for Trial n that is different from that for $n - 1$ if the latter hypothesis is rejected, and they will maintain the hypothesis if it is confirmed. Kemler's task was significantly different from the standard MDL task in that the choice stimuli were line drawings of human figures. Her materials were more concrete, and the problem task was presented to the children as a realistic problem embedded within a story. There were three, four, or five dimensions to the figures in different conditions of her problems, and the dimensions were different pieces of clothing. The subjects were to choose between two figures. Children were told that two twin school-aged girls were difficult to tell apart, so their teacher bought them different hats, necklaces, belts, colored hair ribbons, and glasses. Children were told that the twins often exchanged articles of clothing during the schoolday to fool their friends, but would retain one article of clothing so that the teacher could still tell them apart. The children were to figure out what the girls' secret article of clothing was. Under these realistic conditions, the kindergartners showed some hypothesis-testing behavior. Therefore, caution must be exercised in concluding that kindergartners never exercise rational hypothesis-testing behavior in MDL situations. The success of this task is an illustration of the importance of task demands in assessing cognitive development.

Several factors have been identified as important contributors to hypothesis-testing behavior in children, and thus to absolute MDL. Memory for past trial information has been one factor. Also, coding and recoding of stimulus cues may be important. Ability to shift attention from among the constituent stimulus dimensions can also influence performance, and knowledge of various strategies of learning is important. If a discrimination learning procedure designed to assess

Piagetian concept learning fails to take into consideration developmental changes in these factors, discrimination learning failure may be attributed to these confounding factors, and this attribution may make interpretation problematic.

Memory Factors

One of the task factors that has received attention in the study of MDL is memory. Do children fail to show optimal hypothesis-testing and discrimination learning behavior because they fail to remember past trial information? Research has been focused on two age differences: 8- versus 11-year-olds and 5-year-olds versus older children. This is so because, as described earlier, quantitative differences are seen between second graders (7- to 8-year-olds) and older children and adults, but more dramatic qualitative differences are presumed to exist between children in kindergarten (5-year-olds) and older children.

Eight- versus Eleven-Year-Olds. Eimas (1970) provided evidence for a memory factor in the nonoptimal hypothesis-testing behavior of second graders. Using a standard two-choice multidimensional discrimination task, he gave one group of second graders memory aids concerning the stimuli chosen on past trials, as well as the outcomes of those choices. The stimuli chosen on past trials were kept in the child's view, along with an indicator as to whether the choice was a positive or negative instance. Eimas suggested that 8-year-olds fail to employ focusing strategies not because of basic logical inferential processes, but rather because they would more easily forget the stimuli chosen on past trials as well as the outcome of those choices. As is consistent with the memory deficit hypothesis, children tested with this procedure were more likely to use a focusing strategy.

However, Eimas also produced evidence that a memory deficit was not the only factor. If children were given the same memory aid as described above except that when the child chose a negative instance, the positive instance was marked as positive instead of the chosen negative instance, focusing was enhanced even further. Thus, memory deficits may play a role in constraining children to use less than optimal learning strategies, but they are not the only factor. Another potent factor may be the recoding of a negative instance that is chosen on a particular trial into its complementary positive instance. Failure to recode in this manner is thought to disrupt plausible hypothesis generating and therefore optimal hypothesis testing. The lack of recoding ability postulated by Eimas may be nothing more than the child's failure to look at the positive instance and code its attributes after negative feedback. Thus, in order to use MDL techniques to assess conceptual competence with children it may be necessary to give the children memory aids about past trial outcomes and training in aspects of cue recoding, that is, looking at the positive instance on trials on which negative feedback is received. We will have more to say about the training of learning strategies later.

The Eimas data are not well supported, however, by Kemler's (1978) recent study. Using her very innovative story and game problem task (described above), she tested 7- and 8-year-olds with a two-choice three-, four-, or five-dimensional simultaneous discrimination with various attributes of clothing as relevant under memory-aided and unaided conditions. In the memory-aided condition, she used three cards on which pictures of the stimulus attributes could be placed. On a particular trial, when a child hypothesized that a specific article of clothing (e.g., a red hair ribbon) was the critical one, a representative of that attribute was placed on one of the three differently colored cards. In this case, a red hair ribbon would be moved from one card and placed on the card containing current hypothesized attributes. If the hypothesized attribute was disconfirmed, the child put the attribute representative on a different card. Therefore, there was a card for disconfirmed attributes, one for current hypothesized attributes, and one for attributes whose status was unknown. Young children tended to repeat recently rejected hypotheses by taking attributes from the disconfirmed card and placing them on the card meant to represent current hypotheses. Also, they were observed to alternate between stimulus attributes from the same dimension, for example, the two different colors for the hair ribbon. The memory aid did not enhance the optimality of learning strategies.

It is difficult to resolve the discrepancies between Eimas's positive finding and Kemler's negative finding except in terms of the interactive role of concreteness of materials used for stimuli, and/or the realism of the problem itself. Memory deficits may well be important contributing factors to learning strategies only when the materials and the situation are highly artificial. Indeed, the concreteness/realism of Kemler's task may have enhanced the characteristics of the stimuli to a point where additional memory aids were not needed. Alternatively, however, Kemler's memory aid task may have been so demanding for the children that they did not remember what the different cards meant. This would account for the tendency of Kemler's children to hypothesize attributes already rejected. Although Kemler says that instructions concerning the cards were "continually repeated throughout the problem series," it is not clear how often this was done, or if such instructions were interpreted correctly once problem solving began.

There appears, then, to be *some* direct evidence relating to the role of memory factors in determining the sophistication of learning strategies employed by second graders. Indirect evidence for this factor at this age comes from the interpretation given to the finding that verbalizing hypotheses seems to facilitate second graders' hypothesis testing. Phillips and Levine (1975) compared two different procedures for measuring hypothesis-testing strategies with second and sixth graders, one of which involved overt verbalization of hypotheses before each trial, and the other a nonverbal assessment of active hypotheses after each trial. They found that sixth graders generated hypotheses with equal skill in the conditions, but that second graders were most successful when they were required to verbalize their hypotheses. Specifically, second graders were more likely to rely on the dimension-checking strategy (discussed above) and less prone to choose on the basis of stimulus preferences. The facilitatory effect of verbalizing hypotheses was explained as a result of increases in the use of verbal rehearsal memory strategies. Phillips and Levine suggest that requiring children to verbalize their hypotheses made it more likely that children would spontaneously use verbal rehearsal strategies. An alternative to the rehearsal hypothesis is that the verbalizing explicitly necessitates verbal coding, and verbal coding itself enhances memory. The importance of this finding is that memory factors are implicated in the poor discrimination performance and non-optimal learning strategies of second graders. Requiring second graders to verbalize their trial-by-trial hypotheses facilitates performance.

In contrast to this indirect evidence for memory deficits in the hypothesis testing of second graders, Kemler (1978) has failed to find a facilitatory effect of verbalization of hypotheses. Recall that her task involved the more concrete/realistic story and game situation. Because of her special testing materials, the conflict with standard studies may reside in the already high probability of covert verbalization of hypotheses under her no-verbalization condition.

The experimental analysis of memory factors in second graders' hypothesis-testing behavior can be summarized as, by and large, indicating the presence of such a factor except in conditions where concrete materials and realistic problem situations are involved (Kemler, 1978). No within-experiment analysis has been conducted to test for the interaction between memory requirements and concreteness of materials that is suggested by the comparisons between studies.

Kindergarten Children. The evidence for the role of memory factors in kinder-gartners' much poorer reliance on hypothesis-testing strategies is less compelling than the corresponding evidence for second graders. Only one study bears on this issue directly; however, two studies are somewhat relevant.

Scholnick (1971) found no evidence of improvement in inferential behavior among kindergartners when she made available lists of either all the stimulus choices making up the problems, or all the stimulus values. Nor did she observe differences between conditions where the choice stimuli were presented simultaneously or successively. Scholnick argued that for kindergartners, as for second graders (Eimas, 1970), differences in inferential behavior may be a result of failures to effectively recode negative instances into their positive complementary counterparts. No one, however, has used the Eimas recoding procedure with children this young.

Indirect evidence relevant to the memory deficit hypothesis can again be found in the effect of overtly verbalized hypotheses on hypothesis-testing behavior and discrimination performance. Cantor and Spiker (1977) compared two groups of kindergartners on a standard two-choice three-dimensional simultaneous discrimination task in which size was relevant and color and form were irrelevant. Size was the nonpreferred dimension, as indicated by the fact that the children never stated a size attribute as a hypothesis after the first feedback trial. Thus, the kindergartners were being trained on a nonpreferred stimulus dimension. Contrary to the hypothesis, Cantor and Spiker report that only 29% of the kindergarten children who verbalized their hypotheses met criterion, whereas 69% did so under minimum verbalization conditions. As noted by Cantor and Spiker, verbalization would have facilitated performance if the relevant dimension was their children's preferred dimension, but under the present conditions, kindergarten children fixated on their initially named and preferred dimension. Across trials, their choices alternated randomly between the values of their preferred dimension throughout training. For example, if their preferred dimension was color, they would choose a large red triangle on the basis of red on a trial and a small blue square on the basis of blue on the next trial. Cantor and Spiker's failure to observe facilitating effects of verbalization is contradictory to Phillips and Levine's (1975) findings with second graders discussed earlier. If verbalization functions in the same way for kindergartners and second graders, one implication of this discrepancy is that different cognitive processes are limiting discrimination performance for these different age groups. For example, failure to recode negative instances may impair performance among kindergartners, whereas memory limitations about past trial information may impede second graders' performance. Cantor and Spiker did not provide pretraining for their kindergartners, as Phillips and Levine had done, so the discrepancy may also be a result of differential knowledge about the discrimination problem-solving situation; memory aids will perhaps be of limited value if the reason for poor discrimination learning is failure to understand the task demands of the discrimination learning situation.

Kemler (1978) also reported that kindergarten children in her study were unaffected by a requirement to verbalize their hypotheses. Again, as discussed earlier for second graders, the discrepancy here may lie in the very different kind of materials and task context used by Kemler.

The data from kindergarten children are too fragmentary for us to make strong generalizations, but kindergartners' problems with MDL tasks apparently do not lie in memory deficits alone. This contrasts with the data from second-grade children on memory factors, in which memory for past trial information and recoding of negative instances are apparently important factors.

The memory studies discussed above were conducted in the standard absolute MDL situation. Memory factors may be more important in relational discrimination situations, such as relative number discrimination, because more cognitive processing is required in these tasks. Absolute MDL requires that the child simply encode the cues present in the choice alternatives and integrate present cue information with past trial information. In relative number discrimination learning, the child must encode the cues from the two (or n) choices and then compare the relevant number cues from the choice alternatives in order to ascertain which alternative has more or less. By placing greater processing demands on the limited-capacity information processing system, the relative number discrimination task may enhance the likelihood that memory for past trial information will be lost. Thus, memory aids about past trial outcomes may be especially important for children in relational discrimination learning tasks, such as relative number discrimination.

Learning Strategy Variables

In addition to remembering past trial information, a young child must be able to perform several other subsidiary tasks in order to succeed in MDL, such as shifting choices away from disconfirmed preferred stimulus dimensions and integrating past trial information with present trial information. Evidence exists that young children are not as capable at these tasks, and thus special precautions need to be taken in designing discrimination learning experiments to measure conceptual competence.

Spiker and Cantor (1980) have suggested that the kindergartners' deficits on MDL tasks (when the nonpreferred dimension is relevant) may result from a reduced ability to analyze the stimuli perceptually and verbally into dimensions. Spiker and Cantor (1979) tested this possibility in a pretraining study that included a group of kindergarten children who received pretraining that involved (a) explicit naming of the stimulus dimensions used to construct the choice stimuli, and (b) grouping of similarly constructed multidimensional choice stimuli in a sorting task. That this pretraining did not enhance subsequent performance on a standard MDL task in which the children's preferred dimension was irrelevant casts doubt on the role of dimensional analysis in limiting kindergartners' MDL performance.

Facilitated MDL performance was observed for a group of kindergartners receiving training in which they were "shown" that a cue was correct across trials and that 100% successful performance could be attained. Most standard MDL studies include preliminary procedures designed to train such knowledge (e.g., Gholson et al., 1972), but observed deficiencies in hypothesis testing and discrimination performance may be due to ineffective pretraining of this kind and consequent forgetting by children of important problem characteristics.

Recently, evidence has been produced for the role of another factor in successful learning among kindergarten children. Toppino, Lee, Johnson, and Shishko (1979) tested the possibility that kindergarten children may be deficient in the ability to shift attention from one dimension to other dimensions. Logically, this skill is clearly important in that children in MDL situations will initially choose on the basis of a particular stimulus dimension, and if they do not eventually consider other dimensions as relevant when their presently chosen dimension is disconfirmed, they will not solve the problem. The question addressed by Toppino et al. was whether a general dimension-shifting strategy could be pretrained in kindergarten children. They gave kindergarten children in this study a unidimensional concept formation task using three four-valued dimensions after various types of pretraining. During concept formation, children were shown four different choice stimuli constructed from combinations of the four stimulus values from the three dimensions (color, number of arrow figures, and orientation of arrows), and were then shown a positive stimulus instance. Children were then to indicate which of the four choice stimuli the instance "went with." Verbal feedback about correctness of choice was given for each instance presented, and training continued with different positive instances until criterion level of performance was obtained for a particular concept. Concept-defining dimensions were selected to be nonpreferred by children, as indicated by a separate free-choice matching-to-sample task involving two-dimensional stimuli.

Prior to unidimensional concept learning, groups of children received different types of perceptual pretraining procedures, all of which involved same-different judgments about stimuli differing along only one dimension. The stimulus dimension that differentiated the stimuli was changed from problem to problem so that the children were trained to shift attention between dimensions in the pretraining procedure. Six different kinds of pretraining were given. Toppino et al. found that concept formation was facilitated whether or not the dimensions on which pre-training were given were actually used in the subsequent concept formation task, and whether or not the least preferred dimension, which was subsequently relevant, was included among the pretraining stimuli. In addition, the positive transfer was not observed for a group receiving pretraining in which only one dimension was relevant to pretraining performance. These investigators provide evidence for the importance of a general learning strategy of shifting attention between dimensions in MDL and concept utilization tasks. That positive transfer did not occur with the single-dimension pretraining suggests that the learning involves learning something other than that there is a consistent relationship between cues and feedback stimuli in the problems.

Thus, there is evidence pointing to the importance of knowing that there is a consistent relationship between cue and feedback across trials and that shifting from dimension to dimension is important to problem solving. In addition, Spiker and Cantor (1979) have shown that explicit training of hypothesis generation is im-portant to kindergartners' MDL performance. Spiker and Cantor's pretraining study included a group that received training to shift dimensions, and to generate verbal hypotheses with consideration being given to hypotheses disconfirmed in the past. Pretraining of this sort was effective in enhancing hypothesis testing and discrimi-nation learning.

In agreement with Spiker and Cantor's findings, Tunblin, Gholson, Rosenthal, and Kelley (1979) have shown that first-grade children could be trained to use simple strategies by observing a model use a dimension-checking strategy. However, modeling was ineffective when the model verbally described the use of dimension checking but did not demonstrate it.

The ability of young children to learn more efficient learning strategies, such as hypothesis testing, is not unlimited. Richman and Gholson (1978) presented to second graders a 10-minute videotape of a model who solved four discrimination problems and who stated the operations involved in focusing. These children actually did worse during subsequent MDL than second graders exposed to a model demonstrating and explaining dimension checking. Because the focusing strategy is not spontaneously employed until adolescence, Richman and Gholson argued that the cognitive capabilities necessary for the use of focusing must be present for the modeling to be effective. Presumably, the modeling of dimension checking was effective in the Tunblin et al. (1979) study because the first graders in that study were near the age at which dimension checking normally develops and therefore possessed the prerequisite cognitive abilities. The modeling techniques for training more efficient discrimination learning techniques used by Tunblin et al. (1979) and Richman and Gholson (1978) are limited by the fact that the children are given very limited exposure to training. Failures to find positive training effects of more advanced learning strategies may be attributed to this fact rather than to lack of prerequisite cognitive abilities.

In summary, a variety of factors are important in young childrens' discrimina-tion performance when nonpreferred dimensions are relevant. Inadequate learning can be partially attributed to poor knowledge concerning the consistency of cues and feedback embedded in the structure of these problems, poor spontaneous dimension-shifting behavior, or poor knowledge concerning the relevance of past trial information. There is some evidence that these component processes involved in MDL can be taught to young children. Such training is apparently necessary for these children.

These studies on memory factors and other learning strategies in absolute MDL suggest that nonverbal discrimination assessments using relative discrimination procedures should be designed to minimize the role of memory and learning strategies in causing failure to learn. A false negative error will result if it is concluded from behavioral incompetence that true conceptual incompetence is established. Failures to learn multidimensional discriminations may result for numerous reasons, such as poor memory for past trial information, deficient knowledge and/or utilization of dimension-shifting strategies in seeking the relevant dimension, and deficient knowledge concerning the relevance of past trial information to the generation of hypotheses. Without due regard for these strategy deficiencies, and component process incompetencies, the interpretation of concept learning failures is equivocal.

A recent experiment by McLaughlin (1981) is illustrative. Earlier reports indicated that preschool children could learn relative numerosity discriminations (Estes, 1976; Siegel, 1971a, 1971b). The claim is made by McLaughlin that preoperational children cannot learn a relative numerosity discrimination when relative number is the only relevant dimension and neither item density nor stimulus display length is relevant. This clearly involves training behavioral control to a nonpreferred stimulus dimension; hence, full consideration must be given to the factors discussed above. Because Gholson, O'Connor, and Stern (1976) have shown that preoperational children do not employ optimal hypothesis-testing learning strategies in MDL situations, we must be alert to the need for explicit pretraining techniques that will ensure comparability between preoperational and concrete-operational children on discrimination learning strategies. Even though McLaughlin pretrained the children on a four-dimensional discrimination, the pretraining was conducted with two preferred dimensions, color and form, as relevant. (Kofsky & Osler, 1967, found that color and form were preferred dimensions.) Children reached criterion on at least one of these pretraining problems. However, given the ease with which children can learn multidimensional discrimination problems when preferred dimensions are relevant, one can question whether this pretraining was effective in teaching dimension shifting or optimal hypothesis generating from past trial information. Without this assurance, the failures may result not from inability to judge by relative numerosity, but rather could be a result of nonoptimal discrimination learning strategies.

The point was made earlier that caution needs to be exercised in extrapolating from absolute MDL studies to Piagetian concept learning studies using relational MDL procedures. Specifically, the possibility must be recognized that using absolute cue learning problems in pretraining may not ensure that the effects of pretraining will generalize to relational MDL tasks. Nothing is known about the trainability of these learning strategies in relational cue problems or about transfer from training given in absolute cue problems to relational cue problems. The extra information processing required for successful relational cue learning, discussed above as involving absolute cue encoding and then recoding by comparing the absolute cues, may imply that transfer from absolute cue pretraining to relational cue learning may be limited. Pretraining in the use of strategies with relational learning problems or even pretraining with easier absolute learning problems first followed by slightly more difficult relational learning discrimination problems may be necessary. Further research along these lines will illuminate the constraints operating on the young preoperational child with respect to Piagetian concept learning.

Future Directions for Research

Several lines of research are suggested by the perspective proposed in this chapter. First, further explorations into the assumption that conceptual competence and language, memory, and learning strategies are independent is indicated. Ingenious experimental techniques are needed in order to separate these factors, and investigators of cognitive development must show sensitivity to these confoundings.

Second, the possibility that certain confounding cognitive processes in assessments may be differentially important with different techniques requires experimental verification. For example, the argument was advanced that relative MDL assessment techniques may involve greater information processing loads than absolute MDL tasks, and as a result may enhance the confounding influence of working memory limitations with regard to past trial information. Thus, if one chooses to unconfound a verbal assessment instrument by using a nonverbal relative MDL assessment device, one should know about the new confoundings entailed in the use of the MDL paradigm.

Third, the point of view taken in this chapter concerning the role of learning techniques in assessing conceptual competence entails the idea that cognitive developmental research should consist, at least in part, of learning tasks involving explicit external feedback. We cannot make any claims that these tasks simulate real-world concept acquisition situations. That is an empirical question. But the learning paradigm is one route of access to cognitive development. It should not be ignored and should be used to provide us with valuable information.

Summary

We have discussed the use of the learning paradigm as an alternative to the structural approach of assessing cognitive competence in children. It was argued, following Vygotsky, that the use of controlled learning experiences with children defines a zone of proximal development from within which the direction of cognitive development could be ascertained. In addition, we argued that the learning paradigm can reveal cognitive constraints that operate to limit cognitive development.

Learning studies conducted with very young children in the areas of quantitative concepts, dimensional concepts, and seriation illustrated cognitive competence when confounding linguistic factors are eliminated. Potential confounding factors in the use of the nonverbal learning paradigm were also discussed by reviewing the literature on children's multidimensional discrimination learning. We concluded that although a potentially important information processing difference may exist between this traditional MDL paradigm and the nonverbal learning assessment of Piagetian concepts (i.e., absolute learning vs. relational learning), several cognitive constraints operate in young children that are independent of the conceptual competence under investigation and that limit interpretation of failures to show discrimination learning. Specifically, memory for past trial information, inadequate knowledge about the trial-by-trial consistency of cue-feedback relationships, inability to shift attention between the stimulus dimensions making up the stimuli, and the use of nonoptimal, and in some cases inadequate, learning strategies constrain discrimination learning among young children.

Studies designed to train competence in these subskills were reviewed, and evidence suggests that such training is effective in facilitating discrimination performance among young children. We argued that studies of young children designed to make use of the nonverbal discrimination learning paradigm to assess conceptual competence must pretrain competence in these task subskills and make procedural allowances for these constraints so that discrimination learning failures can be unambiguously interpreted.

Recently, Gholson and Beilin (1979) have argued that nonoptimal learning strategies are constrained by stage-related processes, and that training of these learning strategies would meet with only limited success. For example, they argue that attentional centration and inadequate understanding of class inclusion are among the thought processes limiting the preoperational child's discrimination learning performance. Contrary to this hypothesis, we have seen in our discussion that the training of dimensional attention shifting (Toppino et al., 1979) and proper understanding of class inclusion (Judd & Mervis, 1979) can be affected in young children by special techniques. Therefore, we suggest that precautionary steps, in the form of appropriate pretraining regimes, can be successfully taken to ensure that prerequisite cognitive processes and knowledge are possessed by very young children, with the consequence that (a) failures to learn discriminations can be unambiguously attributed to fundamental conceptual incompetence and (b) greater knowledge will be acquired about the particular cognitive constraints operating to limit the outcome of learning experiences that have the potential to stimulate cognitive development.

Reference Note

1. Smith, L. B. *Young children's understanding of attributes and dimensions: A comparison of conceptual and linguistic measures.* Paper presented at the Psychonomic Society, Philadelphia, November 1981.

References

Borke, H. Piaget's view of social interaction and the theoretical construct of empathy. In L. S. Siegel & C. J. Brainerd (Eds.), *Alternatives to Piaget: Critical essays on the theory*. New York: Academic Press, 1978.

Brown, A. L., & French, L. A. The zone of potential development: Implications for intelligence testing in the year 2000. *Intelligence*, 1979, *3*, 255–273.

Bullock, M., & Gelman, R. Numerical reasoning in young children: The ordering principle. *Child Development*, 1977, *48*, 427–434.

Cantor, J., & Spiker, C. Dimensional fixation with introtracts in kindergarten children. *Bulletin of the Psychonomic Society*, 1977, *10*, 169–171.

Eimas, P. D. A developmental study of hypothesis behavior and focusing. *Journal of Experimental Child Psychology*, 1969, *8*, 160–172.

Eimas, P. D. Effects of memory aids on hypothesis behavior and focusing in young children and adults. *Journal of Experimental Child Psychology*, 1970, *10*, 319–326.

Estes, K. W. Nonverbal discrimination of more and fewer elements by children. *Journal of Experimental Child Psychology*, 1976, *21*, 393–405.

Estes, W. K. Learning theory and intelligence. *American Psychologist*, 1974, *29*, 740–749.

Gholson, B., & Beilin, H. A developmental model of human learning. In H. W. Reese & L. P. Lipsitt (Eds.), *Advances in child development and behavior* (Vol. 13). New York: Academic Press, 1979.

Gholson, B., Levine, M., & Phillips, S. Hypotheses, strategies, and stereotypes in discrimination learning. *Journal of Experimental Child Psychology*, 1972, *13*, 423–446.

Gholson, B., O'Connor, J., & Stern, I. Hypothesis sampling systems among preoperational and concrete operational kindergarten children. *Journal of Experimental Child Psychology*, 1976, *21*, 61–76.

Glaser, R. The future of testing: A research agenda for cognitive psychology and psychometrics. *American Psychologist*, 1981, *36*, 923–936.

Gollin, E. S., Moody, M., & Schadler, M. Relational learning of a size concept. *Developmental Psychology*, 1974, *10*, 101–108.

Greco, P., & Bideau, J. Les opérations cognitives et leur développement chez l'enfant: Rapport de synthèse. *Enfance*, 1980, *45*, 105–113.

Griep, C., & Gollin, E. S. Interdimensional transfer of an ordinal solution strategy. *Developmental Psychology*, 1978, *14*, 437–448.

Judd, S. A., & Mervis, C. B. Learning to solve class-inclusion problems: The roles of quantification and recognition of contradiction. *Child Development*, 1979, *50*, 163–169.

Kemler, D. G. Patterns of hypothesis testing in children's discriminative learning: A study of the development of problem solving strategies. *Developmental Psychology*, 1978, *14*, 653–673.

Kofsky, E., & Osler, S. F. Free classification in children. *Child Development*, 1967, *38*, 927–937.

Larsen, G. Y. Methodology in developmental psychology: An examination of research on Piagetian theory. *Child Development*, 1977, *48*, 1160–1166.

Levine, M. Hypothesis behavior by humans during discrimination learning. *Journal of Experimental Psychology*, 1966, *71*, 331–338.

Levine, M. *A cognitive theory of learning*. Hillside, NJ: Erlbaum, 1975.

Marshark, M. Lexical marking and the acquisition of relational size concepts. *Child Development*, 1977, *48*, 1049–1051.

McLaughlin, J. A. Development of children's ability to judge relative numerosity. *Journal of Experimental Child Psychology*, 1981, *31*, 103–114.

Miller, S. S. Nonverbal assessment of Piagetian concepts. *Psychological Bulletin*, 1976, *83*, 405–430.

Phillips, S., & Levine, M. Probing for hypotheses with adults and children: Blank trials and introtracts. *Journal of Experimental Psychology: General*, 1975, *104*, 327–354.

Richman, S., & Gholson, B. Strategy modeling, age, and information processing efficiency. *Child Development*, 1978, *26*, 58–70.

Saltzman, A. L., & Townsend, D. J. Can children learn to communicate in a word-pair task: Evidence against egocentrism. *Developmental Psychology*, 1980, *16*, 83–84.

Scholnick, E. K. Effects of stimulus availability on children's inferences. *Child Development*, 1971, *42*, 183–194.

Siegel, L. S. The sequence of development of certain number concepts in preschool children. *Developmental Psychology*, 1971, *5*, 357–361. (a)

Siegel, L. S. The development of certain number concepts. *Developmental Psychology*, 1971, *5*, 362–363. (b)

Siegel, L. S. The development of the concept of seriation. *Developmental Psychology*, 1972, *6*, 135–137. (a)

Siegel, L. S. The development of concepts of numerical magnitude. *Psychonomic Science*, 1972, *28*, 245–246. (b)

Siegel, L. S. The role of spatial arrangements and heterogeneity in the development of concepts of numerical equivalence. *Canadian Journal of Psychology*, 1973, *27*, 351–355.

Siegel, L. S. Heterogeneity and spatial factors as determinants of numeration ability. *Child Development*, 1974, *45*, 532–534. (a)

Siegel, L. S. The development of number concepts: Ordering and correspondence operations and the role of length cues. *Developmental Psychology*, 1974, *10*, 907–912. (b)

Siegel, L. S. The relationship of language and thought in the preoperational child. In L. S. Siegel & C. J. Brainerd (Eds.), *Alternatives to Piaget: Critical essays on the theory*. New York: Academic Press, 1978.

Siegel, L. S. The development of quantity concepts: Perceptual and linguistic factors. In C. J. Brainerd (Ed.), *Children's logical and mathematical cognition*. New York: Springer-Verlag, 1982.

Siegel, L. S., & Goldstein, A. G. Conservation of number in young children: Recency versus relational response strategies. *Developmental Psychology*, 1969, *1*, 128–130.

Siegel, L. S., & Hodkin, B. The garden path to the understanding of cognitive development: Has Piaget led us into the poison ivy? In S. Modgil & C. Modgil (Eds.), *Jean Piaget: Consensus and controversy*. London: Holt, Rinehart & Winston, 1982.

Siegel, L. S., McCabe, A. E., Brand, J., & Matthews, J. Evidence of the understanding of class inclusion in preschool children: Linguistic factors and training effects. *Child Development*, 1978, *49*, 688-693.

Spence, K. W. The nature of discrimination learning in animals. *Psychological Review*, 1936, *43*, 427-449.

Spiker, C. C., & Cantor, J. H. Factors affecting hypothesis testing in kindergarten children. *Journal of Experimental Child Psychology*, 1979, *28*, 230-248.

Spiker, C. C., & Cantor, J. H. The effects of stimulus type, training, and chronological age on children's identification and recoding of multidimensional stimuli. *Journal of Experimental Child Psychology*, 1980, *30*, 144-158.

Surber, C. F. Utility of "simplification" as a developmental research strategy. *Child Development*, 1979, *50*, 571-574.

Toppino, T. C., Lee, N. D., Johnson, P. J., & Shishko, S. A. Effect of pretraining on children's concept performance with non-preferred relevant dimensions: Evidence for the role of attentional strategies. *Developmental Psychology*, 1979, *15*, 190-196.

Tunblin, A., Gholson, B., Rosenthal, T. L., & Kelley, J. E. The effects of gestural demonstration, verbal narration, and their combination on the acquisition of hypothesis-testing behaviors by first grade children. *Child Development*, 1979, *50*, 254-256.

Vygotsky, L. S. *Mind in society: The development of higher psychological processes.* Cambridge, MA: Harvard University Press, 1978.

Watson, J. S., & Danielson, G. An attempt to shape bidimensional attention in 24 month old infants. *Journal of Experimental Child Psychology*, 1969, *7*, 467-478.

Watson, J. S., Hayes, L. A., & Vietze, P. Bidimensional sorting in preschoolers with an instrumental learning task. *Child Development*, 1979, *15*, 1178-1183.

3. A Learning Analysis of Spatial Concept Development in Infancy

C. Donald Heth and Edward H. Cornell

Students of learning and students of development have a similar problem: characterizing change in the behavior of an organism. In both domains of inquiry the problem has been so intractable that rather severe limiting assumptions have been required. Although these assumptions were undoubtedly viewed originally as tactical decisions in the emergence of each discipline, over the years they have resulted in two quite different approaches to the study of behavior change.

The orienting attitudes that characterize the study of learning are well known. The historical commitment of learning theory to behaviorism resulted in the specification of change in terms of overt performance. Only a few determinants of change were subject to analysis; maturation was not learning, nor were changes due to physiology. Furthermore, early models of what was changing were quite simple, involving connections between events or between responses and events.

Developmental psychologists have generally included maturation, experience, and the interaction of the two as broad determinants of changes. However, the changes observed in young children are so great and so complex that questions regarding the processes of change were largely deferred in favor of more detailed descriptions of the organism involved. Compilation of age-related abilities was emphasized in developmental laboratories, and "stage" served as a useful heuristic for the organization of temporal patterns of phenomena. Characterizations of the mechanisms of change were by and large borrowed from other domains of inquiry, for example, "assimilation" from biology and "reward" from the learning tradition within psychology.

The research reported herein was supported by Grant A0267 to E. Cornell from the Natural Sciences and Engineering Research Council of Canada.

In addition, there has been a fundamental distinction between the two with regard to the scale of analysis. Learning theory is typically confined to particular episodic experiences; developmental psychology, in contrast, is dedicated to the study of ontogenetic and sometimes phylogenetic events.

The different approaches, assumptions, and scales of analysis of learning and developmental research have tended to obscure a common concern with psychological change. Nevertheless, this common concern is sometimes apparent when both disciplines converge on similar problems. One of these convergences, the role of errors in producing change, is the focus of this chapter. We have chosen this issue because errors and their consequences played an important role historically in learning theory, from Thorndike's law of effect to modern conceptions of concept learning. Similarly, discrepancy between expected and observed outcomes has played a fundamental role in several theories of cognitive development. Thus, the issue of how individuals learn from errors provides an excellent framework for an examination of the relationship between learning theory and developmental psychology.

Our thesis is that there are conceptual and methodological affinities between the two disciplines. These affinities are especially salient in the context of developments in learning theory over the last decade. It appears to us that, at present, there exists significant promise of fundamental synergisms between the two disciplines. We wish to highlight this possibility by examining the role of error information in infants' learning.

Accordingly, our chapter has two main sections. In the first, we discuss certain pivotal issues that characterize the relationship between learning and developmental methodology. We highlight some of the developments that have recently had a strong impact on learning theory, and examine related themes in developmental psychology. We intend this discussion as a prologue to an actual illustration, which forms the second section, in which we present a learning analysis of infants' conceptual ability in a spatial problem.

The Psychologies of Learning and Development

The orienting attitudes of traditional learning theory have been periodically reviewed from a developmental perspective (e.g., Stevenson, 1972; White, 1970). We wish to augment these reviews with a discussion of three general observations. One of these is a reassertion of the fundamental domain of learning theory; for this, we concentrate on the distinction between state and process in the psychology of learning. Our second is a general comment on the way in which state is typically defined and assessed in contemporary learning theory. Finally, we wish to call attention to many recent discoveries in fundamental phenomena of learning that have radically altered the profile of theoretical descriptions of learning. In each of these sections, we will first examine the issue in the context of learning theory, and then try to draw a general reprise relative to issues in developmental psychology.

State and Process in Developing Systems

Any analysis of change begs the question of what is changing. The field of learning has seen a plethora of descriptions of what is learned during various types of experience. Perhaps for this reason, learning has been difficult to define even in methodological surveys of research.

Rozeboom (1965), however, has noted one common thread. Learning has always concerned itself with changes in a special class of psychological variable that Rozeboom terms a "state" variable. Briefly, state variables are, according to Rozeboom's treatment, variables of relatively long temporal constancy that determine the manner in which input variables map to output. This mapping, in turn, is a "process" variable, which in traditional learning theory would relate terms such as stimulus and behavior. Rozeboom likens the state variables of an organism to the program of a computer. Process variables are analogous to the relationship between input and output of the computer. Note that the relationship is wholly determined by the more enduring program. In the psychological domain, Rozeboom (1965) describes his distinction in the following way:

> Epigrammatically, an individual's process properties are what he is doing and what is happening to him or in him, whereas his state properties are what he is. In particular, dispositional attributes characterized in terms of what process properties the individual would have were he to be exposed to a certain input condition . . . are (in general) state properties which persist even when these input conditions are not in fact present. (p. 341)

Learning, in this context, represents a change in psychological state variables. This is reflected in both the usual learning stipulation that changes due to learning are relatively permanent, and the proviso that learning involves changes in the potential for a given behavior. Learning theory has, whatever its commitment to any particular model of state, concerned itself with the specification of the conditions under which states will change.

This methodological partitioning of process and state variables permitted the conceptual distinction of two types of variation in behavior. One class of variation is the local fluctuation of a response, which closely matches the prevailing stimulation. In this category, for example, would be the sudden appearance of an orienting reaction in response to a novel stimulus. This, of course, would represent a process variable in Rozeboom's scheme. Another type of variation could be long-term changes in the functional character of these process variables. We might observe, for example, that at the end of some experiment, a formerly novel stimulus results not in an orienting reaction, but some other response, such as salivation. As before, the functional relationship between the stimulus and the salivation response is a process variable; the relationship itself is different by virtue of a change.

The advantage of this approach is illustrated in Figure 3-1. The symbols O_1, O_2, and O_3 are different behaviors or outcomes observed by the theorist. Ideally, these could be functionally related to certain input conditions, I_1, I_2, and I_3. The upper panel of Figure 3-1 illustrates the prima facie difficulty with a description of the organism solely in such process terms. An organism might exhibit an orienting

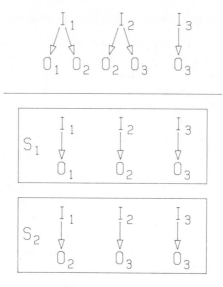

Figure 3-1. Process and state descriptions. Upper panel: Process descriptions without state delineation; I_1, I_2, and I_3 refer to input conditions and O_1, O_2, and O_3 refer to outcome observations. Lower panel: Process descriptions delineated by state descriptions; S_1 and S_2 denote specific dispositional states.

reaction (O_1) to a stimulus (I_1) at the start of an experiment and a salivary reaction (O_2) at the end. The two different outcomes present the theorist with a complex process description.

The state/process solution to this difficulty is illustrated in the bottom panel of Figure 3-1. The theorist partitions different input-outcome relationships into different dispositional states. Therefore, I_1 is functionally related to O_1 when the organism is in state S_1 and is functionally related to O_2 when the subject is in state S_2. The learning theorist adopts the assumption that the organism exhibits different states at different times in the experiment.

Indeed, the bulk of learning theory addresses the conditions that govern these changes in the state exhibited by the organism. There are a number of ways to formally represent how such changes occur. In the most abstract sense, one could consider a theory of learning as a set of permutations or transformations through which a set of states is mapped onto another set of states. Suppose, for example, that we specify a set of three states: S_1, S_2, and S_3. At any given time, we assume that the subject exhibits or possesses one of these states. A learning operation, then, could be considered a transformation of the elements of the original set. We could, for example, define an operation called "reinforcement," which permutes the elements as follows: $S_1 \rightarrow S_2$, $S_2 \rightarrow S_1$, $S_3 \rightarrow S_3$. Thus, if the organism is in state S_1 at the time of reinforcement, it is in state S_2 after the operation. Some possible transitions are illustrated in Figure 3-2. The transformations need not, of course, be completely determined; they could also be probabilistically defined.

To summarize, we wish to present as the basis of our later analysis the view that learning involves the specification of transitions or permutations of underlying dispositional states. These states determine the pattern of input-output correlations that govern the moment-by-moment behavior of the learner.

Reprise. A distinction between state and process is not foreign to developmental psychology. Indeed, in a recent discussion Wilcox and Katz (1981) present a similar analysis in the context of a systems theory approach to development. Their framework is similar to that depicted in Figure 3-1. Differences in input-outcome relationships introduce a "one-to-many" relationship between input and output, because a single environmental input does not have a unique consequence. Wilcox and Katz argue that such a relationship must be rejected if psychological theories are to functionally predict behavior. They suggest developmental states as mediators of input-outcome relationships and propose development as the transition between states.

To envision this schema from a developmental perspective, consider a baby whose task is to search for an object hidden in one of two containers. The concealment of an object within reach is an input to the system. The baby's response to this input, such as reaching with the right hand to the rightmost container, is a process variable mediated by the baby's current state (schemes, organized response dispositions, etc.). Indeed, our description of the state is determined by the form of this input-outcome correspondence. If, for example, the baby opens either container randomly after seeing the object hidden in one, we would ascribe to the baby a particular state description (e.g., "the naive state"). At a later time, the same input conditions might generate a different outcome. We might now observe the baby consistently approaching the container where the object was seen to be concealed. Hence, we postulate a transition from the naive state to some other, such as "discriminative search" (Cornell, 1981).

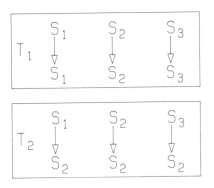

Figure 3-2. State transformation rules. S_1, S_2, and S_3 refer to specific states, such as those defined in Figure 3-1; T_1 and T_2 refer to transformation descriptions that map each state onto another state.

The Specification of States

We have argued for a conceptual view of learning theory that distinguishes the potential for a given behavior (a state) from the actual input-output correspondence governing behavior at any given time (a process). Clearly, the former must be inferred from the latter, given the historical commitment of learning theory to behaviorism. Indeed the necessity of such inference was implicit in our statement that states determine specific processes. This immediately raises the question: What process variables are to be used in identifying specific states?

Historically, the answer looks deceptively simple. State variables in the learning tradition have commonly been inferred from fairly narrowly defined stimulus-response correspondences. We might describe a dog as "conditioned" (i.e., assert that a state transition has occurred) when we observe a salivary response like that to the unconditioned stimulus. Indeed, the method is so prevalent that the outside observer is likely to confuse the description of process with the description of the state. If, for example, the observation is of a stimulus-response process, the state description might be framed solely in terms of stimulus-response dispositions. Such an exact correspondence is valid in only a few learning theories, however; and even for these theories it is only approximately correct (e.g., Hilgard & Bower, 1981). Learning is not restricted to any one theoretical scheme, as evidenced by Tolmanian alternatives to Thorndike.

Although theoretical diversity can be readily appreciated in the abstract, a more general issue is often overlooked. Specific process variables are only the indices of state variables. Learning theories vary widely in the way states are characterized. If latitude is permitted in the state descriptions of the organism, we suggest there should be corresponding latitude in the types of process variables used to index learning.

Attitudes that embody this suggestion are evident in contemporary approaches in learning theory. As recently expressed by Rescorla and Holland (1976), "If our interest is in identifying whether the organism has been modified by the event relations arranged [at the time of acquisition], then *any* index behavior is acceptable" (p. 173). Addressing the traditional descriptions of classical conditioning, Rescorla and Holland (1976) note:

> Of course, one may choose to restrict the word "conditioning" to some subset of the cases here discussed. We are free to place additional restrictions on the types of [unconditioned stimulus] and the types of behavioral changes that are acceptable instances of "conditioning". But then it will only be necessary to find another name for the many other instances of learning about relations that are currently being investigated. Moreover, in our view the placing of such supposedly pretheoretical restrictions can only serve to retard the development of an adequate theory of conditioning. Such restrictions may well grow out of a theory but surely should not precede it. (p. 173)

In this vein, modern conceptions of state transitions include diverse theoretical descriptions of state properties (e.g., Estes, 1973; Seligman & Johnston, 1973). In these treatments, different process variables constitute an organism's current state, and different operations are used to assess "learning." Consequently, reviews of the learning literature since Kimble's (1961) include procedures and paradigms that depart from the traditional Pavlovian and Thorndikian operations. For example, such phenomena as habituation, imprinting, latent inhibition, pseudoconditioning, sensitization, and the learning of intrinsic relations between stimuli are the grist for analysis within Rescorla and Holland's (1976) framework. A broad definition of learning invites substantive insights from these phenomena.

Reprise. In our view, developmental inquiry could profit from a similar liberalization of the construct of learning. Failure to recognize latitude in the specification of state can lead to an unnecessarily narrow theoretical perspective. For example, a recent review of infant learning by Sameroff and Cavanaugh (1979) begins with the assertion that the current usage of the term *learning* "is synonymous with conditioning." By "conditioning" Sameroff and Cavanaugh apparently mean the connection of stimuli and responses. This equating of an important process variable of the conditioning paradigm with the state description itself leads Sameroff and Cavanaugh to questionable conclusions. For example, they consider a heart-rate conditioning study by Stamps and Porges (1975) as anomalous. Stamps and Porges used a trace conditioning procedure, in which the onset and termination of the conditioned stimulus (CS) occur prior to the unconditioned stimulus (US). They found no discernible conditioned response during the CS itself, but did observe a reaction when the US was omitted. In the context of the traditional description of learning as a change in the reaction to a stimulus, Sameroff and Cavanaugh regard this as an empirical dilemma for "S-R classical conditioning," because acquisition and extinction could not be demonstrated in terms of behavior during the CS. Partly because of these results, Sameroff and Cavanaugh suggest that "awaiting a clear demonstration of classical conditioning in the newborn may no longer be worthwhile" (p. 362).

Without taking issue with their more general conclusion, we feel that Sameroff and Cavanaugh are unduly restrictive with respect to the operational specification of conditioning. If one can demonstrate that the response Stamps and Porges observed to the omission of the US depends on pairing the CS and US, then we would argue that it represents a valid demonstration of classical conditioning. Indeed, it is noteworthy that Pavlov himself used this technique to measure a CS. Classical conditioning should be regarded as a change in state brought about by relations between events. Whether the states are S-R in nature or S-S is a different question. Thus, we would suggest that a variety of converging operations be used to assess the efficacy of the Pavlovian conditioning paradigm with respect to infants. Relations between stimuli may indeed alter the newborn's state, provided our assessment of state is sufficiently sensitive.

The more general point is that the specification of state in the developing child need not be restricted to traditional descriptors that were at one time useful to learning theory. A learning analysis of development seeks a relationship between experience and state changes. The analysis is no less valid or valuable if the state is defined in nontraditional ways. For example, a spatial concept could very well be defined as a particular sequence of choices. In principle, it could be defined in such specific terms as "one correct search, followed by two incorrect, followed by three correct." A learning analysis would attempt to relate the acquisition of this type of state to specific experiences. Although the description proposed above might not itself prove useful, it is entirely possible that one based on a sequence of responses might be more amenable to an experimental analysis than one that assesses only one search response. A useful state description might also be one that specifies a certain probability of success, and hence is identifiable only over a series of searches.

To provide a concrete example of the worth of this position, consider the topic of concept learning. There are now many demonstrations that performance in such conceptual tasks as conservation can be enhanced by specific experiences (Brainerd, 1973, 1978). However, the interpretation of these findings is hotly contested. The Genevans in particular have argued that improvement in such tasks cannot be considered as true development unless certain criteria are met. Briefly, such improvements must be lasting, generalizable, and represent new, more complex state properties (Piaget, 1964). As other reviewers have pointed out, these criteria imply an idiosyncratic state description and place severe restrictions on evidence for transition between states (e.g., Brainerd, 1978). In particular, they exclude more molecular state descriptors under the guise of theoretical rigor.

This exclusion is unfortunate in at least two respects. First, the types of performance changes of direct interest to some developmental psychologists and educators are not necessarily the comprehensive changes suggested by the Genevans (e.g., Inhelder, Sinclair, & Bovet, 1974), but rather are the more particular competencies demonstrated as children master componential skills. Second, it is noteworthy that Genevan theory has been generally unsuccessful in isolating the conditions that facilitate concept development. Perhaps a different level of analysis would be more successful.

Against this background, analyses of learning in concept development have much to offer. The chief characteristic of any learning analysis is that it relates state changes to experience. Hence it concentrates on that part of the system that is amendable to modification and control. The chief responsibility of an educator, after all, is not to bide time until his or her students develop, but rather to impart knowledge and induce cognitive changes through some sort of programmatic intervention. Second, learning analyses, especially the more liberalized viewpoint (e.g., Rescorla & Holland, 1976), permit the empirical identification of state transitions without a commitment to any one theoretical description of stable psychological attributes. Hence they allow for both molar and molecular analyses of change. Finally, several mathematical learning theories allow for formal specification of the underlying process of change. We examine the question of state changes in the next section.

Determinants of State Transitions

Although the description of state has played a large role in learning theory, the central focus has always been on conditions that produce changes in these states.

The historical highlights of the field have been those theoretical schemes that manage to group together certain manipulations as effecting change. It would not be feasible to examine each of these efforts here, but it is instructive to contrast two theories, each at one of the endpoints in this history.

As is well known, Thorndike's (1898) original investigation of problem solving led him to conclude that such higher mental phenomena were derivative from the formation of simple habits. These in turn were established through the consequences of a particular action. Thorndike's contempt for cognitive explanations of habit formation is also well known. Nevertheless, simplicity in the operations affecting habit formation did not, for Thorndike, necessarily imply simplicity in the underlying state. Indeed, his successors were to use habits so inventively that their functional difference from expectations and cognition is slight (Kendler, 1952). What does set Thorndike apart from a more "cognitive" theory is the emphasis his theory places on the environmental determination of state transitions. The subject's experience (e.g., a reward following a correct response) accounts for most, if not all, of the determination of state.

In contrast, a recent theory of associative learning by Wagner (1978) attributes a substantial role to the state itself in the determination of transition. Specifically, the probability that two events will be associated is assumed to depend on their conjoint presence in short-term memory. Representation in short-term memory is in turn governed by such factors as prior association of an event with retrieval cues, previous exposure to the event, and the absence of competition for memorial processing. According to this model, contiguity is not sufficient to produce association; association depends necessarily on certain state properties.

Several factors motivated views such as those embodied in Wagner's model. An early influence was noncontinuity discrimination theory, in which attentional and other states govern the acquisition of responses (Levine, 1975). More recently, Kamin (1969) demonstrated that prior conditioning to one element of a compound could attentuate or "block" conditioning to another. Lubow and Moore (1959) found that prior nonreinforced exposures of a conditioning stimulus altered its conditionability. Seligman, Maier, and Solomon (1971) reported severe retardation of avoidance learning when subjects were given prior inescapable shock. Wagner, Rudy, and Whitlow (1973) observed that the presentation of unexpected posttrial episodes could interfere with conditioning. Biologically oriented theorists noted many instances where genotypic characteristics limited transitions (Shettleworth, 1972).

The impact of these demonstrations has been a richer theoretical approach to the specification of transitions. Whereas classical learning theory sought the determinants of transition solely in the structure of the environment, contemporary approaches are much more interactionistic. Within the latter view, an important determinant of change in state is the state itself. This concern with the role of state in the determination of transition has proceeded apace with the more liberalized description of state properties discussed in the previous section. Thus, at the time when theorists were increasingly challenged to recognize the contribution of state properties to transitions of states, their models also reflected a willingness to accept various operations on the specification of states.

Reprise. Historically, developmental psychology has been more receptive than classical learning theory to interactive explanations of state changes. For example, consider the topic of spatial cognition. In this domain, an important developmental state is one characterized by the knowledge that objects can be located in different places at different times. Because this concept is fundamental to our notion of space, its acquisition has been extensively studied. One task that is frequently used in this research requires that infants search for displaced objects. We will use this task as an example.

Suppose we structure the search task in the following way: Several hidings are in one constant place, a cup to the infant's left. As noted in our earlier discussion, the hiding in one location is an input to which we note a corresponding output. What is the stable state variable that governs this correspondence? Does it change? If so, what produces these changes?

We can address these questions by a simple transfer test. After establishing a stable response, we now, in full view of the infant, shift the object to a new location, a box to the infant's right. This procedure is the traditional test for the "Stage IV" error in the development of object permanence (Piaget, 1937/1954). The baby's response to this shift can tell us a great deal about his or her knowledge of spatial relationships. For example, if on the first transfer test the child searches in the previously correct location (the cup), we might conclude that he or she does not realize that objects can exist in different places at different times. Search processes instead appear to be guided by state properties that are dominated by previously successful searches. On subsequent searches, the baby could shift to the currently correct location (the box). Consistently correct searches could reflect two things: (a) the child may have learned to inhibit the old response and/or learned to approach the container where the object is now found; (b) the child understands that objects can be in different places at different times.

In a molecular analysis, both of these possibilities represent transitions to new states. The first is to a state analogous to the original in that the input-output correspondence is governed by cues associated with search. That is, the child chooses a container on the basis of his or her history of previous choices. The observation of the hidings is irrelevant to choice in this state. However, in the second state, the input-output correspondence is governed by cues associated with the act of hiding. The child chooses the container where the occlusion occurred.

Returning to the bottom panel of Figure 3-1, we let the initial searches to the cup on the left define S_1. Consistent search in the box on the right after the displacement defines transfer to some other state. Given such an observation, how can we explain this transfer? We suggest four types of variables affecting state transitions.

Endogenous Determinants. The first type of variable is based on the state properties themselves, producing apparently *endogenous* change. Within this framework, part of the state description is a restriction on the set of possible transformations. For example, although a theory might specify rules T_1, T_2, T_3, and T_4, one particular state might permit only T_3 to occur. The state of the organism would therefore sharply determine additional transformations. Maturation, differentiation, and hierarchic organization reflect such constraints on transition (cf. Werner, 1957).

Input Determinants. Another factor is the *input* variable alone. External stimulation could modify developmental states regardless of any discernible output. Sokolov's (1963) theory of habituation and Gibson's (1969) theory of perceptual learning are good exemplars. In Sokolov's theory, repeated presentations of a stimulus establish its internal representation. A child's subsequent reaction to a novel stimulus is held to be determined by the discrepancy between the novel stimulus and the internal representation. In the framework of Figure 3-1, the repeated stimulation is an input variable. The orienting reaction is governed by the status of an internal representation. Hence, the orienting reaction is a process variable, and the representation a state variable. By postulating the construction of a representation based upon stimulation alone, Sokolov advocates the view that input variables determine state transitions. A similar analysis can be applied to Gibson's (1969) theory, in which attentive mechanisms are shaped by exploration of the environment.

Output Determinants. A third factor is related to the *output* variable. Transitions between states are held to depend intrinsically upon the specific values of the outcome variable—that is, on what the child does. This viewpoint has played a central role in many theories of concept formation (Levine, 1975).

Interactive Determinants. Of course, theories of developmental change are much too sophisticated to accept models in which there are single determinants of change. These may be used to illustrate extreme positions, but they cannot be complete theories of change. Maturation cannot occur in a vacuum, and experience always operates on a biological substrate, so a realistic theory must elucidate the interaction.

Interactions between input, output, and state could result in two types of transition. In one view, transitions between states are a joint function of *input* and *state* variables. Imprinting exhibits state transitions resulting from certain interactions between repeated exposures to the imprinting object and the endogenous state of the organism. Alternatively, transitions could be a function of *state* and *output* variables. Sameroff and Cavanaugh (1979) advocate versions of both of these approaches, based on the concept of biological preparedness (Seligman, 1970). The general idea is that the efficacy of Pavlovian or instrumental conditioning paradigms will depend on existing structures, such as perceptual sensitivities and action capacities. For example, close spatial contiguity between response and reward is more important for 6-month-old infants than for 12-month-olds (Millar, 1974; Millar & Schaffer, 1972), presumably because the older infants possess superior ability to coordinate attentive and manipulative activities. This suggests a situation or task wherein transitions are affected by state-outcome interactions.

Each of the preceding variables represents the basis of a hypothesis relating to developmental change. Furthermore, the latter three represent instances in which experience affects state changes, either as a main or as an interactive variable. They share a common domain with learning theory and indeed are entirely compatible with the more interactive learning models discussed earlier. This common domain presents intriguing possibilities to the developmental theorist. Constructs useful to the learning theorist might be useful to the descriptions of state change that interest developmentalists; and, of special concern to us here, the methodology of learning theory may be relevant to developmental study.

A Markovian Analysis of the Development of a Concept

In the preceding sections we have developed three general themes concerning the psychology of learning. Learning involves changes in enduring state properties; these properties are in turn assessed through certain contingencies between stimuli and behavior. We have noted that contemporary approaches to learning admit a wide variety of processes in the assessment of state. Finally, we suggest that recent theories of state transitions are characterized by greater emphasis on the role of the state itself in determining transitions.

At each point in this survey, we have noted implications of interest to developmental inquiry. In this section, we hope to make these implications more concrete by applying a state transition analysis to a traditional developmental issue. We choose as our example the acquisition of a specific spatial concept—the knowledge that objects can exist in different places at different times, or what we shall refer to as *displacement.* Following our discussion of learning, it is appropriate to ask: What process variables define a state? What is the set of all allowable states? And, what produces specific transformations between states?

As discussed above, we consider search behaviors to be components of specific process variables, and these process variables are considered collectively to define a state. Accordingly, random choices (output) in response to certain episodes could indicate one state. Searches to the right after seeing the object hidden on the right could indicate another state. Searches to the right after seeing the object previously hidden on the left and then switched to the right could indicate a third. Next, as we have argued, it is desirable to consider a variety of possible state descriptions. Once a set of descriptions is established, however, the crux of a learning analysis is to specify the rules of transition. In Figure 3-2, what determines the application of, say, Rule T_1, instead of Rule T_2?

Of course, there has been considerable speculation concerning the application of rules of transition in the development of spatial concepts. An adaptive organism must be responsive to the consequences of a choice. Many theories of development reflect this assumption by emphasizing the conflict between choice and outcome as the mechanism of transition from one state to another. For example, Piaget (1977) suggests that one form of developmental progress is induced when the child notes a discrepancy between an expectancy for the order of events and what actually occurs. Thus, early techniques to facilitate concept development within the

Piagetian perspective involved conflict situations in which children could discover errors in their thinking (e.g., Langer, 1969; Gallagher, 1977). Similar emphases on conflict as a stimulus to change occur within Freudian theory (Freud, 1920/1958) and dialectic approaches (Sameroff & Harris, 1979).

The common concern of these theories is conflict arising from disconfirmed hypotheses. The outcome of a given choice is thus a special focus. An elementary version of a theory that emphasizes conflict would stipulate that the disconfirmation of a hypothesis permutes the state set to produce learning. The theory may allow other outcomes to effect this same transformation, or it might specify different transformation rules for these other outcomes. In the latter case, the theory would identify each kind of outcome with a specific transition rule. It might, for example, stipulate that an error leads to one type of transformation, and a success to another. Finally, it might include the assumption that the outcome interacts with the state of the subject.

An analysis of the acquisition of the displacement concept, then, would ideally meet several requirements. First, it must permit the unambiguous identification of states through the assessment of relevant process variables. The possession or nonpossession of the concept must be indexed in some way by the pattern of searches. Second, to avoid the exclusion of interesting phenomena of both state and process, the methodology must permit just that level of specification that uncovers lawful regularities in transitions. Finally, the traditional concern of the concept acquisition literature with interactionistic approaches encourages an analysis permitting dependencies between state transitions and the prior state of the child.

The general methodological prescription that we have proposed is nicely satisfied by the application of Markovian time series processes to learning data. Briefly, a Markovian process describes a set of discrete stochastic variables across repetitive time periods (see Brainerd, Chapter 1, this volume; and Brainerd, Howe, & Desrochers, 1982). A concise set of parameters determines how these variables change with each period. The initial value of these variables and the transition parameters completely specify the process, and jointly determine a stochastic path known as a Markov chain.

As applied to learning phenomena, Markovian analyses typically assume a small set of variables or "states." The transition parameters specify stochastic changes of these states, usually confined to transitions between two successive periods. The models generated are reasonably tractable mathematically and quite successful in accommodating learning data (e.g., Brainerd, 1979; Greeno & Steiner, 1964; Polson, 1970).

What is particularly attractive for our purpose is that the states of such a process can be strictly defined in terms of observable episodes. Hence, they permit reliability in the assessment of state. In addition, a theoretical process can be formulated that has an established correspondence to the observable iterative description (Greeno, 1967; see also Brainerd et al., 1982, regarding "identifiability"). That is, a theoretical model can be devised in which the states of the Markovian process are theoretical and unobservable; with certain limiting assumptions about performance, these states can then be mapped onto an observed pattern of responses. This feature permits the operational specification of a large domain of possible state descriptions and as such captures the spirit of liberalized approaches to learning. Brainerd and his associates (e.g., Brainerd et al., 1982) in particular have exploited this opportunity, using Markovian analyses to elucidate patterns of memory development.

Finally, we can note the potential for outcome determinant and interactive determinant accounts of state transitions. Markovian models assume that the transition parameters are constant across repeated trials. Within the framework we have described, they permit only a single transformation of states. We wish to allow for the possibility that transformations are sensitive to the outcome of an experience. A common approach within Markovian analyses is to incorporate the outcome of an experience into the state description. For example, to examine the effect of errors on transitions, we distinguish between a state that results in an error on a given trial and one that results in a correct response. We include in our transition matrix a separate rule for transitions following the former state. This strategem increases the size of the state description set and complicates the transformation rule, but it permits the Markovian assumption of a constant transition matrix.

Paradigm and Procedure

We have attempted a Markovian analysis of the acquisition of the displacement concept. We examined infants' ability to retrieve manually a hidden object that had been displaced by an experimenter. Our central question was addressed to changes that occur after the baby has demonstrated the absence of the displacement concept. We infer this from the Stage IV error (Piaget, 1937/1954). Briefly, this error occurs when the baby fails to search first at a new location, even after watching the object being hidden there. Instead, the baby searches at a previously correct location. In the traditional interpretation of this error, the baby has not yet achieved Stage V, which consists of the ability to represent an object in different places at different times.

We tested 64 healthy, full-term infants in a task of this nature. Thirty-two babies were 9 months old (34–40 weeks); the others were 16 months (64–72 weeks). All infants received a hidden object problem in which they could manually search two containers—one to the left, one to the right—on any trial. The general procedure was as follows: When the baby appeared comfortable in the experimenter's presence, a female tester showed the baby a toy, a box, and a cup. This was followed by a series of preliminary trials in which the toy was, in full view of the infant, hidden in one of the containers. The containers were moved toward the baby in a close trajectory (e.g., Cornell, 1981) and on each trial he or she could open both if necessary to retrieve the toy. For the first few trials the hiding place remained the same until the baby opened the correct container on the first attempt on two successive trials. Then another series of trials was begun. During this series, the toy was hidden in the other hiding place until the baby found it five times in a row or failed to reach this criterion in 22 trials. The principal data of the experiment concern searches during the second transfer series.

Proposed Model

As we have argued, one of the attractions of Markovian analysis is that it permits the abstract specification of states that are then identified in terms of certain data patterns. Accordingly, we decided to address the data from this experiment with a Markovian model consisting of three states: One of these, E, represents a state in which search choices are based on previous experiences of finding the object in a particular location. For example, after finding the toy under the cup in the preliminary series, a baby might continue to search under the cup. A baby in this state sometimes makes errors, and sometimes chooses successfully. We therefore distinguish between two different substates, E_e and E_c, where the first is a state wherein the baby makes an error on the trial in question, based on previous experience, and the second is a correct response on the trial, again based on previous experience.

The second two states are those within which the baby is likely to search correctly. We use the flexibility of the Markovian analysis to postulate two separate ways in which the baby might successfully search. One is through the use of certain stable response dispositions. Without limiting this description, these dispositions could be habits, stimulus-response associations, and so on. In this state, the baby searches a particular location based on cues associated with the static location, such as specific characteristics of the container, or the container's position on the table. We designate this state as L, the learned state. The other way the baby could successfully search is through the mastery of a spatial concept that allows the baby to track object displacements. We designate this state as K, knowledge that objects may be in different places at different times.

Associated with these different states is a starting vector specifying the probability of being in each state at the start of the transfer series. We suggest the vector in Table 3-1. The baby begins the first trial with probability k of being in State K. Since all previous experience on preliminary trials has been to the now incorrect hiding place, State L and the success version of E are not possible. Hence, the probability of being in State E_e is $1 - k$.

The next component of the model is a transition matrix specifying how states change from one trial to the succeeding one. We suggest the matrix given in Table 3-2. The process is assumed to be "absorbed" in States K and L; that is, once a baby reaches either state, he or she remains in that state. A more complex pattern of transitions occurs from States E_c and E_e. When in state E_c, for example, the baby can achieve concept mastery with probability a. If the baby does not achieve mastery (with probability $1 - a$), then he or she can enter one of the other states. Probability b is the probability of transition from E_c to L, given that the baby does not achieve the displacement concept. Probability c is the probability of remaining

Table 3-1 Probability of Each State
on the First Trial of the Transfer Phase

State	K	E_c	E_e	L
Probability	k	0	$1 - k$	0

Table 3-2 Probability of Each State after a Trial, Given a Specific State at the Start of the Trial

State at Start of Trial	State After Trial			
	K	E_c	E_e	L
K	1	0	0	0
E_c	a	$(1-a)(1-b)c$	$(1-a)(1-b)(1-c)$	$(1-a)b$
E_e	x	$(1-x)(1-y)z$	$(1-x)(1-y)(1-z)$	$(1-x)y$
L	0	0	0	1

in E_c given that the baby does not move to K or L. Parameters x, y, and z define similar probabilities for transitions from State E_e. The parameters of Table 3-2 therefore describe the baby's transitions across the trials of the transfer series.

The probability of a correct search when the infant is in a specified state is given in Table 3-3. By definition, the probability of a correct search is 1.0 and 0.0 when the baby is in States E_c and E_e, respectively. We also adopt the common assumption that it is 1.0 when the baby is in State L. Successful performance when the infant is in State K, however, depends on the accurate processing of information concerning the initial hiding and its efficient use during search. That is, a child may understand displacement but fail to perform accurately on a particular trial because of memory failure. We represent this dependency by the performance parameter p in Table 3-3. Including this parameter in our model allows us to distinguish between the acquisition of a hypothetical state (State K) and its manifestation in performance.

Tables 3-1, 3-2, and 3-3 define a model with eight independent parameters. Models with this many degrees of freedom typically require some limiting assumptions if they are to meaningfully describe a specific set of data. These considerations will be discussed in more detail later; at this point, however, we introduce one such limiting assumption in the parameters of Table 3-2. In our analysis, we assume $c = z$. That is, given that the infant does not achieve the concept or learn the position, the probability of a correct response is the same following an error as following a correct response. While there is precedent for this limiting assumption in other models of learning (e.g., Brainerd, 1979), we consider it especially appropriate in our search task. Recall that, after making an initially incorrect choice on any trial, the infant was free to open the alternative container, and usually did. Because the last response was generally a discovery of the object, information about the location of the object was consequently available after a correct response and after an

Table 3-3 Probability of a Correct Choice on a Trial, Given a Specific State at the Start of the Trial

State at Start of Trial	K	E_c	E_e	L
Probability of Correct Choice	p	1	0	1

error. Since searches in State E are based only upon previous experience of an object's position, the assumption that $c = z$ seems reasonable.

Tables 3-1, 3-2, and 3-3 provide a compact framework for a model of state transitions. Each trial represents an iterative assessment of the baby's state. In this particular formulation, each iteration is related only to the immediately preceding one. Within each assessment we have defined each state in general terms. Our intention is to provide a methodological analysis that is compatible with a variety of theoretical perspectives. State K, for example, is characterized in terms of concordance between the last hiding of an object and the baby's first search after this hiding. While it includes the important criteria of Piaget's Stage V concept, other behavioral demonstrations, such as the ability to retrace a sequence of hidings (Piaget, 1937/1954), are not necessary to it.

To summarize, with this model we exploit the points developed earlier. First, in Tables 3-1 and 3-2 we delineate several members of the state description set and specify transitions between them; in Table 3-3, we tie these state descriptions to specific behavioral processes of search responses. Our focus is on the states and their transition vectors, but we assess states through the process assumptions of Table 3-3. Second, we have allowed two alternative state descriptions of accurate search. One of these is assessed through a response sequence of perfect accuracy; the other is assessed by accuracy levels fixed by p. Finally, we have provided for state transition rules that depend on the outcome of a search by separating pre-solution error and success states. In this model, we do not address the possibility of interactive determinants, since transitions are only allowed from States E_c and E_e.

Parameter Estimation

We next examined the data of the infant's search task in the context of the model. Our focus was the determination of the individual parameters of Tables 3-1, 3-2, and 3-3. Empirical estimates of these parameters would, for example, allow us to assess the effects of outcomes on state transitions. Nonzero values of b and y would indicate that errors and successes were important determinants of learning; a difference between the two would indicate that one type of outcome was more important than the other. Similar comparisons can be posed with respect to the other transition variables.

Method. This analysis requires two components: an "objective function" relating the parameter vector to the likelihood of the data, and an optimization program that finds the vector maximizing the objective function. In this analysis, we employed as our objective function an iterative algorithm suggested by Polson and Huizinga (1974, Algorithm 1). Given values of the parameter vector of our model (i.e., values for k, p, a, b, c, x, y, z), the algorithm computes the likelihood of a given subject's protocol. Our objective function was then defined as -2 times the sum, across all babies in an age group, of the natural logarithm of that likelihood. This function, in turn, was maximized by a direct search optimization procedure based on the "random leap" heuristic of Curry (1975). The optimization routine randomly perturbates the value of the parameter vector and accepts the new vector as the estimate if it improves the objective function. The amount of perturbation is decreased systematically as the vector converges on a local extremum of the objective function. In our analysis, the optimization program was halted when these perturbations were decreased to less than .001. The only restriction on the values of the parameters was that they vary between 0 and 1 and that $c = z$.

Results

The maximum likelihood estimates of the eight parameters of the model are presented in Table 3-4. These values generated objective function values of 520.489 for the 9-month-olds and 304.064 for the 16-month-olds. Before these estimates can be evaluated, however, it is necessary to determine whether the parameters represented in Table 3-1 are identifiable. The parameters of a Markovian model are said to be identifiable if the data set determines one and only one value for each parameter. Obviously, any discussion of the values given in Table 3-4 demands that the model be identifiable. Using the procedure suggested by Polson and Huizinga (1974), we determined that the model was identifiable.

Process Differences. Having established the identifiability of our model, we begin discussion of it with a general overview. As can be seen in Table 3-4, transitions between states were estimated to be quite low for the 9-month-olds. Transitions seemed more probable in the case of the 16-month-olds. Consequently, we use the data of the older infants for this overview. Later we address developmental trends.

In proposing this model, our intention was to highlight two possible state descriptions that result in successful search. One of these, State L, is a learning process based on certain invariant stimulus properties: The infant responds to a hiding place specified by spatial cues rather than by information gained by watching the experimenter hide the object. The other, State K, represents transsituational knowledge based on spatial concepts that transcend displacements of the hidden object. The infant searches on the basis of where he or she has seen the object last hidden. We assume that L must be learned each time the object is hidden in a new place, but K reflects transfer from previous situations as well as acquisition during the successive hidings.

Table 3-4 Maximum Likelihood Estimates of the Parameters of Tables 3-1, 3-2, and 3-3 as Derived from the Performance of the 32 Infants in Each Age Group

Age (in months)	Parameters							
	k	p	a	b	c	x	y	z
9	.55	.65	.00	.07	.07	.09	.07	.07
16	.55	.83	.05	.05	.14	.29	.22	.14

The parameter estimates indicate how search performance can be explained by these state descriptions. The high value of k in the 16-month-olds indicates that a substantial number of children began the transfer phase within the K state. As we have defined it, knowledge of displacement is therefore appreciable as the child begins the test for the Stage IV error. However, this knowledge is not sufficient to ensure a correct search, as indicated by the fact that p was less than 1.0. Additional performance factors must limit the use of this concept.

Search competency during the transfer stage can improve according to the transformation rules given in Table 3-2. Specifically, transitions can occur from either of the E states to the extent that parameters a, x, b, and y are nonzero. The first two determine whether the child acquires the concept of displacement from either E state; the second two determine whether he or she learns the new position of the object.

As a preliminary test of whether competency does improve in this fashion, we determined the likelihood of a constrained version of the model, in which the four preceding parameters were zero. The negative of 2 times the logarithm of the likelihood was compared to the corresponding value of the model without these constraints. Asymptotically, the difference between the two is distributed as chi square (Brainerd et al., 1982). For this nonspecific test of improvement, we found a significant difference between the constrained and unconstrained models, indicating that the four parameters are not all zero, $\chi^2(4) = 12.99, p < .05$.

Unfortunately, our data were not sufficiently fine grained to isolate individual contributions of a, x, b, and y to improvement in search competency. Likelihood tests of each of the four individual parameters could not reliably establish that any individual parameter was nonzero. However, if we examine the qualitative pattern, out data suggest that outcome determinants are important and that there is similarity in the transition rules governing transitions to both competency states. Given that the infant does not acquire the displacement concept after a search, transitions to State L are moderately probable if the search was unsuccessful and much less likely if the search was correct. Although this difference in magnitude was not reliable, it may indicate that learning the location of the hidden object in terms of invariant stimuli is facilitated by errors but not by successes. This finding is in general accord with studies of concept and conservation learning in children (Brainerd, 1979). Similarly, transitions to State K in the older infants were more likely following an error than a success, although this difference was not reliable either. The pattern may indicate that the acquisition of the concept that an object can exist in different places at different times, like learning its spatial position, depends on the specific outcome of a search.

Finally, the low values of c and z suggest a powerful influence of the pretransfer hidings. Given that the infant stays in either of the presolution states, an error is quite likely.

Age-related Differences. With this general pattern considered, we begin discussion of age differences in the parameters of the model. To test the reliability of differences, we employed likelihood ratio tests of constrained subsets of the general model. For example, to examine the overall age differences, we determined the likelihood of our model under the assumption that, for all eight parameters, each parameter of the 9-month-old group equaled its corresponding parameter of the 16-month-old group. The negative of 2 times the logarithm of the likelihood was compared to the corresponding value of the model without these constraints. For the overall test, this value was $\chi^2(7) = 26.5$, $p < .001$. The likelihood ratio test therefore established that the Markovian process of our model differed between the two age groups. We now turn to a more detailed examination of the individual parameters.

Perhaps the most intriguing result of our analysis concerns the estimate of parameter k, the probability of knowing that an object can be located in different places at different times. The first column of Table 3-4 indicates that 9-month-old and 16-month-old infants were equally likely to possess this spatial concept at the outset of the transfer task. The null result is intriguing, because infants 9 months of age typically perform poorly in such transfer tasks (e.g., the Stage IV error). The younger babies of our study were no different, achieving criterion after an average of 12 trials in comparison to the average of 9 trials required by the 16-month-olds. In light of the similar values of k, many of the younger babies appear to know something but act as if they do not—a classic competence-performance distinction.

The second column of Table 3-4 elucidates this finding. Recall that $1 - p$ is the probability of error even though the baby has achieved the displacement concept. These errors may occur as a result of momentary lapses in attention to the hiding, or forgetting of the most recent hiding, or even a failure to inhibit a previously successful approach to the alternative hiding place. The estimates of p in Table 3-4 indicate that the younger babies who have achieved the displacement concept are likely to perform correctly on 65% of the trials, whereas the comparable older babies do so on 83%, a reliable difference: $\chi^2(1) = 15.45$, $p < .001$.

These results indicate that spatial concept development between 9 and 16 months is more a matter of the efficient execution of knowledge than of its construction. This is not to say that spatial knowledge does not change with age, but that its application appears to be the primary improvement when children encounter situations requiring search for a displaced object. The interpretation is not new; it has been forecast most recently by Cornell (1978) and Lasky, Romano, and Wenters (1980). Nevertheless, up to now there has been no formal method to isolate the differential development of competence and performance.

We are left with the task of explaining how abilities might improve. Two of the parameters of our model, a and x, represent the probability of a transition to knowledge that an object can be located in different places at different times. Although we found some indication of a difference between age groups for both parameters, neither difference was significant statistically. Similarly, no reliable age differences were found to indicate acquisition of a more limited response tendency. Parameters b and y measure the probability of transitions to State L given that the infant does not achieve State K. The likelihood ratio tests of age differences were not significant. Finally, we can note a slight age difference with respect to parameters c and z. Younger babies seem less likely to choose correctly on the next trial, given that they do not exhibit a transition to either State K or State L. Perhaps this reflects greater perseverance of the previously learned choice. The difference, however, was not reliable. In sum, we could find little evidence to suggest that the processes of change are different for these age groups.

Concluding Summary

In this chapter we have stressed the affinities between learning theory and developmental psychology in two ways. We first examined certain conceptual and methodological themes in the analysis of change; we then highlighted these themes with a tentative model of conceptual acquisition. We think it is fitting to conclude our discussion with some general comments.

It is difficult to specify just what characterizes a "learning theory" approach. Here we have argued that a learning theory does three things. It provides an exhaustive list of the possible disposition states of the organism. It then specifies certain process variables by which these states are to be identified. Finally, it stipulates the rules that map one state onto another. In our first section, we examined each of these objectives in turn, and attempted to delineate certain attitudes that characterize contemporary learning theory. We suggest that the developmental analyst might find some of these orienting attitudes useful in the description and explanation of developmental change.

Our Markovian model was intended to illustrate some of the advantages of this approach. A Markovian analysis forces the exact specification of the state description set. In our case, this formal requirement led us to distinguish the attainment of a spatial concept (State K) from the learning of responses to static environmental cues (State L). We also exploited the potential of Markovian models to allow different types of process indices for each state in the set. In our case, we delimited conceptual performance in terms of the free parameter p, while specifying perfect performance for the learned state. Finally, the Markovian approach embeds a list of transformation rules in a quantifiable transition matrix. This matrix allows for interactive transition rules, although we did not make use of this option.

The results were intriguing. We found indications that transitions were similar in both learning the position of an object and acquiring the concept of its possible displacement. Furthermore, we found that the major developmental trend was an increased efficiency in the performance of this displacement conceptual capacity. Although this model is only tentative now, these indications seem worthy of further study.

More generally, we have exploited the potential of Markovian analysis in connection with a relatively basic, Thorndikian, description of state changes. We related state transitions to outcome variables because this has been a historically important theoretical pivot. But use of the method need not be restricted to this issue alone, nor to the state descriptions we have employed. There is a recurrent tendency in theories of cognitive development to suggest that efficient performance is associated with the integration of multiple processes and competencies (cf. Fischer, 1980; Langley & Simon, 1981; Lawler, 1981). We have advocated a compatible analytic framework here. Our focus on one particular state description and transition matrix merely reflects our bias that such fundamental processes may be adequate to account for the baby's progress.

Regardless of this bias, we feel it is timely to emphasize the common concern of learning theory and developmental psychology with transition rules. Although we have chosen to present a highly quantitative analysis of these rules, the more general point is that an analysis of change should seek a functional mapping between a set of states at one time and a set of states at another. Whether one wishes to study a set of functions called "reinforcement" or a set called "equilibration" should not obscure the affinities between the two endeavors. We encourage investigators in both domains to seek these affinities.

References

Brainerd, C. J. Neo-Piagetian training experiments revisited: Is there any support for the cognitive-developmental stage hypothesis? *Cognition,* 1973, *2,* 349–370.

Brainerd, C. J. Learning research and Piagetian theory. In L. S. Siegel & C. J. Brainerd (Eds.), *Alternatives to Piaget: Critical essays on the theory.* New York: Academic Press, 1978.

Brainerd, C. J. Markovian interpretations of conservation learning. *Psychological Review,* 1979, *86,* 181–213.

Brainerd, C. J., Howe, M. L., & Desrochers, A. The general theory of two-stage learning: A mathematical review with illustrations from memory development. *Psychological Bulletin,* 1982, *91,* 634–665.

Cornell, E. H. Learning to find things: A reinterpretation of object permanence studies. In L. S. Siegel & C. J. Brainerd (Eds.), *Alternatives to Piaget: Critical essays on the theory.* New York: Academic Press, 1978.

Cornell, E. H. The effects of cue distinctiveness on infants' manual search. *Journal of Experimental Child Psychology,* 1981, *32,* 330–342.

Curry, R. E. A random search algorithm for laboratory computers. *Behavior Research Methods & Instrumentation,* 1975, *7,* 369–376.

Estes, W. K. Memory and conditioning. In F. J. McGuigan & D. B. Lumsden (Eds.), *Contemporary approaches to conditioning and learning.* New York: Wiley, 1973.

Fischer, K. W. A theory of cognitive development: The control and construction of hierarchies of skills. *Psychological Review,* 1980, *87,* 477–531.

Freud, S. *A general introduction to psychoanalysis.* New York: Permabooks, 1958. (Originally published, 1920.)

Gallagher, J. M. Piaget's concept of equilibration: Biological, logical, and cybernetic roots. In M. H. Appel & L. S. Goldberg (Eds.), *Topics in cognitive development: Equilibration* (Vol. 1). New York: Plenum, 1977.

Gibson, E. J. *Principles of perceptual learning and development.* New York: Appleton-Century-Crofts, 1969.

Greeno, J. G. Paired-associate learning with short-term retention: Mathematical analysis and data regarding identification of parameters. *Journal of Mathematical Psychology*, 1967, *4*, 430–472.

Greeno, J. G., & Steiner, T. E. Markovian processes with identifiable states: General considerations and applications to all-or-none learning. *Psychometrika*, 1964, *29*, 309–333.

Hilgard, E. R., & Bower, G. H. *Theories of learning.* Englewood Cliffs, NJ: Prentice-Hall, 1981.

Inhelder, B., Sinclair, H., & Bovet, M. *Learning and the development of cognition.* Cambridge, MA: Harvard University Press, 1974.

Kamin, L. J. Predictability, surprise, attention and conditioning. In B. Campbell & R. Church (Eds.), *Punishment and aversive behavior.* New York: Appleton-Century-Crofts, 1969.

Kendler, H. H. "What is learned?"—A theoretical blind alley. *Psychological Review*, 1952, *59*, 269–277.

Kimble, G. H. *Hilgard and Marquis' conditioning and learning.* New York: Appleton-Century-Crofts, 1961.

Langer, J. Disequilibrium as a source of development. In P. H. Mussen, J. Langer, & M. Covington (Eds.), *Trends and issues in developmental psychology.* New York: Holt, Rinehart & Winston, 1969.

Langley, P., & Simon, H. A. The central role of learning in cognition. In J. R. Anderson (Ed.), *Cognitive skills and their acquisition.* Hillsdale, NJ: Erlbaum, 1981.

Lasky, R. E., Romano, N., & Wenters, J. Spatial localization in children after changes in position. *Journal of Experimental Child Psychology*, 1980, *29*, 225–248.

Lawler, R. W. The progressive construction of mind. *Cognitive Science*, 1981, *5*, 1–30.

Levine, M. *A cognitive theory of learning: Research on hypothesis testing.* Hillsdale, NJ: Erlbaum, 1975.

Lubow, R. E., & Moore, A. U. Latent inhibition: The effect of nonreinforced pre-exposure to the conditioning stimulus. *Journal of Comparative and Physiological Psychology*, 1959, *52*, 414–419.

Millar, W. S. The role of visual-holding cues and the simultanizing strategy in infant operant learning. *British Journal of Psychology*, 1974, *65*, 505–518.

Millar, W. S., & Schaffer, H. R. The influence of spatially displaced feedback on infant operant conditioning. *Journal of Experimental Child Psychology*, 1972, *14*, 442–452.

Piaget, J. *The construction of reality in the child.* New York: Basic Books, 1954. (Originally published, 1937.)

Piaget, J. Development and learning. In R. E. Ripple & V. N. Rockcastle (Eds.), *Piaget rediscovered: A report on the conference on cognitive studies and curriculum development.* Ithaca, NY: School of Education, Cornell University, 1964.

Piaget, J. Problems of equilibration. In M. H. Appel & L. S. Goldberg (Eds.), *Topics in cognitive development: Equilibration* (Vol. 1). New York: Plenum, 1977.

Polson, P. G. Statistical methods for a general theory of all-or-none learning. *Psychometrika.* 1970, *35*, 51–72.

Polson, P. G., & Huizinga, D. Statistical methods for absorbing Markov-chain models for learning: Estimation and identification. *Psychometrika*, 1974, *39*, 3–22.

Rescorla, R. A., & Holland, P. C. Some behavioral approaches to the study of learning. In M. R. Rosenzweig & E. L. Bennet (Eds.), *Neural mechanisms of learning and memory*. Cambridge, MA: MIT Press, 1976.

Rozeboom, W. W. The concept of "memory." *Psychological Record*, 1965, *15*, 329–368.

Sameroff, A. J., & Cavanaugh, P. J. Learning in infancy: A developmental perspective. In J. Osofsky (Ed.), *Handbook of infant development*. New York: Wiley, 1979.

Sameroff, A. J., & Harris, A. E. Dialectical approaches to early thought and language. In M. Bornstein & W. Kessen (Eds.), *Psychological development from infancy: Image to intention*. Hillsdale, NJ: Erlbaum, 1979.

Seligman, M. E. P. On the generality of the laws of learning. *Psychological Review*, 1970, *77*, 406–418.

Seligman, M. E. P., & Johnston, J. C. A cognitive theory of avoidance learning. In F. J. McGuigan & D. B. Lumsden (Eds.), *Contemporary approaches to conditioning and learning*. New York: Wiley, 1973.

Seligman, M. E. P., Maier, S. F., & Solomon, R. L. Unpredictable and uncontrollable aversive events. In F. R. Brush (Ed.), *Aversive conditioning and learning*. New York: Academic Press, 1971.

Shettleworth, S. J. Constraints on learning. In D. S. Lehrman, R. A. Hinde, & E. Shaw (Eds.), *Advances in the study of behavior* (Vol. 4). New York: Academic Press, 1972.

Sokolov, Y. N. *Perception and the conditioned reflex*. New York: Macmillan, 1963.

Stamps, L. E., & Porges, S. W. Heart rate conditioning in newborn infants: Relationships among conditionability, heart rate variability, and sex. *Developmental Psychology*, 1975, *11*, 424–431.

Stevenson, H. W. *Children's learning*. New York: Appleton-Century-Crofts, 1972.

Thorndike, E. L. Animal intelligence: An experimental study of the associative processes in animals. *Psychological Review: Series of Monograph Supplements*, 1898, *2* (4, Whole No. 8).

Wagner, A. R. Expectancies and the priming of STM. In S. H. Hulse, H. Fowler, & W. K. Honig (Eds.), *Cognitive processes in animal behavior*. Hillsdale, NJ: Erlbaum, 1978.

Wagner, A. R., Rudy, J. W., & Whitlow, J. W. Rehearsal in animal conditioning. *Journal of Experimental Psychology*, 1973, *97*, 407–426. (Monograph.)

Werner, H. The concept of development from a comparative and organismic point of view. In D. Harris (Ed.), *The concept of development*. Minneapolis: University of Minnesota Press, 1957.

White, S. The learning theory approach. In P. Mussen (Ed.), *Carmichael's manual of child psychology* (3rd ed., Vol. 1). New York: Wiley, 1970.

Wilcox, S., & Katz, S. The ecological approach to development: An alternative to cognitivism. *Journal of Experimental Child Psychology*, 1981, *32*, 247–263.

4. Research Strategies for a Cognitive Developmental Psychology of Instruction

Robert Kail

Understanding children's learning and thinking is conceptually distinct from prescribing the conditions under which children will learn and think most effectively. That is, a theory of learning and cognition and a theory of instruction are not the same, a fact noted by many authors. Glaser (1976), for example, argued that "a theory of learning describes, after the fact, the conditions under which some competence is acquired. A theory of instruction is a normative theory in that it sets up criteria of performance and then specifies the conditions required for meeting them" (p. 4).

In a complete theory of instruction, the "conditions" referred to by Glaser (1976) would be defined broadly, and would extend considerably beyond those typically addressed in psychological theories of learning. Such conditions might include, for example, the optimal socioeconomic composition of a student body for maximal achievement by that student body, or the optimal physical arrangement of classrooms. Equally important to a complete theory of instruction would be information regarding (a) optimal structuring of the material to be learned, (b) the kinds and quantity of instruction needed, (c) the knowledge that a student must possess to be able to profit from (a) and (b), and (d) developmental changes in students' abilities that might place important constraints on (a), (b), and (c). "Conditions" (a)–(d) are, of course, those that fall traditionally within the domain of research on children's learning, memory, and cognition, and it is these conditions that are the concern of this chapter.

While recognizing that theories of children's learning and cognition are conceptually distinct from theories of instruction, many theorists (e.g., Rohwer, 1976; Stevenson, Note 1) have argued, nonetheless, that research on the former will gradually give rise to important instructional prescriptions, if not a full-fledged theory of instruction. Rohwer and Dempster (1977) termed this a *resource approach* and described it this way:

> In the resource approach researchers capitalize on the theoretical distinctions, propositions, and empirical information that are their stock in trade. They use these resources to specify relevant domains of educational activity, and to identify factors within these domains that can affect the quality of student achievement. Through this approach, investigators can provide educators with ways of viewing the [memory] demands of tasks analytically, and of estimating for different kinds of students the likely consequences of alternative instructional practices. (p. 409)

Admittedly there are cases in the past three decades where specific instructional practices have fallen out of experimental work on children's learning and memory, with behavior modification being one of the most successful and well-known cases (e.g., Bijou & Ruiz, 1981). Yet, consensus (e.g., Atkinson, 1976) is that research on learning and memory has not had a major impact on educational practice.

It is the thesis of this chapter that the lack of influence reflects in part the fact that theoretically driven and instructionally driven research have distinct though overlapping agenda with different methodological requirements. I assume that the objective of psychological research on instruction is to help a maximum number of students to achieve societally selected objectives as easily as possible from a student's viewpoint, and as efficiently as possible from a teacher's viewpoint. From this assumption, I will argue that many characteristics of the typical experimental study of children's learning and memory make it unlikely that results of much instructional value will accrue.

The organization of the chapter corresponds to the typical temporal sequence in which researchers study instructionally relevant psychological processes. I first discuss selection of experimental tasks, then consider the choice of an appropriate experimental design, and finally discuss methods for analysis of data. In each section I describe the prevailing practices in developmental research, then point to some of the shortcomings of those practices from an instructional perspective, and conclude by suggesting some alternate methods that would help to increase the instructional yield of research.

Many of the criticisms and suggested remedies described in subsequent sections of this paper are not specific to evaluation of cognitive developmental research from an instructional view. Indeed, many of the strategies suggested for improved instructional research turn out to coincide with recommendations for research necessary to generate stronger and broader theories of cognition and its development. Hence, individuals not interested in instruction per se can read this material as a critique of extant methodological practices in research on children's learning, memory, and cognition.

Selection of Tasks

Current Practices

The tasks used by developmental psychologists to study learning and memory in children often strike educators as totally divorced from learning and remembering as they occur in school. Of course, such tasks evolved quite rationally, as part of efforts by child psychologists to study children's learning and memory *experimentally*. The logical basis for the emergence of these tasks was described by Bijou and Baer (1960):

> The essential concept involved in the definition of experimental technique is that of control. In experimental logic phenomena do not change without cause. A statement of cause and effect can be made only when a variation in the supposed effect is coincidental to a preceding variation in the supposed cause, if no other factor has changed. The best guarantee that no other factors have changed is to gain control over them and keep them at fixed values. This essential need for control over all possible causal factors has conferred upon experimental techniques a secondary characteristic of being *laboratory* procedures. (pp. 140–141)

This approach typified the experimental study of children's learning in the 1950s and the study of children's memory in the 1960s and 1970s. Tasks were selected because they allowed the investigator to study some characteristic of learning and memory in isolation, without the contaminating effects of other phenomena that naturally occur with the phenomenon of interest. For example, in the study of children's learning, various transposition and discrimination shift paradigms were used because they were thought to be helpful in tracing the development of language-mediated learning (see Stevenson, 1972a, Chapters 7–9). Similarly, in the study of memory development, different free, cued and probe recall paradigms were used to investigate developmental change in the use of memory strategies (see Hagen, Jongeward, & Kail, 1975; Kail & Hagen, 1982).

The goal of this research was to formulate general theories of children's learning and memory, theories that cut across particular experimental situations. Task-specific components of performance were viewed as an inherent but uninteresting part of the enterprise. Stevenson (1972b), for example, noted that

> psychologists typically evaluate their hypotheses by selecting a certain task as representative of the domain of behavior in which they are interested. . . . Rarely is the task in itself of intrinsic interest. For example, performance on a transposition task is used as an index of relational versus absolute learning, or of the influence of language, instructions, or of the discriminability of the stimuli on learning and transfer. The child's ability or failure to discriminate between two squares or two brightnesses are, in themselves, of no great interest. (pp. 78–79)

In short, performance on specific tasks is of interest primarily as the basis for inferences about more general processes.

Given the nature of the tasks typically used in experimental work, the route from experimentation to instructional prescription is indirect. As noted earlier, one such route is the "resource approach," which involves using "the products of theoretical and empirical analyses as resources for viewing educational practices and for anticipating their consequences" (Rohwer & Dempster, 1977, p. 431). Thus, once some aspect of children's learning and memory is understood, researchers in the resource approach may extrapolate instructional implications from their work.

Research on children's attention during learning can be used to illustrate this approach. Consider, for example, studies of incidental learning derived from serial recall tasks. In this research, children are shown an array of several pictures, with each picture depicting an animal paired with a piece of furniture. Half of the children are told to remember the location in the array of each animal and to ignore the pieces of furniture; half remember the locations of the furniture and ignore the animals. After several trials in which recall of locations is tested, incidental learning is measured by presenting all stimuli, and asking children to pair each animal with the corresponding piece of furniture. Efficient selective allocation of attention can be measured by expressing the number of correct responses on the intentional learning task as a proportion of the total number of correct responses (i.e., intentional recall plus incidental recall). This proportion increases systematically with development (Druker & Hagen, 1969; Hagen, 1967; Hagen & Hale, 1973; Hagen, Meacham, & Mesibov, 1970), a finding interpreted as indicating greater selectivity of attention with development.

Having demonstrated these developmental changes in attentional skill, one then derives recommendations for instruction that are extrapolations from the descriptive findings. For instance, in the present case the implication is that instructional tasks should be constructed so that they provide redundant, relevant cues for correct answers, while minimizing irrelevant cues that may distract a student (Ross, 1976; Stevenson, Note 1). This is particularly true for children in the early elementary school grades, who are most likely to have difficulty spontaneously attending only to task-relevant stimuli. Stevenson (Note 1), for example, pointed out that instructional materials for young children often include irrelevant stimuli to heighten students' interest that may actually impede their learning.

Shortcomings

The resource approach has one major drawback. Recommendations regarding instruction typically are extrapolations from laboratory tasks to what appear to be related instructional tasks. Extrapolations like these are risky because of unknown boundary conditions that may limit the range of applicability of the effects demonstrated in laboratory research. For example, the use of extraneous stimuli to heighten young children's interest in instructional materials (described above) is firmly rooted in findings that novel stimuli often help young children to persist at a task (e.g., Faw & Nunnally, 1968; Odom, 1964). Thus, two lines of research—one concerning the effects of novelty and the second concerning the development of selectivity in learning—generate exactly the opposite recommendations regarding what constitutes effective instructional material. Such inconsistencies in instructional prescriptions from theoretically driven research are not unlikely to occur; they simply reflect the interactive effects of those variables that were controlled so carefully in the laboratory but that are free to influence learning in settings where such control is impossible.

To minimize this risk, some investigators derive instructionally relevant versions of laboratory tasks and attempt to replicate the basic patterns of results established in descriptive research. Willows (1974), for example, created a task in which she could study incidental learning during children's oral reading of brief stories. All stories were printed in black type. In some cases, words printed in red appeared between the lines of text. These distracting words were relevant to the theme of the story but differed from those actually appearing in the stories. For example, in a story about truck drivers who haul dangerous explosives, *dynamite* was one of the distracting words. Willows (1974) anticipated that the skilled readers among the 11-year-olds in her sample would have more developed attentional skill (a hypothesis derived from studies of incidental learning described earlier), and thus would be less distracted by the extraneous words. In fact, to the contrary, skilled readers were much more likely than less skilled readers to use the distracting material to answer questions about the story. For example, when asked "What does he haul that makes his trips dangerous?" skilled readers were more likely than less skilled readers to answer "dynamite" instead of the correct answer, "explosives."

Willows (1974) argued that a skilled reader "simply scans the text, taking in a few fragments of words and phrases here and there to be sure that he is 'on the right track' " (p. 413). The distracting words were readily interpretable because they were semantically consistent with the story, and thus the skilled readers processed them. Less skilled readers, in contrast, are more likely to read word by word and thus were less likely to attend to distractors appearing between the lines. This is a reasonable explanation of interesting data; but it should not obscure the issue at hand. Willows's (1974) experiment illustrates the risks that may be involved in drawing prescriptions for instruction from results that are not derived from children's performance on actual instructional tasks or facsimiles.

The argument developed thus far is that investigators typically simplify the stimulus and response properties of laboratory tasks in order to achieve maximal experimental control. But legitimate instructional tasks such as reading and mathematics are rarely streamlined in their stimulus and response characteristics. Hence, what is often a robust laboratory finding, such as developmental change in incidental learning, will often deteriorate when examined outside of the original or similar contexts. This does not condemn the laboratory findings; it merely demonstrates that the phenomenon is understood only in a particular context from which it may be dangerous to generalize.

An Alternative: Direct Analysis of Tasks

An alternative is to study instructional tasks directly. Rather than studying discrimination learning or paired-associate learning with the hope that ultimately we will understand how children learn to read, we investigate reading per se. In studying instructional tasks (or any complex task for that matter), the priorities are completely reversed from traditional theory-driven research. Now the objective is to understand performance on the chosen task. No longer is performance on a task of interest only as a means toward more general theoretical statements.

In addition, instructional significance, rather than potential analytic value, becomes an important consideration in selecting a task for study. Among the appropriate criteria would be: (a) Does the instructional task represent a fundamental academic skill, one in which all students *should* become proficient? (b) Is the instructional task one in which, despite much instructional effort, some students typically have difficulty achieving the desired level of proficiency? Using these criteria, reading and mathematics (and perhaps to a lesser degree, scientific thinking) typically have emerged as the target tasks for instructional research. The important point, however, is that nonscientific criteria—namely, societal concerns regarding appropriate and important educational objectives—help to define the starting point for the direct approach to cognitive instructional research (Glaser, 1981; Resnick, 1976).

Finally, important instructional tasks are generally more complicated for students than the tasks typically used in research on children's learning and memory. Given this complexity, no longer is it safe—or even reasonable—to assume that all individuals will perform the task in the same way (Simon, 1975). Some individuals' efforts to perform the task will be inadequate; they rarely, if ever, will obtain correct answers. Other individuals may use procedures that result in correct answers for a restricted set of cases. Still other individuals may all perform the task correctly, but differ in the specific approach and, as a consequence, may differ in their efficiency. Hence, in direct analysis of instructional tasks, unlike the case in most theoretically driven work, there is little need to identify the "true" model for performance on a task; instead, the goal of research is to identify a *set* of models that characterize most people's performance on the target task (Kail & Bisanz, 1982b).

Studying complex tasks like those encountered in instruction has not been a popular endeavor in experimental psychology. For most of the 20th century, tasks of choice have been simple, on the grounds that they are more amenable to empirical analyses than are complex tasks. In the last several years, however, the situation has changed drastically, so that now numerous methods are available for analyzing complex, instructionally relevant tasks. I will describe two of these analytic tools, using research on children's subtraction. (See Kail & Bisanz, 1982a, 1982b, for detailed descriptions of these and other methods.)

In one line of this research, *response time* has been used to study children's subtraction of single-digit integers (e.g., $m - n = ?$, where m and n are between 0 and 9). Here children rarely err; the time needed for children to respond is used to infer the processes underlying subtraction. On such problems, most young children apparently use an algorithm based on a mental counter that can be rapidly incremented or decremented, one unit at a time. Second graders, for example, typically set the mental counter to m, then decrement it n times. The final value on the counter is the answer to the problem (Woods, Resnick, & Groen, 1975). Given

"$7 - 4 = $?" the counter is set to 7, decremented 4 times, and the final value on the counter, 3, is the child's answer. For these children, response time on subtraction problems is a function of n, the number of times the counter must be decremented per problem. Problems of the type $m - 2$ are all answered at the same rate, for they all involve decrementing the counter twice, regardless of the value of the minuend. Problems of the type $m - 4$ are also answered at a common rate, but more slowly than $m - 2$ problems, because the counter is decremented four times rather than twice.

Another powerful technique for studying complex tasks is *computer simulation,* in which a theorist creates a working computer program that "behaves" as a person might behave. That is, if a person finds problem A more difficult than problem B, the program should too; if a person answers problem C more rapidly than problem D, the program should as well. Consider, for illustrative purposes, research on children's multicolumn subtraction (e.g., $82 - 53 = $?). Children err much more frequently on these problems than on the single-integer problems discussed earlier. These errors are assumed to reflect consistent application of a faulty algorithm, and the pattern of errors is the data base used to infer this algorithm (e.g., Brown & Burton, 1978; Young & O'Shea, 1981). For example, a common error occurs when the digit in the subtrahend is larger than the digit in the same column of the minuend: Many children apparently subtract the smaller digit in a column from the larger one, regardless of which is the subtrahend and which is the minuend.

Young and O'Shea (1981) used *production systems* to simulate patterns of errors in 10-year-olds' subtraction. The essential unit of Young and O'Shea's systems was a *production,* which consists of a condition (or set of conditions) and an associated action (or set of actions) to be taken whenever the conditions are met. In a production system, the program considers each production in sequence until the conditions of a particular production are met. The actions associated with this production are taken, and then the productions are again considered in sequence, a process that repeats until the problem is solved. (For more detailed descriptions of production systems as they are used to study psychological processes, see Anderson, 1976; Klahr & Wallace, 1976; and especially Newell & Simon, 1972).

Young and O'Shea found that the vast majority of errors (more than 90%) as well as errorless responding were captured in four different production systems. The four systems included 10 productions in common, and varied only in their productions for borrowing. The "correct" system included the 10 productions plus the production "Borrow if the subtrahend (s) is greater than the minuend (m)." The remaining three systems consisted of the 10 productions, plus (a) "Borrow if $s < m$," just the opposite of the appropriate production; (b) "Borrow if $s < m$ or if $m > s$," the correct production plus the reverse; or (c) no productions dealing with the appropriate conditions for borrowing.

Consider, for example, the first of the three faulty systems, which includes the production "If $s < m$, then borrow." Given the problem

$$\frac{\begin{array}{r}74\\-\ 22\end{array}}{}$$

the production system would operate in the following sequence:

1. Read the m and s from the right-hand column.
2. Compare m and s.
3. Finding that $s < m$, borrow, which means adding 10 to the one's column and decrementing the digit borrowed from (i.e., 7) by 1.
4. Find the difference, 12.
5. Because $12 > 10$, write the 2 and "carry" the 10 to the subtrahend in the left column.
6. Write the difference, 3.

In this manner, the program simulates one common type of error in children's subtraction. Furthermore, as noted earlier, correct subtraction results from a minor change in the system: Substituting the correct production (borrow if $m < s$) in Step 3.

Computer simulation, as exemplified in Young and O'Shea's (1981) analysis of subtraction, is but one of the many analytic tools now available with which to analyze performance on complex instructional tasks with the same degree of rigor and precision that has characterized analysis of children's learning of discrimination shifts or their recall of categorized lists of words. Given the potential dangers involved in instructional prescriptions derived from theoretically driven work, plus the inevitable wait for instructionally relevant work of this sort to accumulate, direct analysis of instructional tasks emerges as the preferred approach for a cognitive developmental psychology of instruction.

Experimental Designs

Current Practices

Selection of tasks is a conspicuous difference between theory-driven and instructionally driven research, but it is not the only difference. Another important distinguishing characteristic concerns the choice of independent variables in designing an experiment. This issue deserves exploration in some detail, for many researchers who claim to do instructional research—and in fact are doing so based on their choice of tasks—revert to methods derived from theory-based research when it comes to the selection of independent variables.

The logic of most theoretically driven research is that psychological processes can be revealed by examining performance under a variety of conditions, noting differences in performance, and associating such differences with the corresponding conditions. The simplest case involves comparing the performance of an experimental group with that of a control group. More complicated versions involve multiple experimental groups in which the impact of many variables is examined at once. Still more complicated are developmental designs in which the focus is possible age-related changes in the influence of combinations of variables.

Implicit in the current state of the art is the assumption that ordinal relationships among performance in different conditions are sufficient to test most psychological theories. That is, predictions involve statements that a particular mean should be greater than or less than other means. The absolute values of means (or other statistics) are generally irrelevant to the enterprise, as is, by extension, the exact size of the differences in performance between conditions. Where more than a single independent variable is involved, predictions are often made regarding the significance (or nonsignificance) of interactions as well as main effects, but here too predictions typically are ordinal. One such prediction would be that an independent variable will produce differences in means under some levels of a second independent variable, but not other levels. A particularly important instance of this prediction for developmental work is the Age X Condition interaction, where age differences in performance are expected in some conditions but not others (or where conditions will produce differences at some ages but not others).

Consider, for example, a study by Hagen and Kail (1973) that concerned developmental change in the use of memory strategies. We tested 7- and 11-year-olds on a serial position probe task in which seven pictures were presented individually for 2 seconds, then turned face down. Following the seventh picture, a duplicate of one of the seven pictures was shown and the child was asked to point to the matching picture in the array of face-down cards. Our predictions regarding children's performance were derived from two facts. First, rehearsal—a strategy of repetitively naming stimuli to be recalled—typically improves retention of pictures seen early in a series, a finding usually referred to as the "primacy effect." Second, in prior developmental research, 11-year-olds were likely to use memory strategies like rehearsal to improve retention, but 7-year-olds were not. Hence, our prediction of an Age X Condition interaction involved the appearance of a primacy effect for 11-year-olds but not 7-year-olds, a prediction that was confirmed. Note, however, that we made no predictions regarding exact values of the means or their differences, nor was there any theoretical basis for doing so.

The fact that ordinal relations are typically sufficient for evaluating theories of children's learning and memory underlies another common practice in developmental work. In most work on children's learning and memory, developmental psychologists sample just a few levels of an independent variable, and typically in an ad hoc manner. Others (e.g., Brown & DeLoache, 1978) have deplored the ubiquitousness of the 2 X 2 design in developmental psychology. What is not recognized is the link between this practice and the state of theory testing in cognitive developmental psychology. If ordinal relations suffice for theory testing and the effects of an independent variable are monotonic, then performance for *any* two levels of that independent variable provides the necessary data. Suppose, for example, that we predict that rate of presentation affects children's ability to learn a list of words, as in serial, paired-associate, or free recall learning. As long as we assume that the function relating learning to presentation rate is monotonic, then any two presentation rates will be equally informative with regard to the prediction, because the prediction is exactly the same for all presentation rates: Learning should be better at the slower of the two rates. The *size* of the difference in performance will vary depending on the two presentation rates selected if the underlying function is nonlinear, but that simply means that some pairs of points would provide statistically more powerful tests of the predictions, assuming that the number of children is fixed. But other than for the purposes of statistical power, the size of a difference is typically irrelevant for much theory-driven research.

Thus far our discussion has concerned independent variables that vary quantitatively. A parallel case can be made, however, when levels of an independent variable differ qualitatively. Here, of course, there is no underlying function that relates performance to an independent variable, and thus two levels of an independent variable provide data about only one ordinal relation. Other comparisons of interest must be tested rather than inferred from a continuum. On this basis, one might expect that the norm would be to sample many qualitatively different levels of an independent variable (either within or across experiments), but this is probably the exception rather than the rule. In many lines of research on children's learning and memory, one typically encounters two levels of a qualitative independent variable in the ubiquitous 2 X 2 design. Illustrative examples would include comparisons of (a) violent and "neutral" films in the study of learning of aggressive behavior; (b) learning of relevant versus irrelevant stimuli; (c) responsive versus unresponsive individuals in studies of social reinforcement; (d) children told to label the names of stimuli in a learning and memory task versus those not so instructed; and (e) recall of organized information versus recall of disorganized information.

Shortcomings

Ordinal relations among means are sufficient to evaluate most current hypotheses regarding children's learning and memory, and the 2 X 2 X $\cdots$ X n design (where n refers to the number of age groups) will usually provide the needed data. However, these practices have several shortcomings from an instructional perspective. If one is interested in identifying conditions that facilitate instruction, a statistically significant ordinal difference between means will almost always be inadequate as the principal criterion upon which to evaluate research. In its place are one or two socially agreed-upon criteria. First, instructional objectives are often formulated in absolute terms. For example, at the end of first grade, a child should attain socially specified levels of achievement in reading, arithmetic, and the like. Thus, in evaluating conditions of instruction, one needs to know if achievement in that condition equals or exceeds the chosen criterial level of achievement. Second, because some costs are almost certainly associated with implementation of a new instructional "condition" (i.e., a new method for teaching reading), that method must be tangibly better than existing conditions, where tangible refers to a socially agreed upon value for the increase in achievement that merits the cost of the new system.

If the precise value of a mean and the size of a difference between means are often the critical data in instructional research, then the standard 2 X 2 design will rarely be appropriate in instructional research, for the observed means (and differences between means) will depend entirely on the ad hoc selection of particular levels of an independent variable.

Alternatives

A better approach is to sample levels of an independent variable broadly (i.e., selecting many levels). In this way, one can estimate the influence on performance associated with each value of an independent variable as well as estimate the exact sizes of differences in performance between conditions. With these data, one could then decide what levels of an independent variable should be used to achieve desired performance goals. In addition, one could decide if the increase in performance merits the associated costs.

Let us return to the study of learning and memory strategies to illustrate what might be done. It is well established in the developmental literature that teaching students to use appropriate strategies for learning and remembering improves their performance on academic tasks. The results of a study by Pressley and Levin (1978) are typical in this regard. The task was to learn 18 elementary Spanish vocabulary words. Some of the sixth graders in the study were taught to use a keyword mnemonic: Children were first taught to associate the foreign word to a similar-sounding English word (i.e., the keyword). For example, *carta,* meaning letter, might be associated to *cart.* Children were then told to form a mental image of this keyword interacting with its English equivalent. So, for example, the student might imagine a letter resting inside a shopping cart. Children taught this strategy recalled nearly twice as many words (68%) as children of comparable age and ability who were left to their own devices to learn the words.

Based on this facilitation and other positive features, several investigators (e.g., Levin, in press) have argued that the keyword method has much instructional merit. Unfortunately, most of the extant work in the descriptive theoretical tradition has simply focused on showing that the keyword method is powerful relative to appropriate control conditions and provides few specific guidelines regarding the manner in which the keyword method should be implemented in classrooms for greatest effectiveness. For example, one would need to know how much the keyword-generated images should be reviewed in order to maximize retention. Certainly retention would be expected to increase as a function of the opportunities for review. If that were a pressing theoretical question, it could be tested by comparing retention of words rehearsed once or twice with those rehearsed several times. As an instructional matter, however, the important data are changes in level of learning associated with various frequencies of review: Because successive reviews require additional time, whether we decide to allocate instructional time for additional review would be determined, in part, by the resulting increments in retention. If, for example, there is a point beyond which successive reviews yield negligible gains in retention, they would represent a poor investment in instructional time.

Such data were provided in a study by Kail, Collier, and Hale (Note 2). Undergraduates as well as junior high and high school students were taught the keyword method and then asked to use it to learn the names of various products manufactured in different cities. Subjects were given from one to four trials (five in the case of undergraduates) to study each city-product pair. The maximum number of study trials was set at four for junior high and high school students and five for under-

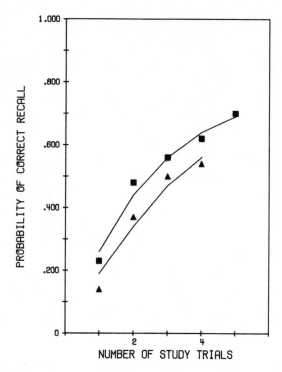

Figure 4-1. Probability of recall as a function of the number of study trials. Data for junior high and high school students are represented by triangles; data for undergraduates are represented by squares. The functions represent predicted performance for the two groups of students derived from the best fitting exponential equations.

graduates, for the practical reason that this represented the upper limit in terms of the length of time that students were willing to devote to the task.

Probability of recall (collapsed across several different retention intervals) is depicted in Figure 4-1 as a function of the number of opportunities for review. Two aspects of these findings are noteworthy. First, approximately three to four reviews yielded nearly asymptotic levels of recall for junior high and high school students, whereas four or five reviews yielded asymptotic recall for undergraduates. Second, the asymptotic level of recall is reasonably accurate: Individuals learned most of the products.

Obviously these results are only a small step toward specifying the conditions under which the keyword method could best be used in classrooms. A number of other variables would have to be examined in isolation and in interaction before one could generate, with much confidence, specific guidelines regarding the classroom use of the keyword method. The study, however, does represent some of the elements of the research strategy that is needed. The quantitative relationship between the amount of review and various levels of recall was identified for the entire practical domain of this independent variable. Hence, it provides a strong starting point from which to make recommendations regarding effective use of review of keyword-generated images in instructional settings.

Summary

Only ordinal predictions can be derived from most existing theories of children's learning, memory, and thinking. Hence, 2 X 2 designs are sufficient to test these theories. The shortcomings of these designs for instructional purposes are that (a) absolute values of parameters are ignored, as are absolute values of differences between parameters; and (b) values of independent variables are selected arbitrarily, with the result that boundary conditions of effects are often unknown. The suggested alternative is to study the level of performance associated with a broad range of values of an independent variable. In this way absolute levels of performance and the domain of the independent variable are central rather than incidental to the research.

Analysis of Data

Current Practices

Associated with the experimental designs of theoretically driven research in cognitive developmental psychology is a distinctive and generally familiar set of analytic methods. Traditionally this approach involves the use of analysis of variance to determine if means differ in the predicted manner at a statistically acceptable level. Thus, in Hagen and Kail's (1973) study of children's rehearsal (described earlier), one focus of the analysis was the interaction of age and the position of the picture tested. The fact that this interaction was significant, in conjunction with post hoc analyses to identify the locus of the interaction, led us to conclude that only the older children were rehearsing.

Shortcomings

This type of analysis could be conducted in research with an instructional focus, but it is not the most useful approach. For instructional purposes, analysis of variance and its associated procedures have several limiting features. First, the usual focus of analysis of variance is the statistical significance of differences between means. It is, however, quite conceivable—some would say routine—that an independent variable can produce statistically significant effects and yet have a relatively minor influence on the dependent variable (i.e., account for a relatively small percentage of variance in the dependent variable). Second, the analysis of variance typically does not provide information about the likely values of those means or the likely values of differences between means. Third, in most applications, analysis of variance requires that an investigator combine the data of individuals; it is often ill suited for analyzing the data of individuals separately.

Alternatives

For each of these shortcomings there is an alternative approach that is well established in textbooks, if not in actual practice.

Percentage of Variance. For a variable to be worthy of serious study by instructionally oriented psychologists, it must produce reliable (i.e., statistically significant) effects in the dependent variable. But all independent variables that yield significant differences are not of equal instructional import, for some account for greater variance in the dependent variable than others. Because implementation of instructional variables represents an investment of instructional resources, it is important to concentrate research efforts on those variables that yield significant and large effects.

Hence, we need some measure of the variance accounted for by an independent variable to gauge the potential instructional import of that variable. In the analysis of variance framework, ω^2 (Hays, 1973) or η^2 (Cohen & Cohen, 1975) are indices of proportion of variance. These measures, like R^2, range from 0 to 1 and indicate the proportion of variance in a dependent variable that is associated with a main effect or interaction. For example, for the data presented in Figure 4-1, ω^2 for the main effect of number of study trials was .19 for junior high and high school students and .17 for undergraduates. Thus, the number of study trials accounts for a reasonable amount of variance in the recall data, enough to merit further study.

Measures of strength of association like ω^2 and η^2 rarely appear in cognitive developmental research. As argued previously, this no doubt reflects the fact that the statistical significance of a predicted effect is critical for formulating and evaluating hypotheses, while the strength of such an effect is less important or even irrelevant. There is, perhaps, another reason for the absence of such measures in the literature, one worth discussing briefly. The size of an association between two variables is influenced by the specific values of the independent variable. Hence, psychologists who do correlational research typically make sure that samples include the entire range of possible values of variables. As we argued in the previous section, quite the opposite practice prevails in experimentation on children's learning and memory: Investigators typically sample a few levels of an independent variable and the same levels are not necessarily used in successive experiments or by different investigators. A result of this practice is that ω^2 or η^2 would be expected to vary across experiments, depending on the chosen levels of the independent variable, and the data from any single experiment is probably a poor basis from which to estimate the strength of the relation between the independent variable and the dependent variable in the population.

This fact alone should not preclude the use of ω^2 or η^2. These indices do reflect the influence of a variable relative to others in the experiment and relative to within-cell (i.e., subject) variance. As Cohen and Cohen (1975) put it:

> We find such measures to be quite useful, provided that their dependence on the levels and relative sample sizes of the research factor is understood. When necessary, one simply attaches to them, as a condition or qualification, the distribution of the research factor. We find such qualifications no more objectionable, in principle, than the potentially many others (apparatus, tests, time of day, subjects, experimenters) on which research results may depend. (pp. 5-6)

Furthermore, if, as I suggested previously, investigators would sample values of independent variables broadly, estimates of ω^2 and η^2 would vary less from experiment to experiment, because they would always reflect the entire range of the independent variable.

Estimating Means and Their Differences. Inferences about the values of population means may be made on the basis of confidence intervals. If we compute 95% confidence intervals for the data from junior high and high school students presented in Figure 4-1, the best estimate of mean recall for the population is between .08 and .21 following one study trial, .30–.40 for two study trials, .44–.56 for three study trials, and .47–.60 for four study trials.

The drawback to confidence intervals is that they provide minimal information about the relations among means. Such information comes from an equation that expresses the dependent variable as a function of an independent variable (or set of independent variables). Orthogonal polynomials are often used to detect linear, quadratic, or other higher order relationships among means. For example, use of the method of orthogonal polynomials with the data for junior high and high school students presented in Figure 4-1 reveals significant linear components, $F(1, 96) = 85.06$, $p < .001$, plus significant nonlinear components, $F(1, 96) = 8.77, p < .01$.

One way to determine the nature of this nonlinear component in the data would be to fit successively higher order polynomials (e.g., quadratic, cubic) until the residual is no longer statistically significant. Another approach would be to select a specific nonlinear function derived from a mathematical model of the processes under investigation, should such a model be available. For example, the amount of learning over time (i.e., the learning curve) is well described by exponential functions of the general form

$$y = a(1 - e^{-tr}) \qquad (4\text{-}1)$$

where y is a measure of learning and t is the amount of time (or some correlate, such as the number of trials) on the learning task (Mazur & Hastie, 1978). This equation includes two free parameters: a is the asymptotic level of learning (i.e., learning when time is infinite) and r is a rate parameter indicating how rapidly a subject reaches asymptotic levels of learning.

As can be seen in Figure 4-1, the fit of Equation 4-1 to the keyword data is quite accurate. With such an equation, instructional goals could be formulated in terms of a number of items to be learned, and one could then estimate the number of study trials needed to achieve that objective. Such an equation, computed for these and other independent variables, would provide an empirically derived way of organizing course material in a manner that should maximize students' learning. Further, because of the wide applicability of the exponential function to learning data, there is the added benefit that the present findings can be readily compared with other relevant data (e.g., Mazur & Hastie, 1978).

Analysis of Individuals' Data. There is a final prescription for analysis of data obtained in instructional research: The level of analysis should always be data from single individuals rather than a group of individuals. As noted earlier, individuals typically differ in their solutions to complex tasks like those encountered in instruction. Hence, reliance upon aggregate data can often yield a pattern that reflects a mix of solution strategies and does not represent a strategy used by any individual (Simon, 1975), and so instructional recommendations derived from the analysis would be entirely misleading.

Most of the analytical tools described here can be applied successfully to the data from individual subjects—if one plans such analyses from the outset and consequently collects sufficient data per individual. Many examples could be cited where the methods discussed here have been used to characterize the performance of individual children on instructionally relevant tasks. Instances would include the use of computer simulation to reveal students' scientific and mathematical reasoning (Anderson, Greeno, Kline, & Neves, 1981; Baylor & Gascon, 1974; Klahr & Siegler, 1978) and the use of response time to determine individuals' solutions to problems like those appearing on psychometric tests (e.g., Kail, Pellegrino, & Carter, 1980; Sternberg & Rifkin, 1979; Carter, Pazak, & Kail, in press).

An emphasis on analyzing data for individuals does not mean that the number of models of performance must be as large as the number of individuals performing the task. To the contrary, typically only a small number of models is necessary to explain the performance of the majority of individuals. Nor does the focus on individuals signal an abandonment of the search for general psychological laws and general instructional recommendations. Instead, I am simply suggesting that the surest route to truly general laws and recommendations is first to explain the performance of individuals, then to look for commonalities across individuals in these explanations (see Underwood, 1975, for a related view).

Summary

The traditional preoccupation in descriptive theoretical work with significance testing is insufficient for instructional research. The latter would be better served (a) by increased emphasis on the proportion of variance accounted for by independent variables; (b) by determining confidence intervals for means, and expressing dependent variables as a function of an independent variable or combination of independent variables, and (c) analyzing data for individuals rather than for groups of individuals.

Concluding Remarks

The thesis of this chapter has been that the goals of descriptive theoretical research result in methodological practices that are often poorly suited for attaining the aims of instructional research, which I defined as determining how all students can achieve socially determined levels of achievement. I have shown that with regard to (a) choice of experimental tasks, (b) experimental designs, and (c) methods of analysis, the dominant methodological practices of cognitive developmental psychology tend to minimize the likely impact of this work on instruction.

Given the extent of these differences, what can be said about the future relationship between descriptive theoretical work on children's learning, memory, and thinking, and instructional work with children? Differences in terms of experimental design and methods of analysis are most easily addressed, for these seem to reflect the current state of theoretical work in cognitive development psychology. While the 2 × 2 design and its concomitant analytic modes have been sufficient to evaluate many extant theories, this need not always be the case. Indeed, there are many recent instances in which more elaborate experimental designs and analytic techniques have been used in cognitive developmental work (e.g., Brainerd, in press; Gitomer, Pellegrino, & Bisanz, 1983; Sternberg & Rifkin, 1979, Wilkinson, DeMarinis, & Riley, in press). As cognitive developmental theory becomes more sophisticated, the predictions of such theories should become more precise: Predictions about the significance of main effects and interactions will be supplemented with predictions about values for particular parameters and the form of functions relating dependent variables to independent variables.

The experimental tasks of descriptive theoretical research have traditionally been selected because (a) they are representative of some characteristic of children's learning, memory, or thinking; and (b) they afford considerable experimental control. However, I argued earlier that sophisticated methods now exist that allow us to study complex behaviors with considerable precision. Hence, if experimental control no longer necessitates the use of a distinctive class of tasks that are streamlined in their stimulus and response characteristics, then we can pay greater attention to ensuring that our tasks indeed be representative of the broad domain of children's learning, memory, and thinking (see Chapter 6 in this volume for related arguments). One general approach that follows from this conclusion would be to identify the important settings in which children learn (e.g., schools, neighborhoods) and then devise ways to investigate in depth the learning that occurs there.

In sum, then, we have come full circle: No longer is it necessarily the case that instructional prescriptions must follow (and have secondary status to) descriptive theoretical work. To the contrary, because of methodological advances that allow us to investigate complex behaviors with precision, instructional tasks now represent one of the important proving grounds of such work.

Reference Notes

1. Stevenson, H. *Learning and cognition.* Unpublished manuscript, 1975.
2. Kail, R., Collier, D. S., & Hale, C. A. *Maximizing the effectiveness of the keyword method.* Unpublished manuscript, 1981.

References

Anderson, J. R. *Language, memory, and thought.* Hillsdale, NJ: Erlbaum, 1976.
Anderson, J. R., Greeno, J. G., Kline, P. J., & Neves, D. M. Acquisition of problem-solving skill. In J. R. Anderson (Ed.), *Cognitive skills and their acquisition.* Hillsdale, NJ: Erlbaum, 1981.
Atkinson, R. C. Adaptative instructional systems: Some attempts to optimize the learning process. In D. Klahr (Ed.), *Cognition and instruction.* Hillsdale, NJ: Erlbaum, 1976.
Baylor, G. W., & Gascon, J. An information-processing theory of the development of weight seriation in children. *Cognitive Psychology,* 1974, *6,* 1–40.
Bijou, S. W., & Baer, D. M. The laboratory-experimental study of child behavior. In P. H. Mussen (Ed.), *Handbook of research methods in child development.* New York: Wiley, 1960.
Bijou, S. W., & Ruiz, R. *Behavior modification: Contributions to education.* Hillsdale, NJ: Erlbaum, 1981.
Brainerd, C. J. Young children's mental arithmetic errors: A working-memory analysis. *Child Development,* in press.
Brown, A. L., & DeLoache, J. S. Skills, plans, and self-regulation. In R. S. Siegler (Ed.), *Children's thinking: What develops?* Hillsdale, NJ: Erlbaum, 1978.
Brown, J. S., & Burton, R. R. Diagnostic models for procedural bugs in basic mathematical skills. *Cognitive Science,* 1978, *2,* 155–192.
Carter, P., Pazak, B., & Kail, R. Algorithms for processing spatial information. *Journal of Experimental Child Psychology,* in press.
Cohen, J., & Cohen, P. *Applied multiple regression/correlation analysis for the behavioral sciences.* Hillsdale, NJ: Erlbaum, 1975.
Druker, J. F., & Hagen, J. W. Developmental trends in the processing of task-relevant and task-irrelevant information. *Child Development,* 1969, *40,* 371–382.
Faw, T. T., & Nunnally, J. C. The influence of stimulus complexity, novelty, and affective value on children's visual fixations. *Journal of Experimental Child Psychology,* 1968, *6,* 141–153.
Gitomer, D., Pellegrino, J. W., & Bisanz, J. Developmental change and invariance in semantic processing. *Journal of Experimental Child Psychology,* 1983, *35,* 56–80.

Glaser, R. Components of a psychology of instruction: Toward a science of design. *Review of Educational Research*, 1976, *46*, 1–24.

Glaser, R. The future of testing: A research agenda for cognitive psychology and psychometrics. *American Psychologist*, 1981, *36*, 923–936.

Hagen, J. W. The effect of distraction on selective attention. *Child Development*, 1967, *38*, 685–694.

Hagen, J. W., & Hale, G. H. The development of attention in children. In A. D. Pick (Ed.), *Minnesota symposia on child psychology* (Vol. 7). Minneapolis: University of Minnesota Press, 1973.

Hagen, J. W., Jongeward, R. H., & Kail, R. V. Cognitive perspectives on the development of memory. In H. W. Reese (Ed.), *Advances in child development and behavior* (Vol. 10). New York: Academic Press, 1975.

Hagen, J. W., & Kail, R. V. Facilitation and distraction in short-term memory. *Child Development*, 1973, *44*, 831–836.

Hagen, J. W., Meacham, J. A., & Mesibov, G. Verbal labeling, rehearsal, and short-term memory. *Cognitive Psychology*, 1970, *1*, 47–58.

Hays, W. L. *Statistics for the social sciences* (2nd ed.). New York: Holt, Rinehart, & Winston, 1973.

Kail, R., & Bisanz, J. Cognitive development: An information-processing perspective. In R. Vasta (Ed.), *Strategies and techniques of child study*. New York: Academic Press, 1982. (a)

Kail, R., & Bisanz, J. Cognitive strategies. In C. R. Puff (Ed.), *Handbook of research methods in human memory and cognition*. New York: Academic Press, 1982. (b)

Kail, R., & Hagen, J. W. Memory in childhood. In B. B. Wolman (Ed.), *Handbook of developmental psychology*. Englewood Cliffs, NJ: Prentice-Hall, 1982.

Kail, R., Pellegrino, J., & Carter, P. Developmental changes in mental rotation. *Journal of Experimental Child Psychology*, 1980, *29*, 102–116.

Klahr, D., & Siegler, R. S. The representation of children's knowledge. In H. W. Reese & L. P. Lipsitt (Eds.), *Advances in child development and behavior* (Vol. 12). New York: Academic Press, 1978.

Klahr, D., & Wallace, J. G. *Cognitive development: An information-processing view*. Hillsdale, NJ: Erlbaum, 1976.

Levin, J. R. The mnemonic 80's: Keywords in the classroom. *Educational Psychologist*, in press.

Mazur, J. E., & Hastie, R. Learning as accumulation: A reexamination of the evidence. *Psychological Bulletin*, 1978, *85*, 1256–1274.

Newell, A., & Simon, H. *Human problem solving*. Englewood Cliffs, NJ: Prentice-Hall, 1972.

Odom, R. Effects of visual and auditory stimulus deprivation and satiation on children's performance in an operant task. *Journal of Experimental Child Psychology*, 1964, *1*, 16–25.

Pressley, M., & Levin, J. R. Developmental constraints associated with children's use of the keyword method of foreign language learning. *Journal of Experimental Child Psychology*, 1978, *26*, 359–372.

Resnick, L. B. Task analysis in instructional design: Some cases from mathematics. In D. Klahr (Ed.), *Cognition and instruction*. Hillsdale, NJ: Erlbaum, 1976.

Rohwer, W. D. An introduction to research on individual and developmental differences in learning. In W. K. Estes (Ed.), *Handbook of learning and cognitive processes* (Vol. 3). Hillsdale, NJ: Erlbaum, 1976.

Rohwer, W. D., & Dempster, F. N. Memory development and educational processes. In R. V. Kail & J. W. Hagen (Eds.), *Perspectives on the development of memory and cognition.* Hillsdale, NJ: Erlbaum, 1977.

Ross, A. O. *Psychological aspects of learning disabilities and reading disorders.* New York: McGraw-Hill, 1976.

Simon, H. A. The functional equivalence of problem solving skills. *Cognitive Psychology,* 1975, *7,* 268-288.

Sternberg, R. J., & Rifkin, B. The development of analogical reasoning. *Journal of Experimental Child Psychology,* 1979, *27,* 195-232.

Stevenson, H. W. *Children's learning.* New York: Appleton-Century-Crofts, 1972. (a)

Stevenson, H. W. The taxonomy of tasks. In W. W. Hartup & J. deWit (Eds.), *Determinants of behavioral development.* New York: Academic Press, 1972. (b)

Underwood, B. J. Individual differences as a crucible in theory construction. *American Psychologist,* 1975, *30,* 128-134.

Wilkinson, A. C., DeMarinis, M., & Riley, S. J. Developmental and individual differences in rapid remembering. *Child Development,* in press.

Willows, D. M. Reading between the lines: Selective attention in good and poor readers. *Child Development,* 1974, *45,* 408-415.

Woods, S. S., Resnick, L. B., & Groen, G. J. An experimental test of five process models for subtraction. *Journal of Educational Psychology,* 1975, *67,* 17-21.

Young, R. M., & O'Shea, T. Errors in children's subtraction. *Cognitive Science,* 1981, *5,* 153-177.

5. Social Learning, Causal Attribution, and Moral Internalization

David G. Perry and Louise C. Perry

For the past two decades much of the research concerned with the effects of socialization practices on the child's personality and social development has been inspired by learning theory. It is thus not surprising that learning-theory explanations figure prominently in contemporary accounts of the effectiveness of such practices as punishment, social reinforcement, and modeling (e.g., Parke, 1970, 1974; Walters & Grusec, 1977). Over the last several years, however, psychologists working within the framework of attribution theory have presented an alternative conceptualization of the effects of socialization practices on the child's development and have begun to muster substantive support for their position.

The time is ripe for a review of the recent attribution research and for an assessment of the degree to which the attribution research poses a threat to our previous understanding of the socialization process based on learning-theory principles. Such a review is the purpose of this chapter. We have chosen to center our discussion on recent attribution research about moral internalization. Moral internalization is the learning process by which children come to adhere to society's rules even when they are free of external surveillance or the expectation of rewards or punishments from socializing agents. We examine this process because many of the attribution theorists' more influential experiments have addressed issues of internalization. Furthermore, when trying to understand processes of moral development, we confront a set of issues that are basic to understanding the socialization process more generally.

Our chapter begins with a summary of the predictions and rationale that characterize the attribution perspective on moral internalization; an overview of modern social learning theory follows. We then review recent attribution research on each of five socialization practices (punishment, reasoning, reward, direct verbal attribution, and modeling), discussing for each practice the extent to which the attribution research contributes to our understanding of the socialization process. In a third section we examine the role of the child's age in attributional analyses of moral development. Fourth, we discuss a paradox in the socialization literature: Although in field studies firm parental control is associated with good moral internalization in children, recent attribution research has been taken to suggest that firm control undermines moral internalization. We discuss how various theorists have tried to resolve this issue. Finally, we present our conclusions. We propose that the attribution research furnishes several principles that help us understand the internalization process and also offers valuable suggestions for practical child rearing. However, we believe modifications to the prevailing attribution account of internalization are necessary if the theory is to constitute a viable account of how moral internalization typically occurs (and can best be facilitated by socializing agents) under naturalistic conditions.

The Attributional and Social Learning Analyses of Moral Internalization

The Attribution Perspective

To achieve internalization of society's values by their children, most parents, teachers, and other socializing agents agree that a first step involves inducing children to comply behaviorally with these values. The assumption seems to be that children are unlikely to internalize a norm if they are allowed to behave in ways that violate it. Thus most parents do what they can to prevent their children from telling lies, breaking promises, disobeying prohibitions, stealing, and engaging in other negative behaviors; and they try to get their children to practice positive behaviors, such as sharing with a friend in need, showing concern for others, complying with requests for mature behavior, and delaying gratification. Naturally a great many of a parent's initial attempts to induce his or her child to comply with social norms will involve some sort of external control: The parent may threaten the child with loss of affection or some privilege, may offer an attractive reward (a bribe) for compliance, may plead with the child until the child complies, and so on. But it is hoped that with age children will come to accept the values as their own, that they will inhibit unwanted behaviors and practice desired ones even when not under the watchful eyes of adults. How, according to attribution theory, does this occur?

According to the attribution perspective on internalization (e.g., Lepper, 1981), when children are induced to comply with a norm, they seek to explain their behavior to themselves ("Now why did I go along with that?"). Furthermore, children can justify their behavior in any of a number of ways. Suppose a father has been successful in persuading his son to watch a family-type television program rather than a rerun of *The Untouchables,* a program the child would prefer to watch.

Afterward, according to attribution theory, the boy will try to justify his counter-attitudinal behavior. He may conclude, "I didn't watch *The Untouchables* because Dad would have spanked me if he caught me watching it." Or he may conclude, "I really don't like *The Untouchables* all that much anyway," or even, "Good people don't watch programs like *The Untouchables,* and I am a good person."

Moreover, the specific causal attribution a child generates for complying with a request is believed to influence the probability of the child's internalizing the value. Internalization is expected to be strongest when children generate an "internal" attribution for their initial compliance—when they believe their conformity stems from their own intrinsic motivation to be good or when they believe the behavior they have been induced to avoid is inherently wrong or undesirable. In contrast, internalization is thought to be weakest when children generate an "external" attribution for compliance—when they attribute their compliance to the operation of an external contingency, such as the fear of getting caught and punished or the anticipation of an attractive material reward for compliance. The theory is that when children who attribute their compliance to internal factors are confronted with a later temptation to break the rule in the absence of external surveillance, they will not be able to do so without violating their own attitude or their own self-image of being a "good person." The prospect of dissonance, guilt, or dashed self-esteem for transgressing motivates them to conform. In contrast, external attribution children, when tempted to break a rule, first simply scan the external environment to see if anyone is watching. If they can assure themselves that they are free of surveillance, they go ahead and deviate. In sum, children's perceptions of what is motivating them to follow a rule influence how diligently they strive to follow the rule when external contingencies are lifted.

According to the attribution analysis, children are most likely to generate internal attributions when compliance has been induced in a way that minimizes the children's perception of external control. In other words, children who have observed themselves to obey a rule and cannot pinpoint any salient factor in the external environment that forced them to behave the way they did are likely to conclude that they must have been (and still are) intrinsically motivated to adhere to the standard in question (Bem, 1972). Thus a major prediction is that parents who use heavy-handed disciplinary techniques that draw the child's attention to the operation of an external contingency (e.g., threat of physical punishment, promise of attractive material rewards) to induce compliance are preventing their children from generating internal attributions. In fact, the use of such techniques is thought to foster external attributions for compliance that undermine internalization.

The attribution account of moral internalization is not in any significant sense a "developmental theory." That is, the theory does not explicitly recognize that the effects of socialization practices depend on the child's developmental level (e.g., cognitive abilities). Nor does the theory regard moral internalization as the outcome of a sequence of events or processes that typically span an appreciable length of time (months, years) in the child's natural development. Moral internalization is thought to occur immediately upon the child's initial compliance with a social value in the absence of perceived external control.

To what extent are the attribution predictions at odds with learning-theory explanations of the effects of parental discipline? We cannot furnish a simple answer to this question, for there is no single, generally agreed-upon learning theory of socialization. Instead, there exists a variety of learning-theory explanations of socialization and moral development. Rather than try to compare the attribution account with each of these learning-theory accounts, we have elected to compare the attribution account with what we perceive to be the most influential of contemporary learning-theory accounts of socialization—Bandura's (1977) social learning theory.

The Social Learning Perspective

According to social learning theory, behavior that accords with a social norm but occurs in the absence of external surveillance is primarily under the control of cognitive self-regulatory processes. Bandura suggests that as children get older they develop and continuously refine their conceptions of what society deems to be appropriate and inappropriate conduct for people like themselves. Children base these conceptions on a variety of social learning experiences—their personal history of rewards and punishments for various behaviors, the consequences they see similar others receive for their actions, direct verbal tuition from socializing agents, and so forth. At the same time as children are synthesizing information from these various sources in order to arrive at standards of blameworthy and praiseworthy behavior, they start to see that it would be to their advantage to regulate their own behavior in terms of these standards. Children can gain this insight in a variety of ways. Perhaps children observe their parents and other persons regulating their behavior so as to achieve desired outcomes, and the children infer that they can do the same for themselves. Or perhaps children are verbally tutored in ways to self-regulate (e.g., "If you spend 15 minutes each night studying your spelling words, you'll get your spelling tests right;" "If you remember to clean up your room each morning before going to school, we'll take you to the movies on Saturday"). Thus children begin to regulate their behavior so as to bring it into line with standards of appropriate conduct. For example, a child may choose to forgo watching television in favor of studying because she views such self-regulation as a stepping stone to greater, though perhaps temporally remote, personal and social benefits. In the process, the child may set subgoals that require self control, rewarding herself when she matches her subgoals and criticizing herself when she falls short of them.

Furthermore, once children observe themselves successfully executing difficult self-controlling responses, their confidence in their ability to self-regulate should be strengthened. (Or, to use Bandura's term, their "perceived self-efficacy" in self-regulation is bolstered.) Bandura suggests that once children believe themselves capable of self-regulation, they should increase their attempts at self-regulation in the future, persist longer at self-regulation in the face of obstacles, and—if their attempts at self-regulation prove successful—adjust their standards upward to become more exacting and challenging. The children might even generalize their self-regulation to new areas of social and personal functioning.

It is instructive to highlight some points of difference between the attribution and the social learning perspectives. First, attribution theorists stress the *negative* role that external controls and incentives, such as external punishments and rewards, play in the socialization process. In fact, some attribution researchers (e.g., Lepper, 1981) suggest that parents should do whatever they can to eliminate external incentives and substitute more subtle ways of inducing compliance in children that will prevent children from making external attributions of motivation. Lepper, for example, suggests that a major goal of future research should be the discovery of new socialization techniques that allow parents to manipulate children into displaying desired behavior without their realizing that they are being externally pressured (1981; Lepper & Gilovich, 1982). In contrast, social learning theorists see a positive, constructive role for salient external incentives in the establishment and maintenance of self-regulation. In social learning theory, contingent external outcomes serve the essential function of informing children about the sorts of behaviors that it is important to self-regulate. For example, when children see that a certain form of behavior reliably produces an aversive outcome (e.g., social disapproval, punishment, failure), they are motivated to initiate the self-controlling responses that will help them avoid the negative outcome. Furthermore, as we intimated earlier, if children find that their self-regulation brings the desired external outcome, their attempts at self-regulation in the future are strengthened, not diminished. In essence, external incentives can motivate and maintain self-control.

A related point is that social learning theorists do not paint the same sharp dichotomy between perceptions of internal causation and perceptions of external causation that attribution theorists do. Attributionists often express the opinion that perceived internal motivation and perceived external motivation for a behavior are mutually exclusive. In contrast, social learning theorists stress that self-regulation is often in the service of an external end. This implies that children can fuse internal and external attributions into a single self-statement that motivates self-regulation (e.g., "I am a good boy because I made my bed every morning this week so I could get my allowance"; "I am a good girl—I managed to go a whole week without disrupting the class so the teacher wouldn't send me to the principal's office"). In this analysis, external and internal attributions can be compatible, even mutually reinforcing, and it is difficult to say that one sort of attribution is more important than the other in sparking and maintaining self-control. It is partly for this reason that social learning theorists prefer to speak of "self-regulation" rather than "internalization." (For a detailed discussion of how internal and external factors play "reciprocally determining" roles in self-regulation, see Bandura, 1978.)

There are also points of compatibility between the attribution and the social learning positions on disciplinary practice and internalization. Like the attribution theorists, the social learning theorists argue that external incentives can sometimes be hazardous to the socialization process. For example, social learning theorists point out that unnecessarily harsh discipline (e.g., severe physical punishment) can teach the child aggressive and impulsive habits that compete with self-controlled behavior, and that material reward can distract children to the point where they lose interest in a rewarded activity (Bandura, 1977). Also, in his theory of self-regulation, Bandura (1978) incorporates some principles of causal attribution. He suggests, for example, that when children observe themselves successfully engaging in self-regulation, they are most likely to increase their confidence in their ability to self-regulate (and hence continue to self-regulate) if they have performed the self-regulating responses without excessive external assistance. A mother who constantly reminds her child to study or clean up, then, should be less likely to promote her child's self-perceived efficacy in self-regulation than if she somehow manages to motivate her child to perform the desired behaviors regularly without the external reminders. In other words, self-regulation is most likely to become self-perpetuating if the child can conclude that the self-regulation flows from his or her own skills.

Is social learning theory a developmental theory? Although social learning theorists do not emphasize developmental factors (e.g., age-related changes in the child's cognitive apparatus that influence the way the child synthesizes social information), it is apparent that social learning theorists consider internalization to be the product of cumulative developmental experiences. For instance, the child's standards of appropriate conduct are believed to represent the integration of diverse social learning experiences. This implies that the social learning theorists regard moral internalization as a process requiring considerable time and undergoing considerable change. That self-regulation is regarded as the outcome of a sequence of social learning experiences (formulating personal standards, observing the benefits of self-regulation in others, initiating preliminary self-controlling responses oneself, estimating one's competence at self-regulation) also suggests that social learning theorists regard internalization as a gradually evolving process.

Having now summarized the attribution and social learning perspectives on internalization, we turn to the recent empirical work carried out to evaluate the attribution position.

Techniques of Socialization: Recent Attribution Research

Punishment

The prediction from attribution theory is that use of unnecessarily powerful and punitive control techniques to produce compliance with parental demands undermines internalization of the values underlying those demands. An early study by Aronson and Carlsmith (1963) bears on this issue. Young children were asked to refrain from playing with a toy they had previously rated as attractive. Some children were threatened with mild punishment for deviation (the experimenter said she would be a little annoyed); others were threatened with more severe consequences (they were led to believe that the experimenter would become extremely angry and might leave the school). All children complied with the request to avoid playing with the toy. Afterward, when children were asked to judge the attractiveness of the toy again, children who received the mild threat devalued the toy, whereas those receiving the severe threat did not. Later research showed that children who received the mild threat also were more likely to avoid the forbidden toy when they were unexpectedly given an opportunity to play with it several weeks later (Freedman, 1965).

Aronson and Carlsmith interpreted their result in terms of cognitive dissonance theory, but Lepper (1973) pointed out that the result also confirms attribution theory. In his view, children receiving the mild threat lacked sufficient external justification for their avoidance of the toy during the temptation period and thus, in an effort to explain their behavior, concluded they must have avoided the toy because they did not like it. In contrast, children threatened severely could readily explain their behavior in terms of the strong external contingency and thus did not take their avoidance of the toy to imply dislike of it. Other explanations have been offered to account for the devaluation by mildly threatened children (Ebbesen, Bowers, Phillips, & Snyder, 1975; Dembroski & Pennebaker, 1975; Hom & Maxwell, 1979; Ostfeld & Katz, 1969). However, it is clear that the results are consistent with attribution theory.

In an important study, Lepper (1973) used Aronson and Carlsmith's "forbidden toy paradigm" to test another implication of the attribution model. Lepper reasoned that because mildly threatened children lack external justification for their compliance with the experimenter's request to resist temptation, they should be more likely than severely threatened children to conclude that they complied because they are by nature good, honest, and obedient. He thus predicted that mildly threatened children should be more likely to behave morally in a new situation than severely threatened children. In this study, second-grade children initially resisted the temptation to play with a forbidden toy under a threat of either mild or severe punishment. Later, all children were tested for honesty in a different situation: Children were given an opportunity to falsify their scores secretly on a game in order to win a prize. As predicted, midly threatened children cheated less than severely threatened children, even though the test for cheating followed the initial compliance by several weeks and was conducted by a different adult in a different room of the children's school. This experiment is an important one, for it suggests that the ways adults solicit initial compliance from children can influence the probability of the children's forming a generalized moral disposition.

In Lepper's analysis, when children comply with adult values without obvious external coercion, they are likely to conclude that they are "good people." These internal attributions are thought to mediate further moral action. To test more directly the hypothesis that attributions mediate the effects of induced compliance, Lepper took the commendable step of assessing children's self-perceptions after the children had complied with either mild or severe threat (but before the cheating test). Specifically, half the children in each threat condition rated themselves on adjectives chosen to reflect an honesty-dishonesty dimension. Mildly threatened children's self-perceptions were more positive than those of severely threatened children, although the difference reached significance only when one child's aberrant data were excluded from analysis. Thus the hypothesis that minimally coercive techniques are more likely to promote self-perception of intrinsic goodness was modestly supported.

Better support for the hypothesis that salient external control undermines self-perceptions of goodness comes from a study by Smith, Gelfand, Hartmann, and Partlow (1979). Seven- to nine-year-old children were initially encouraged to donate some of their earnings from a game to another child. For some children, donation was elicited by threat of material punishment (monetary fines) for non-compliance; for other children, donation was solicited without reference to external consequences. Afterward, children were asked to provide reasons for their having shared during the game. Children in the punishment group tended to mention the external contingency as their reason for sharing, whereas children in the no-consequences group more often expressed their sharing in terms of a personal disposition (e.g., "I didn't want to be selfish"; "I guess I just like to share").

To determine if attributions for induced sharing are related to later noncoerced sharing, Smith et al. also gave the children another opportunity for altruism. In this phase, children were told they could donate but did not have to, and the children were tested without adult supervision. The results gave ambiguous support to the attribution position. The no-consequences children as a group did not share significantly more than the punishment children. However, when the relationship between attributions and anonymous sharing was examined within each group, children who had given an external attribution for sharing in the first phase shared less in the test phase. Thus we have suggestive but not overwhelming evidence that salient external contingencies undermine attributions of intrinsic prosocial motivation and that intrinsic attributions are associated with better moral internalizations.

An important attribution perspective on the role of punishment in moral internalization was offered by Dienstbier, Hillman, Lehnhoff, Hillman, and Valkenaar (1975). Dienstbier et al. proposed that the likelihood of children's withstanding temptation in the absence of external surveillance is a function of the causal attributions children generate in order to explain the emotional arousal they experience when faced with the temptation to do something they have previously been punished for doing. The authors suggest that virtually all children become aroused (anxious) when faced with an opportunity to break a prohibition. Such anxiety may stem from a conditioning process (association of deviation with punishment), from the approach-avoidance conflict the child faces, from the child's uncertainty over the outcome of deviating, or from something else. But, Dienstbier et al. argue, a child's perception of the cause of his or her anxiety determines whether the child will deviate or not. Specifically, if children believe they feel anxious because they are worried about getting caught and punished (an external attribution), then the chance of deviation in the absence of external surveillance is high. Presumably, such children reason like this: "The only reason to fear deviating is the possibility of being found out and punished; I know nobody is watching right now, so I might as well deviate." In contrast, children who believe their anxiety is due to contemplating something that is inherently wrong or who are afraid of violating their self-image of being a good person should be unlikely to deviate even in the absence of adult surveillance.

Dienstbier et al. proposed that the way parents cognitively structure the punishment they administer to their children for transgressing can influence the children's causal attributions for the arousal they experience during subsequent temptations. To gather support for this position, Dienstbier et al. first induced children to break a prohibition: After the child had agreed to perform a tedious task in the experimenter's absence, the experimenter distracted the child from performing the task by activating some attractive toys by remote control. The experimenter then confronted the child with his or her deviation, but phrased his criticism differently for two groups of children. To one group, he remarked that the children were probably feeling upset because they had done something they had known to be wrong (internal attribution condition). To the other, he remarked that the children were probably feeling upset because they had been caught deviating by the experimenter (external attribution condition). Later, both groups were given another chance to perform the boring task in the face of distraction from the toys. (Pains were taken to assure the children that this time no one would be able to tell if they deviated or not.) Children in the internal attribution condition deviated only half as much as their counterparts in the external attribution condition, thus supporting the authors' formulation. The Dienstbier et al. research has its shortcomings; for example, attributions were not directly assessed and there is no guarantee that internal and external attribution children actually experienced the same degree of anxiety during the final temptation. However, the results are in line with the authors' attributional analysis.

We have reviewed the scant laboratory-experimental evidence linking punishment, attribution, and internalization. Attributional theorists point out that findings from field research also sometimes confirm attribution predictions. In numerous interview and observational studies, for example, parents who favor frequent and severe "power-assertive" discipline (in which parents gain compliance through a show of force, such as actual or threatened physical punishment or deprivation of privileges) have children who score low on several indices of internalization, especially resistance to deviation, remorse following transgression, and inhibitions against expressing aggression outside the home (see Hoffman, 1977, and Martin, 1975, for reviews). This is just what one would predict on the basis of attribution theory. Forceful parental discipline presumably sensitizes children to the fact that their behavior is governed by external contingencies, leaving the children with no motivation for conforming when the external contingencies are lifted. A field study linking parental style of discipline to children's attributions for moral conduct would be of interest. If asked to explain the behavior of story characters who are depicted as adhering to social values, will children whose parents favor power assertion tend to attribute the story characters' conformity to external concerns (e.g., "The boy didn't cheat because he was afraid he'd be found out if he did")?

Traditionally, research on punishment carried out by learning theorists has taken a very different tack from that of the attribution theorists. In the 1960s and early 1970s, learning theorists conducted numerous experiments aimed at determining the conditions under which contingent aversive stimuli (e.g., a buzzer) could serve to inhibit certain of children's responses (e.g., touching attractive toys, punching a Bobo doll) in the later absence of adults. Typically, external punishment has little effect on a child's inhibition of a response unless the punishment is administered in such a way that the child is able to discriminate punished from unpunished behavior and is motivated to remember the punished responses. For example, little response inhibition will occur unless either the physical properties of the punishment are arranged to motivate learning (i.e., the punishment is sufficiently intense to arouse anxiety, is judiciously timed, is applied consistently, etc.) or the punishment is accompanied by verbal reasoning that clarifies which responses are deviant and why. In other words, learning-theory research has provided information on how punishment should be administered if it is to inhibit responses at all.

The objective of the attribution research on punishment, of course, is quite different. Attribution theorists have been primarily concerned with demonstrating that the use of unnecessarily severe punishment to motivate initial compliance can undermine internalization. Thus learning-theory research and attribution research have been addressed to understanding different aspects of the disciplinary process. We see from the attribution research, however, that children's thoughts during and following a period of induced compliance need to be taken into account if we are to gain a fuller appreciation of the internalization process.

Reasoning

The learning-theory research on punishment and resistance to deviation carries a curious footnote. In the late 1960s and early 1970s, learning theorists discovered in laboratory experiments that when adults accompanied their punishment with a verbal rationale indicating why the punished behavior is undesirable, children's subsequent performance of the punished behavior fell to extraordinarily low levels—so low, in fact, that there was little room for factors previously found to influence punishment effectiveness (e.g., punishment timing and intensity) to contribute anything extra to the effect (e.g., Parke, 1969). One might have expected these dramatic effects to have stimulated vigorous research efforts to understand just why reasoning is so effective in inhibiting undesirable behavior. This was not the case. Of course, the effectiveness of different types of verbal reasoning was explored in several studies (Cheyne, 1972; LaVoie, 1974; Parke, 1974). One finding was that accompanying a buzzer with a concrete rationale ("The toy is fragile and might break") was more effective than a more abstract rationale ("The toy belongs to another child") at producing response inhibition in 3-year-old children but that the relative effectiveness of these two rationales was reversed for 5-year-olds (Parke, 1974). However, the flurry of interest in experimental investigations of reasoning was short lived. The lack of interest in possible psychological mechanisms mediating the effects of reasoning is all the more odd when we consider that several field researchers were reporting strong positive correlations between the parents' use of reasoning and indices of moral internalization in children (see Hoffman, 1970b).

Why was there so little sustained interest on the part of learning theorists in researching the effectiveness of reasoning? We suggest that contemporary learning theory lacked an adequately developed conceptual framework for generating hypotheses relevant to understanding the impact of verbal reasoning on moral development. A decade ago, social learning theory was just beginning to advertise that it was "going cognitive" (e.g., Mischel, 1973), and the theory could offer little insight into how children process information contained in parental reasoning. In consequence, learning theorists couched their explanations of rationale effectiveness in conditioning concepts. For example, Parke (1974) wrote that

> verbal rationales initially may acquire their inhibitory capacities by being paired with anxiety-arousing stimuli. . . . The socializing agent may pair a rationale with punishment, particularly with younger children. Through classical conditioning the child may eventually learn to inhibit when he hears the rationale. Another related possibility is the use of punishment for noncompliance with the rationale-based prohibition. The child learns to anticipate punishment for non-conformity to a verbal rationale. . . . In addition the child may learn to comply with verbal rationales by observing the inhibitory impact of rationales on the behavior of other children. (p. 119)

Although Parke acknowledged that rationale effectiveness depends on cognitive processes, there was little attempt by the learning theorists to put together a coherent account of what these processes might be. Unfortunately, the same can be said of contemporary social learning theory. For example, in his recent statements of socialization process, Bandura (e.g., 1977) makes only passing reference to parental reasoning.

Does attribution theory offer any new insights into how verbal reasoning aids moral internalization? Hoffman (1977) proposes an explanation for the effectiveness of reasoning that draws on principles of attribution. Based on field research, Hoffman emphasizes that the sort of reasoning found to correlate most consistently with measures of children's internalization is *other-oriented induction,* or reasoning in which the parent points out to the child the causal relationship between the child's behavior and positive or negative consequences for other people (e.g., "You can see Paul is sad; you can make him feel better by letting him play with your toy"; "Don't ever bite! You can see how much it hurts. How would you like it if someone did that to you?"). Hoffman suggests that inductive reasoning helps children learn to anticipate guilt for failing to adhere to a social norm. In his view, guilt is an empathic response to another's distress coupled with the belief that one is responsible for initiating or prolonging the distressed other's state. Like Dienstbier et al. (1975), Hoffman seems to suggest that children become emotionally aroused when confronted with an opportunity to deviate. If children interpret their arousal as empathic distress to another's plight and if children perceive themselves to play a causal role in the other's distress, then arousal turns to guilt, which persists until the children take some prosocial or moral action.

Hoffman speculates further that when children who have experienced inductive discipline are confronted with a later opportunity to deviate, they may recall the inductive message but may dissociate the message from its original external source, the parent. In other words, when children find themselves trying to talk themselves out of deviating (e.g., "Don't do it—if you hurt him you'll have no one to blame but yourself"), they may perceive the message to have originated within themselves. Hoffman cites evidence that such dissociation of the semantic content of a message from its original context would be consistent with memory theory (e.g., Tulving, 1972). Of course, according to attribution theory, if children find themselves espousing a social value without apparent external pressure, they should consider themselves intrinsically disposed to adhere to the standard.

Unfortunately, little evidence bears directly on Hoffman's speculations. Induction does seem to make children more aware of the feelings and thoughts of other people. For example, Bearison and Cassel (1975) report that parents who justify their disciplinary actions with statements that focus on the intentions and feelings of others (e.g., "Your teacher will feel said if you . . ."; "You could make her feel better if you . . .") rather than with statements that focus on the power of the parents, on status factors, or on appeals for conformity (e.g., "All children should . . ."; "Do it because I said so!") have children who are skilled at role taking (deciphering the private experiences of others). But Hoffman's suggestions that induction strengthens children's empathic reactions to other people's emotional states and helps children appreciate the causal role they can play in alleviating or aggravating such states remain untested. Furthermore, to date most evidence linking induction to children's behavior comes from correlational field studies, making statements of cause and effect difficult.

A recent study by Perry, Bussey, and Freiberg (1981) offers experimental evidence that induction facilitates internalization. In this study, 7- to 8-year-old children were first asked to share half their winnings from a bowling game with children who would not get a chance to play. For one third of the children, the request to share was accompanied by a short inductive appeal in which the experimenter emphasized that sharing makes other people happy and makes oneself feel good for having caused the other people's happiness. A second group heard a power-assertive appeal emphasizing that sharing is necessary because adults expect it and get angry when they find out that children have failed to practice it. A third (control) group was asked to share but was not given any accompanying rationale. After the children completed the initial phase of instructed sharing, they were given a further opportunity to share without adult supervision and without direct instructions to share. In this phase, children who had initially shared in compliance with the inductive appeal were roughly three times as generous as children in either of the other two conditions.

Although the Perry et al. study indicates the effectiveness of inductive reasoning, it leaves important questions unanswered. No measures were taken of children's attributions for donating in either phase of the study. Furthermore, the inductive appeal was complex, and which aspect of the appeal was responsible for its effectiveness is not known. Did induction work because it alerted children to the fact that sharing could make them happy, because it emphasized that sharing could make others happy, because it stressed the causal link between the other's happiness and one's own, or for some other reason? Because research from both field and laboratory now attests to the importance of induction in facilitating internalization, we believe the time has come to undertake systematic experimental work in order to elucidate the mechanisms underlying the effectiveness of inductive reasoning.

Induction is not, of course, the only form of reasoning with implications for children's attributions. As we saw in the previous section, the ways adults interpret to children the emotional upset they experience following transgression can also influence the children's internalizations (Dienstbier et al., 1975). Some additional hypotheses regarding reasoning can be derived from Kelley's (1973) attribution model. Kelley surmised that when people perceive "high consensus" for an actor's behavior (or believe that the actor's behavior would have been performed by almost everyone in similar circumstances), they are inclined to locate the cause of the actor's behavior in the external environment rather than in some personal quality of the actor. One implication of this principle is that if children feel they must conform to a social norm just because everyone else conforms to it, they may feel their compliance is externally forced and they may fail to internalize the norm. This prediction was confirmed in an experiment by Lepper, Zanna, and Abelson (1970). Children were asked to refrain from playing with an attractive toy. Before the temptation period, an adult told one group of children that all the other children who had been tested had complied with the request not to touch the toy. A second group was not given this information. (Both groups were threatened with mild punishment for deviating.) All children resisted the temptation, after which they were asked to evaluate the forbidden toy. Children given the consensus information failed to devalue the toy, presumably because they attributed their compliance to external pressures and had no need to explain their avoidance of the toy in any other terms.

Kelley also suggested that people are likely to attribute an actor's behavior to an enduring personal disposition if they see the actor consistently display the behavior across many situations rather than in only one or two situations. One implication of this hypothesis is that if adults can help make children aware of cross-situational consistencies in their prosocial conduct, then children should be likely to perceive themselves as possessing an intrinsic disposition to perform the desired behavior. We shall return to this point later when we discuss direct verbal attribution of moral dispositions.

An important benefit of reasoning is that it helps reduce children's perceptions of external coercion when parents must resort to force to motivate children's compliance. Dix and Grusec (Note 1), for example, found that the ill effects of power assertion on children's attributions may be minimized if the power assertion is accompanied by inductive reasoning, at least for girls. In this study, children heard stories in which characters performed acts of helpfulness under various combinations of parental influence techniques; then children were asked to explain the characters' helpfulness. Girls were less likely to nominate an external cause for an actor's helpfulness if it was depicted as motivated by both power assertion and inductive reasoning than if it was motivated by power assertion alone. No parallel effect occurred for boys. Dix and Grusec suggest that girls are more sensitive to statements about the needs of others.

When parents have little choice but to employ power assertion to gain compliance, it is probably a good idea for them to accompany it with induction, since doing so may help reduce external attributions. But it is also worth reemphasizing a point about reasoning made by learning theorists (e.g., Parke, 1974): Reasoning is unlikely to be very effective unless parents teach their children that they "mean business" when reasoning with them. Research confirms that parents who are the most effective "reasoners" are those who back up their words with action and firm enforcement—even physical punishment, if necessary (Baumrind, 1973; Hoffman, 1970a; Lytton & Zwirner, 1975; Walters & Grusec, 1977; Zahn-Waxler, Radke-Yarrow, & King, 1979). This does not imply that reasoning should always be accompanied by power assertion. On the contrary, if reasoning will succeed alone, it probably should be used alone; but if children begin to drift toward noncompliance with reasoned requests, power-assertive backup may be called for. In conclusion, it seems that both attribution theory and learning theory contribute to our understanding of the effectiveness of parental reasoning.

Reward

Attribution research on the role of reward in moral internalization began with an early study by Lepper, Greene, and Nisbett (1973), in which material reward led children to lose intrinsic interest in an activity. In this study, young children were promised and given a prize for engaging in an activity (drawing pictures with felt pens). Compared to children who were neither promised nor given a reward for drawing, the "bribed" children later avoided drawing during free play periods when rewards were no longer available. Lepper et al. labeled this the "overjustification effect": By adding unnecessary external motivation, the reward undermined the children's intrinsic interest.

Although reward-induced decreased play effects can be interpreted without reference to attribution processes (Feingold & Mahoney, 1975; Karniol & Ross, 1979; Perry, Bussey, & Redman, 1977; Ransen, 1980; Reiss & Sushinsky, 1975; Smith & Pittman, 1978), the attribution explanation remains viable. Furthermore, in research conducted since the Lepper et al. study, children's interest in a wide variety of activities (solving puzzles and mazes, playing musical instruments, working on arithmetic problems) has been undermined by a wide variety of material rewards (money, toys, food). However, there are at least three important circumstances in which rewards do not undermine, and may in fact enhance, intrinsic interest in an activity. First, reward does not undermine intrinsic interest unless it takes the form of a material bribe. Social reinforcement (praise, compliments) does not undermine interest. In fact, social reward often increases the motivation for performing an activity in the later absence of adults, possibly because social rewards engender feelings of competence and pride in performing the activity (Anderson, Manoogian, & Reznick, 1976; Dollinger & Thelen, 1978). Second, reward does not undermine intrinsic interest if it carries information to children that they are competent at the activity. Indeed, when children are told that receiving a material reward signifies that they are doing a competent and successful job, the reward may enhance children's tendencies to engage in the activity when rewards are withdrawn (Boggiano & Ruble, 1979; Karniol & Ross, 1977). Third, rewards do not undermine intrinsic interest if children participate in determining the contingencies of reward delivery (Bandura & Perloff, 1967; Weiner & Dubanoski, 1975; Enzle & Look, Note 2).

Although there has been considerable research into the effects of reward on children's intrinsic interest in activities, attribution research examining the effects of reward on children's moral internalization is meager. Recall that in the Aronson-Carlsmith forbidden toy paradigm, children who comply with a request to refrain from playing with a toy under a mild threat of punishment for deviation tend to devalue the toy afterward, presumably because they fail to see their avoidance of the toy as externally caused; hence they conclude that they must have avoided the toy because they did not like it. Perry, Bussey, and Fischer (1980) found that promising children a "present" if they resisted temptation prevented mildly threatened children from devaluing the toy. The attribution explanation is that reward led children to attribute their conformity to the external incentive rather than to dislike of the toy. However, the promise of reward in the Perry et al. study may have distracted children from being tempted to play with the forbidden toy, making interpretation of the results rather difficult.

Smith et al. (1979; cited in our section on punishment) examined the effects of rewarding children for sharing on the children's attributions for having shared. Children who were rewarded with pennies for sharing were less likely to attribute their sharing to a personal disposition to help or to a concern for the other child than were children who were requested to share without any external incentive. Not surprisingly, children rewarded materially clearly viewed their sharing as motivated by the external incentives. However, when children were given social reward (praise) rather than material reward for sharing, they tended to produce internal attributions for their altruism. Furthermore, when children were asked to recall the experimenter's behavior, children rewarded materially were more accurate than children rewarded socially, suggesting that social controls are less salient than material ones.

Smith et al. also related children's attributions for induced sharing to their tendencies to share during a subsequent, anonymous opportunity. Within each condition, children who had explained their initial sharing in terms of a personal disposition shared the most during the anonymous test. However, as groups, the material reward, social reward, and no-consequences conditions did not differ significantly in anonymous sharing. If the attribution theory of internalization is to remain viable, clearer evidence is required that external incentives produce external attributions that in turn undermine internalization.

Future research might profitably explore more of the conditions under which reward incentives undermine or foster internalization. Possibly, if children are led to believe that receiving a material reward indicates that the child is exceptionally good or competent at self-control, the reward will promote internalization. Another direction for study would involve assessing the effects of involving children themselves in the reward process. Several studies conducted with the behavior modification tradition already indicate that when children are taught to observe their own behavior and to deliver material rewards to themselves contingently upon successful periods of relative self-control, enduring self-improvements may result (e.g., Drabman, Spitalnik, & O'Leary, 1973). Considering the central role that the concept of reinforcement plays in contemporary accounts of socialization, it is surprising how little we know about reward and moral internalization.

Direct Verbal Attribution

Thus far we have discussed how children decide on the presence or absence of an intrinsic disposition to engage in moral conduct: When children observe themselves behaving morally in the apparent absence of external control they conclude, as if by default, that an internal disposition must be responsible. Several researchers, however, have proposed that children can also arrive at internal dispositional attributions of goodness more directly by being told by adults that they are the kind of people who by nature like to practice moral conduct.

There is now substantial evidence that children are receptive to direct verbal attributions of goodness. In fact, a broad range of prosocial and moral behaviors—including neatness, academic achievement, altruism, delay of gratification, friendliness, and cooperation—can be elicited in children simply by telling them that they are intrinsically disposed to display the behaviors (e.g., "I know you're the kind of kid who likes to help others"; Grusec, Kuczynski, Rushton, & Simutis, 1978; Grusec & Redler, 1980; Jensen & Moore, 1977; Miller, Brickman, & Bolen, 1975; Toner, Moore, & Emmons, 1980). We should also note that in some studies, verbal attribution of prosocial disposition has been more effective in generating and sustaining the desired behavior than other techniques, such as verbal persuasion or social reinforcement (e.g., Grusec & Redler, 1980; Miller et al., 1975).

There are several possible explanations for the finding that children endeavor to display or "live up to" prosocial qualities attributed to them by adults. When adults hold certain expectations for children, the adults may behave toward children in ways that serve to fulfill their prophecies. Another possibility is that attributions of goodness make children more aware of adults' expectations of them, and children seek to conform to these expectations in order to gain the adults' approval and to avoid their censure. But it is also possible, as the attribution theorists suggest, that when children are told they possess desirable attributes they come to believe the information. The resultant increases in self-perceptions of goodness should cause the children to have higher self-expectations for good behavior. Furthermore, children who hold higher self-expectations for moral conduct should anticipate greater dissatisfaction and self-recrimination for behaving improperly than children who never particularly expected the behavior of themselves in the first place. This should help sustain moral conduct.

Perry, Perry, Bussey, English, and Arnold (1980) tested the hypothesis that children who have been told they are especially good are likely to punish themselves particularly severely when they misbehave. Third and fourth graders in one group were given a standard attribution-of-goodness treatment in which an adult explained that, in her opinion, the child was one who both wanted to and was able to carry out instructions, follow rules, work hard, avoid distraction, and do what he or she is told to do in the absence of adults. Children in a second group received no attribution treatment. Subsequently all the children were set to work on a tedious task, were prepaid a sum of 30 tokens (exchangeable for small prizes) for performing the task, and were left alone to complete it. All the children were distracted from completing the task by a television set playing a lively cartoon. A different experimenter confronted the children with their failure to finish their task and gave them an opportunity to punish themselves by letting the children decide (anonymously) how many, if any, of their tokens they should relinquish. However, before letting children punish themselves, the experimenter told one group of children that other children had deviated too (high consensus), told a second group that other children had not deviated (low consensus), and gave a third group no information about how their behavior compared with other children's. The main finding was that children who received verbal attributions of goodness and low-consensus information about their deviation punished themselves substantially more than children in any other condition. The results were interpreted as supporting the attribution hypothesis that children who are told by adults that they possess desirable moral characteristics experience particularly strong remorse when they fail to exercise self-control in temptation situations, so long as they feel that they have nothing to blame but themselves for deviation. (Presumably, children in both the high-consensus and no-consensus conditions could more easily attribute their misbehavior to something in the environment and thereby reject responsibility for their lack of self-control.)

Perry et al. (1980) suggested that it may be worthwhile to include concepts from both attribution theory and social learning theory when conceptualizing the role of self-evaluation in children's self-control. As shown in their study, causal attributions influence children's self-reactions following misbehavior or conformity: The more internal the attribution, the more guilt for misbehavior or pride for conformity the individual should feel. According to social learning theory, however, a critical determinant of people's resistance to deviation is the degree to which people *anticipate* rewarding themselves for conforming or punishing themselves for deviating. Combining the attribution and social learning principles, we can surmise that a critical determinant of resistance to temptation will be the causal attribution a child anticipates for deviation or conformity. As they develop, children probably become more adept at predicting their causal attributions following contemplated transgression or obedience and therefore the degree of self-blame or self-praise they are likely to experience (e.g., "I know I'll feel terrible if I do that because everyone else was able to resist the temptation"; "I'll feel great if I master this task because nobody helped me and nobody else has done well at it"). Such a formulation is consistent with Hoffman's suggestion that moral behavior is frequently a function of anticipated guilt, or causal attribution of one's empathic arousal to one's own lack of effort to help a distressed other. In sum, resistance to deviation may often result from anticipated causal attributions and the sign and strength of the self-reactions they mediate.

Modeling

Research conducted within the social learning tradition provides ample demonstrations that a variety of prosocial and moral behaviors—including resistance to deviation, altruism, delay of gratification, and expressions of remorse after transgression—can be transmitted by example. Children who witness a model forgo an attractive but prohibited activity, for instance, are subsequently more likely themselves to resist a similar temptation than children not exposed to a resisting model (Bussey & Perry, 1977; Grusec, Kuczynski, Rushton, & Simutis, 1979; Perry, Bussey, & Perry, 1975). Attribution researchers, notably Grusec, have proposed that modeling may have the advantage not only of causing children to adopt moral conduct but also of leading children to generate internal attributions for their imitative moral behavior. The theory is that after children have imitated a model's behavior, they may not be aware, or perhaps do not like to admit, that their behavior is attributable to imitation of another; lacking anything external to which to attribute their behavior, the children turn to an internal explanation. Conformity induced by modeling, then, may be especially conducive to internalization.

Several experimental results are consistent with this suggestion. Bussey and Perry (1977) found that children who freely imitated a model's resistance to deviation were more likely afterward to express a dislike for the avoided activity than children who resisted deviation because an adult had insisted on it. Presumably, children in the modeling condition lacked external justification for their resistance to temptation and therefore interpreted their avoidance of the activity to imply intrinsic dislike of it.

Grusec et al. (1978) hypothesized that when children have imitated a model's conformity, they experience uncertainty over the cause of their conformity. Hence children who have just imitated conformity should be susceptible to adult-supplied explanations of their behavior. In their study, children initially were induced to share with another child, either through modeling or through direct instructions. Immediately afterward, an adult remarked to one group, "I guess you shared because you're the kind of person who likes to help other people" (internal attribution) and to another group, "I guess you shared because you thought I expected you to" (external attribution). A third group received no attribution. Then the children had a final, anonymous opportunity for noninstructed donating. The internal attribution enhanced, and the external attribution depressed, noninstructed sharing among children whose original sharing was induced through modeling. However, when sharing had been induced by direct instructions, noninstructed sharing was comparable in the three conditions. Presumably, when children are explicitly told to do something, they attribute their compliance to the external request and find an adult-supplied internal attribution implausible.

To determine if children do sometimes spontaneously attribute imitated actions to personal dispositions, Dix and Grusec (Note 1) asked children to explain the actions of various story characters who had performed altruistic acts. Children were indeed likely to say that a story character who imitated a parent's helpfulness did so because the character possessed an altruistic trait. Perhaps children make similar attributions when they imitate the actions of others.

Research on modeling and causal attribution is supportive of the attribution perspective on moral internalization. However, there may be important occasions when children do not generate internal attributions for their imitative behavior and hence fail to internalize an attitude or motive consistent with their imitation. For example, children's imitative performance is frequently under the control of anticipated external consequences (e.g., Bandura & Barab, 1971). This can be seen in research on the effects of "vicarious consequences" on children's imitation: Children frequently strive to imitate actions they have seen lead to reward for a model and they strive to inhibit actions they have seen produce punishment for a model (Bandura, 1965; Flanders, 1968). Such effects are strongest when children believe they are subject to the same reinforcement contingencies as the model (Bussey & Perry, 1976; Thelen & Rennie, 1972). The question is whether imitation elicited under such conditions is conducive to internalization. If, for instance, children refrain from imitating a model's aggression because they fear the same severe punishment they have seen the model receive for behaving aggressively, will they internalize a negative attitude or disposition toward aggression? The attribution perspective suggests not. The social learning perspective, however, suggests that seeing a model punished for a behavior may motivate children to attempt self-regulation of the behavior. Our understanding of the role of modeling in socialization would benefit from further research on the links between children's causal attributions for their imitation and their propensities to internalize the imitated responses.

Developmental Factors in Attribution

Thus far we have been speaking as if the attribution effects we have reviewed apply equally to children of all ages. This would be a false impression. Although few attribution theorists have formally incorporated developmental factors into their accounts of moral internalization, there is enough evidence now to suggest that this is probably necessary. Age plays a role in children's attributions in at least two important ways—in determining the likelihood that children will discount intrinsic motivation in the face of an external incentive and in determining children's ability to understand that behavior may be caused by stable, underlying dispositions and traits. We discuss each of these points.

Age and Children's Use of the Discounting Principle

Suppose that children of varying ages are asked, "Who is the kinder child: Susan, who just got up one morning and decided to share a favorite toy with her brother, or Mary, who shared a favorite toy with her brother because her mother promised her a dollar for doing so?" Children of elementary school age and older will answer "Susan." They are said to be using a "discounting principle": They take the mother's bribe as a sufficient explanation for Mary's behavior and discount intrinsic motivation on Mary's part. Preschool children, however, do not usually take the presence of an external incentive to imply the lack of intrinsic motivation. In fact, many preschoolers will say Mary is the kinder child. Curiously, these children seem to be using the presence of an external cause to imply the presence rather than the absence of an internal cause. They are not just responding randomly, for they show a similar style of reasoning across other story examples. These children are said to be using an "additive principle" because they see extrinsic inducements as adding to the strength of intrinsic factors (Cohen, Gelfand, & Hartmann, 1981; DiVitto & McArthur, 1978; Karniol & Ross, 1976; Kun, 1977; Leahy, 1979). We might note that preschoolers' use of an additive principle is not limited to the case where the external incentive is reward; preschoolers also take aversive external controls (e.g., threats of punishment or deprivation of privileges) to imply the presence rather than the absence of intrinsic motivation.

Finding that preschool children fail to use the discounting principle poses a puzzle for attribution researchers, because some of the other research findings that we have reviewed (e.g., the failure of children to devalue a forbidden toy under severe threat, the undermining of intrinsic interest by extrinsic reward) have been discovered in work with children as young as 3 or 4 years of age, and these findings were interpreted in terms of the children's use of the discounting principle. Some authors have attempted to resolve the puzzle by suggesting that young children fail to discount only when asked to judge or explain hypothetical actions of other people and that they are quite capable of using the discounting principle when it applies to their own behavior in real-life situations (Shultz & Butkowsky, 1977; Wells & Shultz, 1980). At present there simply is not enough evidence to establish whether preschool children discount their own intrinsic motivation when subjected to external sanctions. More research is needed to determine the precise roles that the discounting and additive principles play in children's moral internalization at different points in development.

Age and Children's Understanding of Dispositions and Traits

Earlier we saw that children endeavor to display prosocial and moral motives attributed to them. In research on the development of "person perception," however, children younger than 7 or 8 years have a great deal of difficulty conceptualizing themselves (as well as other people) in terms of underlying, relatively enduring personality traits or dispositions that produce consistency in their behavior across time and situations. For example, when children are asked to describe themselves (or other people), children younger than 8 focus on observable surface characteristics such as their appearance, possessions, environment, and typical activities (Livesley & Bromley, 1973; Peevers & Secord, 1973). Older children more often describe themselves in terms of stable personality dispositions and other underlying psychological dimensions that organize their personality and social habits. If young children do not conceive of themselves in terms of general traits, then perhaps verbal attribution of prosocial traits will not have very powerful effects on their behavior.

In a study designed to test this possibility, Grusec and Redler (1980) first asked 5-, 8-, and 10-year-old children to donate some of their winnings from a game to another child. Afterward some of the children of each age were told: "You know, you certainly are a nice person; I bet you're someone who is helpful whenever possible." All the children were then given additional tests for altruism, both in the same situation in which they had already been observed (i.e., they had another opportunity to play the game and share their winnings) and in a new situation (they were given an opportunity to collect craft materials for sick children in the hospital). When the test situation was the same as the original situation, children who had been told that they were helpful were more generous than children who had not been told this at all age levels. However, when children were tested for altruism in the new situation, the benefit of the attribution treatment was evident only for children aged 8 or older. Presumably only the older children saw the relevance of the trait attribution for new situations. This finding does not mean that adults should feel free to refrain from making prosocial attributions until children reach 7 or 8 years, but it does suggest that children's tendencies to behave in ways that accord with self-perceived traits increase with age.

A Paradox: Conflicting Laboratory and Field Evidence on the Effects of Firm Control

According to the attribution perspective and the laboratory work conducted in support of it, salient external controls undermine moral internalization. Yet according to several field studies (Baumrind, 1973; Hoffman, 1970a), parents who exercise "firm control" over their children—who make age-appropriate demands on their children for moral and prosocial action and strictly enforce these requests (with external sanctions, if necessary)—have children who score high on indices of morality and altruism.

One approach to resolving this paradox involves reinterpreting the field studies, which are correlational in design and do not permit cause-and-effect conclusions. Lewis (1981), for example, suggests that firm parental control is associated with effective socialization not because of the firm control itself but rather because of other parenting variables that covary with firm control, such as parental warmth, use of reasoning to justify requests, and a respect for and responsiveness to the child's arguments and opinions. She also suggests that the parent-child behavior sequences that researchers have interpreted as reflecting firm parental control may in fact reflect the child's willingness to obey rather than the parent's determined effort to exercise control. In essence, then, Lewis concludes that effective socialization is probably not dependent on the parent's exercise of firm control. We do not share Lewis's view, as we shall elaborate later.

Lepper (1981) suggests a different resolution to the paradox. According to Lepper, parents who receive high scores on "firm control" in field studies are not parents who use unnecessarily harsh discipline but rather are parents who are skilled in using the minimum degree of external control necessary to ensure that their children comply with requests for mature behavior. To understand Lepper's point, it is useful to differentiate among three styles of parental control. Let us say a parent initiates a social control sequence (e.g., asks her child to share with a friend, or to turn off the television set) and that the child dodges the request. One parent may ignore the child's noncompliance or fail to apply sufficient follow-up pressure to make sure that the child eventually complies (permissive or "insufficient" discipline). A second parent, refusing to tolerate noncompliance, will persist until compliance is achieved but will be careful not to apply more external pressure than necessary to achieve compliance ("minimally sufficient" discipline). A third parent will elicit compliance through a show of force stronger than that necessary to gain compliance ("oversufficient" discipline).

Lepper (1981) proposes that parents identified in field studies as using firm control come closer to the minimally sufficient style of discipline than to either of the other two. He suggests that these parents are skilled in eliciting desirable behavior from children in ways that do not make salient to the children the fact that their behavior is under external control. It is true that many parents who exercise firm control employ a style of discipline that sometimes may help reduce external attributions. For example, they tend not to enforce sanctions arbitrarily and erratically, they justify their disciplinary action with reasoning, they engage their children in verbal give-and-take, and they are willing to modify their disciplinary action when their child's arguments merit it (Baumrind, 1973).

Thus Lepper concludes that parents identified in field studies as using firm control are furnishing the two critical ingredients that, according to attribution theory, promote moral internalization. First, these parents are taking pains to ensure that their children actually engage in desired forms of behavior. Lepper reminds us that a cornerstone principle of attribution theory is that people are unlikely to perceive themselves as internally motivated to perform a behavior unless they have first observed themselves to engage in it (Bem, 1972). (This is why permissive or insufficient discipline cannot lead to moral internalization.) Second, in Lepper's view, parents identified in field studies as using firm control are effective in eliciting the desired behavior without letting the child feel externally coerced into performing it. Remember, according to attribution theory, it is when one perceives oneself performing a behavior in the absence of external control that one is likely to internalize the behavior.

Lepper (1981) argues that a major thrust of future research should be the discovery of disciplinary tactics that allow parents efficiently to elicit desired behavior from children without letting the children draw external attributions. He points out that there may be ways of gaining compliance without arousing the child's suspicions that he or she is being manipulated (1981; Lepper & Gilovich, 1982). For example, parents may increase their chances of gaining compliance by giving the child an illusory choice (e.g., "Would you like to take your shower upstairs or downstairs?") or by packaging a request as a puzzle, a game, or a challenge (e.g., pretending one is on a treasure hunt while cleaning up one's room). The implication in Lepper's stance is that moral internalization is undermined if the child realizes that external pressures are contributing to his or her conformity.

Although Lepper's analysis is appealing in its simplicity, we do not find it satisfying. We are not convinced that it is possible simply to equate "firm control" as it has been assessed in field studies with a minimally sufficient style of discipline that avoids attributions of external control. Although parents who exercise firm control may favor auxiliary techniques that occasionally help minimize the child's perception of external coercion (e.g., reasoning), we are skeptical about the suggestion that firm enforcement of parental demands can typically be accomplished in a way that precludes the child's drawing an external attribution of motivation. Under naturalistic conditions of child rearing, even minimally sufficient discipline often entails sufficient force to provoke an external attribution on the child's part. In other words, we do not feel it justified to claim that parents identified in field studies as high on the variable of firm control are consistently, or even very often, achieving compliance in their children in ways that avoid perceptions of external control on the part of their children.

Moreover, several important recent findings suggest that disciplinary practices carefully designed to avoid perceptions of external control may not be the most advantageous for promoting moral internalization. Specifically, there exist several studies in which discipline that would be classified as "oversufficient" by attribution theorists was found to be more conducive to moral internalization than (the theoretically preferable) minimally sufficient discipline. In our view, these studies pose a threat to the attribution theory of moral internalization. We shall consider these findings here.

One of these studies is an experiment by Israel and Brown (1979), who found that the more explicitly and forcefully an adult phrased a request to share, the more likely children were to continue sharing after the instructions were discontinued. In this study, children who were given a *command* to share ("You must share . . .") in an induced sharing phase shared more during a later anonymous non-instructed test than children for whom initial sharing had been induced through a less coercive *suggestion* ("You might want to share, but you don't have to . . ."). There is other evidence that internalization is facilitated when adults solicit initial compliance in a way that forcefully brings home to children the message that the behavior in question is expected and required conduct. Earlier, when discussing the modeling research, we reviewed a study by Grusec et al. (1978) that was interpreted as supporting the hypothesis that children are more likely to accept an internal attribution for their prosocial behavior if it has been induced through modeling than if it has been induced through direct instructions. Although results in line with this specific prediction were found, an unexpected yet important finding from this study was that direct instructions consistently led to high levels of generosity on a subsequent internalization test. Also, when the effectiveness of direct instructions is directly compared in the same experimental design with more "internal" techniques for eliciting moral behavior (e.g., modeling), direct instructions usually produce superior internalization (Lepper, Sagotsky, & Mailer, 1975; White, 1972; White & Burnam, 1975). Finally, the results of field studies also indicate that making it clear to children that altruism is absolutely required of them facilitates altruistic development. Zahn-Waxler et al. (1979), for example, found that the most altruistic preschoolers were ones whose mothers forcefully ordered them to engage in altruism when playing with other children, and who scolded them (in a voice charged with indignation) when they failed to do so spontaneously.

In all the studies just cited, socializing agents successful at instilling internalization of prosocial conduct seem to be communicating to children, in one way or another, the following message: "You have no choice but to help others. It is very important behavior. Noncompliance is not an option and will not be tolerated." In none of these studies were children's attributions for engaging in altruism directly assessed, but it seems likely that in each study children who complied in response to the command would have generated external rather than internal attributions for their obedience (assuming that they generated attributions at all). Our interpretation of these findings is that forceful commands to children to engage in prosocial behavior facilitate rather than undermine internalization of the behavior—even though the commands may (initially at least) elicit attributions of external motivation. This conclusion is not compatible with the prevailing attribution perspective on internalization. As we have already noted, Lepper (1981; Lepper & Gilovich, 1982) has proposed that parents phrase their requests to children in subtle and delicate ways that are designed to play down the coercive nature of the requests (e.g., by giving the child an illusory choice of activity, by introducing an activity as a game). The findings we have reviewed here challenge Lepper's suggestion that requests for compliance should be carefully engineered to prevent perceptions of external control. More generally, the findings suggest that the prevailing attribution account of internalization is in need of revision, or at least qualification.

Our hunch is that attribution does play a role in moral internalization, but not exactly in the way that most contemporary attribution theorists believe. In the following (final) section, we sketch an alternative account of the development of moral internalization that draws on principles of both social learning theory and attribution theory.

The Development of Moral Internalization: An Integration of Social Learning and Attribution Principles

In our view, moral internalization is a developmental process that involves gradual changes in the child's causal attributions for conforming to the values and norms of society. We suspect that internalization typically originates in habits of desirable behavior that are at first clearly externally motivated. However, as children mature, they also generate internal attributions for conformity that may gradually assume a dominant role in mediating moral behavior but that probably never entirely supplant external attributions for conformity. We believe that principles of social learning play an important role in initiating the process as well as in guiding internalization in its later phases. We suspect that the attribution-theory component of internalization (i.e., inferring an intrinsic motivation to be good when conforming in the absence of salient extrinsic incentives) is more important at later stages of the process than at early ones.

Our argument that internalization rests on establishing early habits of moral and prosocial conduct should not come as a surprise. We have already cited field evidence that prosocial development depends on "firm control," or the parents' unwavering enforcement of demands for prosocial behavior in the early years of the child's life (Baumrind, 1973; Olejnik & McKinney, 1973; Whiting & Whiting, 1975; Zahn-Waxler et al., 1979). Experimental studies confirm this conclusion. For example, children who are drilled in role playing make-believe altruistic acts over a course of several weeks come to display altruism in new (i.e., unrehearsed) situations (Friedrich & Stein, 1975; Skarin & Moely, 1976; Staub, 1971).

Contrary to the attribution perspective, we doubt that these initial habits must be established in ways that prevent attributions of external motivation. In fact, we are not convinced that establishing early habits in ways carefully crafted to avoid perceptions of external coercion is even particularly desirable. We base these statements on several pieces of evidence. Studies reviewed in the preceding section revealed that forceful insistence on desirable behavior promotes rather than diminishes internalized control of the behavior. Also, as we concluded earlier, there is no thoroughly convincing evidence that young children (preschool age) who are forced to conform to social norms by oversufficient discipline generate external attributions that interfere with their internalization of the behavior.

Our thesis, then, is that effective socialization begins by imparting to the child a clear understanding of proper and improper behavior and by requiring the child to conform behaviorally to these standards. Almost certainly this approach will frequently entail external control *and* external attributions on the child's part, but this does not, we believe, interfere with the origins of internalization. In fact, we suspect that a great deal of what passes for internalized behavior by young children (i.e., conformity to social norms in the absence of external surveillance) is actually motivated by external concerns, such as a fear of getting caught and punished for misbehaving. Most of us can remember times as children when we were absolutely convinced that nobody was watching while we did something naughty only to be quickly found out and punished. Such experiences may shake young children's belief that they are ever truly free of external surveillance and may help motivate firm habits of "internalized" behavior. However, as children grow older and improve their skills at detecting the presence or absence of real surveillance, they probably begin to see themselves perform prosocial and moral acts even when no one is watching (assuming that such habits have been established). It is at this time, we believe, that children can update their attributions to be more internal (e.g., "If I am doing this even though I don't have to, then I must want to do it"), and the foundation for a more mature variety of internalization is laid. In sum, we imagine that internal attributions assume importance in moral internalization primarily after habits of moral action have been implanted by external means.

The foregoing analysis suggests that social learning theory may more accurately account for the origins of internalized behavior than attribution theory. Recall that social learning theory includes the prediction that external ends can serve as powerful incentives for self-regulatory responses. Furthermore, according to social learning theory, the more clearly a child conceptualizes the contingency between an activity and a substantial external consequence (e.g., a reward or punishment), the more motivated the child should be to self-regulate the activity. This view accords with the findings that forceful insistence on prosocial behavior facilitates internalization of the behavior.

The notion that moral behavior often has its roots in externally implanted habits does not constitute a green light for parents to focus exclusively on external incentives in order to obtain compliance in the early years of their child's life. Numerous field studies reveal that forceful insistence on prosocial and moral behavior is effective only if the parents generally maintain an atmosphere of warmth and respect for the child, justify their disciplinary actions with inductive reasoning, encourage verbal give-and-take with the child, and are responsive to the child's point of view (e.g., Baumrind, 1973). In addition, the ills of using certain varieties of unnecessarily harsh "oversufficient" discipline (e.g., severe physical punishment) have been amply demonstrated.

Although we believe our emphasis on establishing habits of desirable behavior through firm control fits better with the social learning than the attribution perspective, the two points of view accord in recommending against permissive or insufficient discipline. In fact, attribution theory provides the basis for an important prediction concerning the effects of insufficient discipline. Lepper points out that if a child is permitted to get away with noncompliance with a parental request, the child may develop internal attributions for noncompliance (e.g., "I don't have to do what Mom says unless I want to"; "I didn't share even though Dad asked me to, so I must really hate sharing"). Such attributions may not only prevent internalization of the specific norm in question but also seriously interfere with the likelihood of the child's complying with parental requests on later occasions (Lepper, 1981).

Although internal attributions may begin to play an increasingly important role as children develop, we subscribe to the social learning view that external and internal attributions are not necessarily antagonistic. As we noted in our introduction to the social learning perspective, children may perceive themselves to be good people or competent self-regulators precisely because they are achieving success in regulating behaviors that society considers important and that lead to powerful external outcomes. We suspect, then, that with age children do not come entirely to supplant external attributions with internal ones. Instead, we imagine that internal attributions simply assume greater salience for the individual with age, but that one of their primary functions continues to be that of regulating the self toward some more distal external goal.

Still, there is a considerable amount that parents can and should do to help their children add internal attributions to their repertoire of cognitions that aid internalized behavior. For example, to foster children's confidence in their ability to self-regulate, parents might institute external contingencies aimed to teach the child to perform desirable actions without first being told to do so by adults. To illustrate, parents might threaten to withhold some privilege from the child unless the child spontaneously remembers to clean up his or her room each morning. The aim is to get children to perform desirable actions without reliance on immediate external prodding. Moreover, once children do spontaneously perform the behavior, parents can offer social reinforcement and verbal attributions of prosocial dispositions (e.g., "Did you see how you helped Tom without anyone telling you to? I know you like to make your friends feel better whenever they are unhappy").

Our theory is developmental in the sense that it specifies a hypothesized sequence of events and processes in internalization. In our analysis, internal attributions are not assumed to play a major role in internalization until some time after firm habits of desirable behavior are implanted through external means. The finding that children do not come to think of themselves as possessing generalized prosocial and moral traits until 8 or 9 years of age is compatible with our view that internal attributions contribute to internalization relatively late in the process. Also, if future research confirms that preschool children fail to use the discounting principle (to infer reduced intrinsic motivation in the face of external incentives), then we will have more support for our thesis that parents need not painstakingly avoid applying external sanctions in order to achieve initial compliance by their young children.

Our account of internalization as a gradually evolving process suggests that research on internalization might benefit from examining changes in children's thought and behavior over considerable lengths of time. Do children's causal attributions for conforming to society's standards actually shift from predominantly external to a blend of the internal and the external? To what naturally occurring child rearing experiences are such shifts related? Is self-regulation really ever in the service of long-term external ends, yet at the same time facilitated by self-cognitions focusing on one's desire and ability to be "good" in the shorter term? Can researchers operationalize the social learning construct of self-perceived efficacy at self-regulation, and do children's scores on this variable actually influence their moral behavior? It is worth reminding ourselves that although causal attributions have been hypothesized to mediate the effects of discipline on moral internalization, children's attributions following compliance under various conditions of control have actually been measured in only two studies (Lepper, 1973; Smith et al., 1979). Furthermore, it is not clear that children always do spontaneously engage in causal attributions following their behavior (cf. Diener & Dweck, 1978, 1980). If any single message emerges from this review, it is this: There exists considerably more theory on moral internalization than definitive evidence, and this state of affairs is unlikely to change until theorists document the mediating links in the process they are striving to explain.

Reference Notes

1. Dix, T., & Grusec, J. E. *Parental influence techniques: An attributional analysis.* Unpublished manuscript, University of Toronto, 1982.
2. Enzle, M. E., & Look, S. C. *Self versus other reward administration and the overjustification effect.* Unpublished manuscript, University of Alberta, 1980.

References

Anderson, R., Manoogian, S. T., & Reznick, J. S. The undermining and enhancing of intrinsic motivation in preschool children. *Journal of Personality and Social Psychology*, 1976, *34*, 915–922.

Aronson, E., & Carlsmith, J. M. The effect of the severity of threat on the devaluation of forbidden behavior. *Journal of Abnormal and Social Psychology*, 1963, *66*, 584–588.

Bandura, A. Influence of models' reinforcement contingencies on the acquisition of imitative responses. *Journal of Personality and Social Psychology*, 1965, *1*, 589–595.

Bandura, A. *Social learning theory*. Englewood Cliffs, NJ: Prentice-Hall, 1977.

Bandura, A. The self system in reciprocal determinism. *American Psychologist*, 1978, *33*, 344–358.

Bandura, A., & Barab, P. G. Conditions governing nonreinforced imitation. *Developmental Psychology*, 1971, *5*, 244–255.

Bandura, A., & Perloff, B. Relative efficacy of self-monitored and externally-imposed reinforcement systems. *Journal of Personality and Social Psychology*, 1967, *7*, 111–116.

Baumrind, D. The development of instrumental competence through socialization. In A. D. Pick (Ed.), *Minnesota symposia on child psychology* (Vol. 7). Minneapolis: University of Minnesota Press, 1973.

Bearison, D. J., & Cassel, T. Z. Cognitive decentration and social codes: Communication effectiveness in young children from differing family contexts. *Developmental Psychology*, 1975, *11*, 29–36.

Bem, D. J. Self-perception theory. In L. Berkowitz (Ed.), *Advances in experimental social psychology* (Vol. 6). New York: Academic Press, 1972.

Boggiano, A. K., & Ruble, D. N. Perception of competence and the overjustification effect: A developmental study. *Journal of Personality and Social Psychology*, 1979, *37*, 1462–1468.

Bussey, K., & Perry, D. G. Sharing reinforcement contingencies with a model: A social-learning analysis of similarity effects in imitation research. *Journal of Personality and Social Psychology*, 1976, *34*, 1168–1176.

Bussey, K., & Perry, D. G. The imitation of resistance to deviation: Conclusive evidence for an elusive effect. *Developmental Psychology*, 1977, *13*, 438–443.

Cheyne, J. A. Punishment and reasoning in the development of self-control. In R. D. Parke (Ed.), *Recent trends in social learning theory*. New York: Academic Press, 1972.

Cohen, E. A., Gelfand, D. M., & Hartmann, D. P. Causal reasoning as a function of behavioral consequences. *Child Development*, 1981, *52*, 514–522.

Dembroski, T. M., & Pennebaker, J. W. Reactions to severity and nature of threat among children of dissimilar socioeconomic levels. *Journal of Personality and Social Psychology*, 1975, *31*, 338–342.

Diener, C. I., & Dweck, C. S. An analysis of learned helplessness: Continuous changes in performance, strategy, and achievement cognitions following failure. *Journal of Personality and Social Psychology*, 1978, *36*, 451–462.

Diener, C. I., & Dweck, C. S. An analysis of learned helplessness: II. The processing of success. *Journal of Personality and Social Psychology*, 1980, *39*, 940–952.

Dienstbier, R. A., Hillman, D., Lehnhoff, J., Hillman, J., & Valkenaar, M. C. An emotion-attribution approach to moral behavior: Interfacing cognitive and avoidance theories of moral development. *Psychological Review,* 1975, *82,* 299–315.

DiVitto, B., & McArthur, L. Z. Developmental differences in the use of distinctiveness, consensus, and consistency information for making causal attributions. *Developmental Psychology,* 1978, *14,* 474–482.

Dollinger, S. J., & Thelen, M. H. Overjustification and children's intrinsic motivation: Comparative effects of four rewards. *Journal of Personality and Social Psychology,* 1978, *36,* 1259–1269.

Drabman, R. S., Spitalnik, R., & O'Leary, K. D. Teaching self-control to disruptive children. *Journal of Abnormal Psychology,* 1973, *82,* 10–16.

Ebbesen, E. B., Bowers, R. J., Phillips, S., & Snyder, M. Self-control processes in the forbidden toy paradigm. *Journal of Personality and Social Psychology,* 1975, *31,* 442–452.

Feingold, B. D., & Mahoney, M. J. Reinforcement effects on intrinsic interest: Undermining the overjustification hypothesis. *Behavior Therapy,* 1975, *6,* 367–377.

Flanders, J. P. A review of research on imitative behavior. *Psychological Bulletin,* 1968, *69,* 316–337.

Freedman, J. L. Long-term behavioral effects of cognitive dissonance. *Journal of Experimental Social Psychology,* 1965, *1,* 145–155.

Friedrich, L. K., & Stein, A. H. Prosocial television and young children: The effects of verbal labeling and role playing on learning and behavior. *Child Development,* 1975, *46,* 27–38.

Grusec, J. E., Kuczynski, L., Rushton, J. P., & Simutis, Z. M. Modeling, direct instruction, and attributions: Effects on altruism. *Developmental Psychology,* 1978, *14,* 51–57.

Grusec, J. E., Kuczynski, L., Rushton, J. P., & Simutis, Z. M. Learning resistance to deviation through observation. *Developmental Psychology,* 1979, *15,* 233–240.

Grusec, J. E., & Redler, E. Attribution, reinforcement, and altruism: A developmental analysis. *Developmental Psychology,* 1980, *16,* 525–534.

Hoffman, M. L. Conscience, personality, and socialization techniques. *Human Development,* 1970, *13,* 90–126. (a)

Hoffman, M. L. Moral development. In P. Mussen (Ed.), *Carmichael's manual of child psychology* (Vol. 2). New York: Wiley, 1970. (b)

Hoffman, M. L. Moral internalization: Current theory and research. In L. Berkowitz (Ed.), *Advances in experimental social psychology* (Vol. 10). New York: Academic Press, 1977.

Hom, H. L., Jr., & Maxwell, F. R., Jr. Methodological considerations in the forbidden toy paradigm. *Developmental Psychology,* 1979, *15,* 654–655.

Israel, A. C., & Brown, M. S. Effects of directiveness of instructions and surveillance on the production and persistence of children's donations. *Journal of Experimental Child Psychology,* 1979, *27,* 250–261.

Jensen, A. M., & Moore, S. G. The effect of attribute statements on cooperativeness and competitiveness in school-age boys. *Child Development,* 1977, *48,* 305–307.

Karniol, R., & Ross, M. The development of causal attributions in social perception. *Journal of Personality and Social Psychology,* 1976, *34,* 455–464.

Karniol, R., & Ross, M. The effect of performance-relevant and performance-irrelevant rewards on children's intrinsic motivation. *Child Development*, 1977, *48*, 482–487.

Karniol, R., & Ross, M. Children's use of a causal attribution schema and the inference of manipulative intentions. *Child Development*, 1979, *50*, 463–468.

Kelley, H. H. The processes of causal attribution. *American Psychologist*, 1973, *28*, 107–128.

Kun, A. Development of the magnitude-covariation and compensation schemata in ability and effort attributions of performance. *Child Development*, 1977, *48*, 862–873.

LaVoie, J. C. Cognitive determinants of resistance to deviation in seven-, nine-, and eleven-year-old children of low and high maturity of moral judgment. *Developmental Psychology*, 1974, *10*, 393–403.

Leahy, R. L. Development of conceptions of prosocial behavior: Information affecting rewards given for altruism and kindness. *Developmental Psychology*, 1979, *15*, 34–37.

Lepper, M. R. Dissonance, self-perception, and honesty in children. *Journal of Personality and Social Psychology*, 1973, *25*, 65–74.

Lepper, M. R. Intrinsic and extrinsic motivation in children: Detrimental effects of superfluous social controls. In W. A. Collins (Ed.), *Minnesota symposia on child psychology* (Vol. 14). Minneapolis: University of Minnesota Press, 1981.

Lepper, M. R., & Gilovich, T. Accentuating the positive: Eliciting generalized compliance from children through activity-oriented requests. *Journal of Personality and Social Psychology*, 1982, *42*, 248–259.

Lepper, M. R., Greene, D., & Nisbett, R. E. Undermining children's intrinsic interest with extrinsic rewards: A test of the overjustification hypothesis. *Journal of Personality and Social Psychology*, 1973, *28*, 129–137.

Lepper, M. R., Sagotsky, G., & Mailer, J. Generalization and persistence of effects of exposure to self-reinforcement models. *Child Development*, 1975, *46*, 618–630.

Lepper, M. R., Zanna, M. P., & Abelson, R. P. Cognitive irreversibility in a dissonance reduction situation. *Journal of Personality and Social Psychology*, 1970, *16*, 191–198.

Lewis, C. C. The effects of parental firm control: A reinterpretation of findings. *Psychological Bulletin*, 1981, *90*, 547–563.

Livesley, W. J., & Bromley, D. B. *Person perception in childhood and adolescence*. London: Wiley, 1973.

Lytton, H., & Zwirner, W. Compliance and its controlling stimuli observed in a natural setting. *Developmental Psychology*, 1975, *11*, 769–779.

Martin, B. Parent-child relations. In F. D. Horowitz (Ed.), *Review of child development research* (Vol. 4) Chicago: University of Chicago Press, 1975.

Miller, R. L., Brickman, P., & Bolen, D. Attribution versus persuasion as a means for modifying behavior. *Journal of Personality and Social Psychology*, 1975, *31*, 430–441.

Mischel, W. Toward a cognitive social learning reconceptualization of personality. *Psychological Review*, 1973, *80*, 252–283.

Olejnik, A. G., & McKinney, J. P. Parental value orientation and generosity in children. *Developmental Psychology*, 1973, *8*, 311.

Ostfeld, B., & Katz, P. A. The effect of threat severity in children of varying socioeconomic levels. *Developmental Psychology*, 1969, *1*, 205–210.

Parke, R. D. Effectiveness of punishment as an interaction of intensity, timing, agent nurturance, and cognitive structuring. *Child Development*, 1969, *40*, 213–235.

Parke, R. D. The role of punishment in the socialization process. In R. A. Hoppe, G. A. Milton, & E. C. Simmel (Eds.), *Early experience and the processes of socialization*. New York: Academic Press, 1970.

Parke, R. D. Rules, roles, and resistance to deviation: Recent advances in punishment, discipline, and self-control. In A. D. Pick (Ed.), *Minnesota symposia on child psychology* (Vol. 8). Minneapolis: University of Minnesota Press, 1974.

Peevers, B. H., & Secord, P. F. Developmental changes in attribution of descriptive concepts to persons. *Journal of Personality and Social Psychology*, 1973, *27*, 120–128.

Perry, D. G., Bussey, K., & Perry, L. C. Factors influencing the imitation of resistance to deviation. *Developmental Psychology*, 1975, *11*, 724–731.

Perry, D. G., Bussey, K., & Fischer, J. Effects of rewarding children for resisting temptation on attitude change on the forbidden toy paradigm. *Australian Journal of Psychology*, 1980, *32*, 225–234.

Perry, D. G., Bussey, K., & Freiberg, K. Impact of adults' appeals for sharing on the development of altruistic dispositions in children. *Journal of Experimental Child Psychology*, 1981, *32*, 127–138.

Perry, D. G., Bussey, K., & Redman, J. Reward-induced decreased play effects: Reattribution of motivation, competing responses, or avoiding frustration? *Child Development*, 1977, *48*, 1369–1374.

Perry, D. G., Perry, L. C., Bussey, K., English, D., & Arnold, G. Processes of attribution and children's self-punishment following misbehavior. *Child Development*, 1980, *51*, 545–551.

Ransen, D. L. The mediation of reward-induced motivation decrements in early and middle childhood: A template matching approach. *Journal of Personality and Social Psychology*, 1980, *39*, 1088–1100.

Reiss, S., & Sushinsky, L. W. Overjustification, competing responses, and the acquisition of intrinsic interest. *Journal of Personality and Social Psychology*, 1975, *31*, 1116–1125.

Shultz, T. R., & Butkowsky, I. Young children's use of the scheme for multiple sufficient causes in the attribution of real and hypothetical behavior. *Child Development*, 1977, *48*, 464–469.

Skarin, K., & Moely, B. E. Altruistic behavior: An analysis of age and sex differences. *Child Development*, 1976, *47*, 1159–1165.

Smith, C. L., Gelfand, D. M., Hartmann, D. P., & Partlow, M. P. Children's causal attributions regarding help giving. *Child Development*, 1979, *50*, 203–210.

Smith, T. W., & Pittman, T. S. Reward, distraction, and the overjustification effect. *Journal of Personality and Social Psychology*, 1978, *36*, 565–572.

Staub, E. The use of role playing and induction in children's learning of helping and sharing behavior. *Child Development*, 1971, *42*, 805–816.

Thelen, M. H., & Rennie, D. L. The effect of vicarious reinforcement on imitation: A review of the literature. In B. H. Maher (Ed.), *Progress in experimental personality research* (Vol. 6). New York: Academic Press, 1972.

Toner, I. J., Moore, L. P., & Emmons, B. A. The effect of being labeled on subsequent self-control in children. *Child Development,* 1980, *51,* 618–621.

Tulving, E. Episodic and semantic memory. In E. Tulving & W. Donaldson (Eds.), *Organization of memory.* New York: Academic Press, 1972.

Walters, G. C., & Grusec, J. E. *Punishment.* San Francisco: Freeman, 1977.

Weiner, H. R., & Dubanoski, R. A. Resistance to extinction as a function of self- or externally determined schedules of reinforcement. *Journal of Personality and Social Psychology,* 1975, *31,* 905–910.

Wells, D., & Shultz, T. R. Developmental distinctions between behavior and judgment in the operation of the discounting principle. *Child Development,* 1980, *51,* 1307–1310.

White, G. M. Immediate and deferred effects of model observation and guided and unguided rehearsal on donating and stealing. *Journal of Personality and Social Psychology,* 1972, *21,* 139–148.

White, G. M., & Burnam, M. A. Socially cued altruism: Effects of modeling, instructions, and age on public and private donations. *Child Development,* 1975, *46,* 559–563.

Whiting, B. B., & Whiting, J. W. M. *Children of six cultures.* Cambridge, MA: Harvard University Press, 1975.

Zahn-Waxler, C. Z., Radke-Yarrow, M., & King, R. A. Child rearing and children's prosocial initiations toward victims in distress. *Child Development,* 1979, *50,* 319–330.

6. Ordinary Learning: Pragmatic Connections Among Children's Beliefs, Motives, and Actions

Scott G. Paris and David R. Cross

Children's learning is the core of their everyday experiences. The principal tasks of childhood include learning physical skills for play and work, social conventions for interaction, and cognitive understanding of the environment. These tasks require a tremendous amount of children's time and energy and are concerns of parents, teachers, and scientists alike. Our common goals are to understand and to facilitate children's learning because it is so vital to their education and development. In this chapter we sketch a conceptual framework of children's learning and describe motivational factors that shape children's acquisition and refinement of various skills. We begin with several intuitive tenets about children's learning that help to define the scope of our inquiry and to chart the paths of our proposal. We are concerned with children's learning that is ordinary, socialized, functional, and adventurous.

Ordinary learning involves common tasks mastered over long time periods. Learning how to sew, to read, to play soccer, and so forth are culturally prescribed activities in which many children participate. Common tasks are the target of our proposal because they are the principal activities of children and afford the most ecologically valid observations of learning. Because of our concern for everyday tasks, we emphasize contextual and temporal variables neglected in some past theories. Ordinary learning involves tasks that fit into the child's total fabric of existence; the relevance and value of tasks vary for individuals across contexts. Ordinary learning usually is not accomplished in minutes or hours but may require months or years and become a lifetime vocation or avocation. Analyses of unusual tasks or of children who acquire idiosyncratic knowledge and skills with exceptional speed are cases of *extra*ordinary learning.

Learning is a socialized activity for most children. They observe other people performing everyday tasks and interact with family and friends to master activities that are salient for them. Significant others present these tasks to young learners and establish goals, give feedback, and encourage children to discover task solutions on their own. Tutorial help is needed most by young children, novices, and people undergoing training or remediation. Although social reciprocity may become less evident as skilled learners acquire greater control over their own performance, a broad framework of learning has to allow for the recurrent influence of other people on the learner's attitudes, interests, and skills (cf. Vygotsky, 1978).

Learning is usually functional; it serves a purpose. If a task is ordinary and socialized, then mastering it probably has some utility for other endeavors. Functional learning typically includes a sense of intentionality for achieving goals that have value for the individual. Ordinary learning also involves affect and beliefs, so that purpose is charged with feelings. Goal-directedness is a cornerstone of children's learning. Conversely, failures to understand, articulate, select, or pursue appropriate goals can interfere seriously with learning.

Learning is often adventurous and self-perpetuating. Children do not just perform under stress and watchful eyes, nor do they simply obey regimented rules. They choose how to spend their time pursuing some activities rather than others. Social competition, personal challenge, and risk of failure make ordinary learning adventurous. Satisfaction provided by mastering tasks of work and play is crucial for continuing motivation and lifelong learning (Maehr & Nicholls, 1980). Hence, we need to develop a conceptual framework in which central roles are assigned to challenge and adventure as ingredients of self-initiated learning.

Our intent is to sketch a framework of ordinary learning that helps up to understand the intuitively important qualities of children's learning. We try to synthesize some exciting new research from educational, social, developmental, and cognitive psychology into a cohesive account of children's learning and motivation that has a more expansive frame of reference than previous views. Specifically, we propose a temporal framework of recursive learning cycles in which learners are motivated to pursue some tasks, strategies, and actions over others. We focus on the pragmatic value of learning that guides the learner's choices and allocation of effort. Our major goal is to establish an empirically testable framework for describing and explaining factors that control learning. Our synthesis is an attempt to be bold but not fanciful, and to be grand but not grandiose.

Recursive Motivated Learning

Psychological investigations of children's learning have seldom analyzed "ordinary learning." Instead, isolated bits of behavior have been studied in brief and artificial circumstances. Although this tactic has been valuable, we think that the resulting conceptualizations of learning have been unduly narrow. Theories and research have often been predicated on particular tasks. This kind of centration and methodological inbreeding has led to criticisms that the tasks and theories are not "ecologically valid." This accusation raises two issues that need to be stated explicitly.

First, most tasks used to study learning in psychological laboratories have been dull. These tasks have often involved repetitive, boring actions (e.g., dropping marbles in a box, sorting objects, moving cranks and levers, memorizing nonsense syllables). Tasks were often selected so as to minimize interest, affect, and motivation and to disguise the purpose of learning. Skill and will were intentionally separated and subsequent characterizations of learning were often remarkably sterile. Second, these tasks have usually required elementary responses that could change in frequency, speed, or contingency within brief testing sessions. Performance changes in well-prepared responses are impoverished instances of learning and appear considerably different in quality than everyday experiences that demand purpose and persistence for the acquisition of new behavior.

In the course of constructing our framework we have sought to overcome these weaknesses by building on a foundation of repeated practice and motivation. We discuss the first of these themes in the section "Learning Cycles: Time Lines, Loops, and Spirals," where we highlight the recursive nature of learning for most tasks. This aspect of our framework is designed to portray learning in everyday contexts such as the home, playground, or school, where tasks are repeated almost daily and skills are mastered over long time periods. We discuss the second theme in "Fusing Skill and Will," where we reassert the role of motivation in children's learning. This aspect of our framework draws attention to both cognitive and motivational factors that determine children's learning. Both of these themes— learning cycles and fusing skill and will—are elaborated and consolidated within a temporal scheme in "Marshaling and Distributing Resources for Learning," where both knowledge and effort are characterized as resources for learning. Next we emphasize the functional nature of learning in the section "Pragmatics of Ordinary Learning." In the remaining sections we discuss empirical studies that illustrate the usefulness of our approach for understanding children's learning.

Learning Cycles: Time Lines, Loops, and Spirals

Our framework is based on temporal divisions in task-oriented behavior. We take the thoughts, feelings, and actions of task-engaged learners as the object of scrutiny rather than beginning with a psychological characterization of learning mechanisms (e.g., reinforcement) or outcomes (e.g., conservation). In this manner we can observe, for example, metacognitions, attributions, and attitudes as they function together in concrete situations. Throughout our temporal framework we emphasize the context of learning and social transactions among people because learning may vary greatly across different situations (Rogoff, 1982). We divide task-oriented behavior into three categories: antecedents to the task, engagement on the task, and consequences to performance.

Antecedent activities involve preparation for responding. Learning depends on a person's existing skills, knowledge, and dispositions to pursue particular goals.

These factors influence decisions about whether to engage a task and how to approach it. Choices must be made about the relative importance of the outcomes, strategies to be employed, and costs of the required effort. This phase of decision making includes attachment of values to relevant variables (e.g., time, effort, and ability) and selective allocation of resources. *Task engagement* consists of the application and self-regulation of requisite responses. That is, learners implement chosen strategies and monitor their own activities to ensure that their plans are followed. Learners may also abandon or revise plans and goals during the course of task engagement. *Consequent activities* include evaluations of performance, rewards, attributions for success or failure, and related consequences. These consequences may alter the learners' knowledge and beliefs and set the stage for subsequent pretask activities when the task is encountered again.

Figure 6-1 illustrates the recursive relations among the learner's activities before, during, and after task engagement. Although most current approaches to learning emphasize the time line of events in part A of the figure, considerably less attention has been paid to the effects of repeated learning cycles. Cycles of task engagement, as depicted in part B of Figure 6-1, focus our analyses on alterations in the learner's plans, strategies, persistence, and satisfaction with each successive trial. By charting progressive systematic changes in thoughts and feelings throughout the

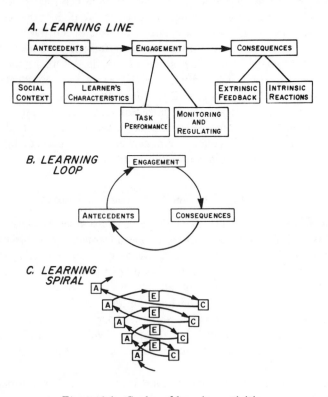

Figure 6-1. Cycles of learning activities.

course of ordinary learning, we can identify patterns of causes and consequences in behavioral development. We have represented this progress as a spiral in part C to highlight improvement with practice and new conditions for learning. Each cycle of learning affords opportunities for the individual to receive help and direction from other people as well as a chance to practice, reconsider, integrate, and refine the skill. The notion of a "learning spiral" is borrowed from Soviet psychologists, who use it to describe how successive quantitative changes in behavior eventually result in qualitatively new developments (Wertsch, 1981). The actual behavior described by a learning spiral will vary according to the detail of skill being analyzed, but we can use the metaphor to portray learning *processes* (e.g., successively better use of planning or memorizing strategies) as well as learning *products* (e.g., progressively richer concepts).

The temporal model of processing is not novel and can be readily translated into S-R or information-processing terminology (Kail & Bisanz, 1982). It serves as a unit for learning loops and learning spirals. We do not view learning as a linear process or one-pass system. Most ordinary learning requires considerable time and practice— literally thousands of repetitions in order to learn the alphabet, how to swim, or how to type. Thus, a model of learning should be recursive and cyclical. But this iterative aspect of learning is not just repetition of the traditional time-line model. Indeed, redundancy of similar antecedents, engagement, and consequences defines *nonlearning*. The recursive loop requires change in one or more of the variables as a necessary condition for learning. Which changes are sufficient, of course, is an empirical question.

Fusing Skill and Will

Motivation is essential throughout cycles of learning. Dispositions to respond are influenced by incentives and task considerations prior to engagement as well as by rewards and attributions following performance. No matter how capable the individual is, desire and purpose must fuel behavior for ordinary learning. Yet, great desire cannot guarantee learning if the individual does not have the requisite physical or mental prowess. Thus, both skill and will are necessary for ordinary learning—neither alone is sufficient—and we must be able to describe their inter-action during learning. To begin, we focus our attention on the role of will. The social-psychological constructs of belief, attitude, and value offer helpful insights into the concept of "will." We start with definitions of these constructs and then describe how they fit into our framework of learning.

Beliefs reflect a person's understanding of the dynamic and static properties of the environment. They are the product of repeated experiences with family and social groups as well as with inanimate objects. But they are more than mere knowledge; they are convictions about the way things are or ought to be. According to Rokeach (1979), beliefs are expectancies about (a) *existence* (e.g., "There is a monster in my closet" or "Objects fall at a constant speed"), (b) *evaluation* (e.g., "Jogging is boring" or "Reading mysteries is fun"), (c) *prescription* (e.g., "I must not hit other children" or "People should pay their bills on time"), and (d) *causa-*

tion (e.g., "John writes well because he is smart" or "The tree fell on my car because I didn't go to church last week").

Existential, evaluative, prescriptive, and causative beliefs are clearly interrelated. They tend to be organized around salient features of people's lives and to reflect emotional investments that may or may not appear reasonable to others. Consider, as one example, the fact that children often impart animate qualities to inanimate objects such as clouds. Their existential beliefs, that clouds have feelings and will-power, give rise to causative beliefs such as, "The cloud cried and rained all over us because it was sad." In many ways this is a rational, if not accurate, explanation of a phenomenon that could be difficult to explain to a young child. It is the *reasonableness* of beliefs, within ecological contexts for particular individuals, that imbue them with power to shape behavior. Part of children's learning involves understanding that some prior beliefs are not really sensible; there are alternative and better ways of conceptualizing the world. Thus, learning involves more than just the accumulation of facts and beliefs; it reflects persuasive reasons for changing one's mind.

Relatively stable sets of beliefs organized around objects, events, or behaviors form attitudes (Rokeach, 1979). Thus, children's attitudes toward mathematics could involve existential beliefs about their abilities, evaluative beliefs about mathematics, prescriptive beliefs about parents' expectations, and causative beliefs about the factors necessary for success. Children's attitudes are often shared by their families, friends, and teachers. These shared beliefs constitute values that characterize cultures and subcultures, and these values, like more idiosyncratic attitudes and beliefs, can exert powerful influences on the ordinary learning of children.

How are beliefs and attitudes related to children's learning? They are personally significant aspects of children's knowledge that give rise to meaningful goals and intentions. Beliefs and attitudes energize and guide learning. Consider that most ordinary learning is self-initiated and directed toward particular ends. Goals provide rationales for the behavior. Many incentives, intrinsic and extrinsic, may accompany the goals. The values of those incentives can determine the degree of one's desire and striving. This translates behaviorally into effort and persistence toward a goal.

Plans for action involve decisions about cost/benefit ratios and the utility of various means to reach goals. An attitude is an evaluation of the behavior in question that results in pragmatic judgments of intentions (Fishbein, 1979). Positive evaluation, and hence favorable attitudes, are formed from expectations that effort will lead to generally positive outcomes. Conversely, negative evaluations and unfavorable attitudes accompany behavior that is expected to lead to generally negative outcomes. Accordingly, a child who expects a negative outcome from taking a mathematics test will have an unfavorable attitude, whereas a child with optimistic expectations will have a more favorable attitude. However, intentions to act are determined by several forces, including the individual's prescriptive beliefs about normative behavior. Beliefs concerning other people's expectations and the individual's motivation to comply with these significant others determine subjective norms and behavioral intentions. As a result, if our child with the unfavorable attitude were sufficiently motivated to comply with his teacher's desire that he take the test, he would take the test despite low expectations for success.

Goals and plans involve *skill* as well as *will*. The formulation of a goal reflects not only one's beliefs, but also one's knowledge of the skills necessary to achieve the goal. Hence, effective learning requires self-management of resources and realistic goal setting. Self-management refers, in part, to knowing how particular variables influence learning. For example, good readers know that important ideas in text serve as good retrieval cues for later recall (Brown, 1980). Similarly, good memorizers understand that they should study information that is not yet learned rather than studying information that has been mastered already (Masur, McIntyre, & Flavell, 1973). Of course, we could list many kinds of relevant knowledge of this sort; the important point is that information about variables and processes that affect learning is a critical part of cognitive skills.

Many researchers have referred to knowledge about self-management as *metacognition*, the understanding and orchestration of one's own cognitions (Flavell, 1978). Metacognition includes understanding how performance is affected by task difficulty, personal abilities, and cognitive strategies. Although metacognition may reflect awareness of mental processing constraints only sometimes, it is manifested in strategies such as predicting, estimating, and monitoring one's own thinking (Brown, 1978). Metacognition is involved in assessments of one's mental states as well as in the dynamic translation of knowledge into action. Evaluating, planning, and regulating one's own problem solving improve dramatically during childhood for diverse skills such as reading, memory, attention, and communication (Paris & Lindauer, 1982). Part of this developmental accomplishment reflects children's sensitivity to the need to be planful and to appreciate the benefits of cognitive strategies (Brown, 1980). Cognitive development also reflects affective reactions or "metacognitive experiences" (Flavell, 1979) such as uncertainty, confidence, bewilderment, and pride that accompany children's learning. The interrelationships among metacognition, motivation, and affect are at the heart of cognitive development and effective education (Glaser, 1982; Resnick, 1981). In our view the fusion of skill and will is essential for a complete analysis of learning and is at the foundation of our proposal.

Marshaling and Distributing Resources for Learning

Beliefs, knowledge, and social supports can be regarded as resources available to learners as they prepare for task engagement, actually engage tasks, and react to consequences of their performance. We view the learner as a self-manager who marshals and distributes resources in response to task demands. Self-management is a skill that becomes more efficient, autonomous, and attuned to the needs, interests, and aptitude of the learner with development. Within various information processing models of learning, expertise is accompanied by parallel processing and automaticity (e.g., LaBerge & Samuels, 1974). Learning to use strategies concurrently or automatically frees additional cognitive resources for other endeavors (Case, 1978; Shatz, 1978). In our temporal scheme, each recursive loop could pro-

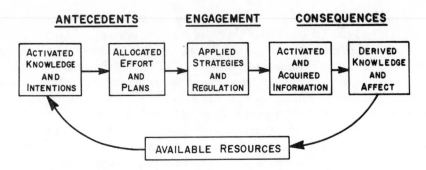

Figure 6-2. Marshaling and distributing resources for learning.

vide new cognitive and motivational resources or each trial could activate different kinds of knowledge and dispositions as relevant. We have illustrated the distribution of resources for learning across our temporal schematic in Figure 6-2.

Available resources include personal abilities, attitudes, social supports, and external influences that are potentially of use to the learner. Available skill and effort represent the learner's dynamic competence (cognitive, physical, motivational, social). Only some knowledge will become important and activated before task engagement. For example, instructions given before the task may direct the person's attention to time constraints, relevant features of the task, the major goal, or suitable strategies to employ. Incentives, desire, fear of failure, and motivational variables may also be emphasized. These activated bits of information are integrated by the person into decisions and plans for action.

Activated information must be managed, since it cannot be acted upon simultaneously or haphazardly. Choices must be made about the relative importance of goals, behavioral strategies to be employed, and costs of the required effort. This phase of decision making includes attachment of values to activated variables and selective allocation of effort. The resulting intentions are applied subsequently to the task. During engagement on the task, good learners also monitor their own activities to ensure that their plans are followed.

The consequences phase of learning cycles includes activation of new information following task engagement by personal reflection or by feedback from others. For example, after a test students may receive praise that signals excellent performance and adds to their knowledge and motivation. However, the person must construct meaning from evaluations of performance. Two students who each receive B grades may react quite differently, depending on their expectations, efforts, abilities, and attributions. The knowledge, affect, and motivation derived from task involvement can alter the learner's approach to future learning loops. Speed, accuracy, and efficiency of learning, the skills of experts and wills of craftsmen, can be indexed by management of the individual's resources for learning. Activation of information, allocation of effort, application, and derivation of knowledge are distinct components of learning cycles that can each be improved through experience to enhance continued learning, motivation, and task involvement.

Pragmatics of Ordinary Learning

Skill and will are fused in ordinary learning to promote continued task involvement and mastery. Isolated measurements of an individual's amount of knowledge or motivation reveal little about the dynamics of learning cycles and improvements in performance and understanding. Our framework emphasizes the functional aspects of learning over time because we believe that children's efforts to learn about the world are often guided by their pragmatic considerations. Their goals, expectations, and standards for performance are influenced by other people and the consequences of learning. Children often choose to invest effort in some learning activities rather than others based on the value or utility of the activities. Positive outcomes of learning thus help children adapt to the evolving social and cognitive demands of their environment.

Learning is usually functional but this does not mean that functions are uniform or normative. The utility of different learning processes or products may vary according to characteristics of the learner, goals of the task, contexts, and available strategies. These four factors have been identified as the tetrahedral model of learning (Jenkins, 1979), but they do more than introduce additional variables to consider. Functionalism is a doctrine in which utilitarianism, purpose, and pragmatics are criteria of learning (Beilin, Note 1). Despite an early emphasis on these factors by Tolman, Lewin, Binet, Thorndike, and others, the constructs have been ignored too often in cognitive accounts of learning. We believe that a framework for analyzing learning that includes a functional emphasis on learners' beliefs, attitudes, and values—those personally significant and constructed thoughts about one's self and the world—can help to ameliorate this problem.

We have synthesized diverse variables that influence learning according to the timing and operation of their influence. The temporal, functional approach circumvents problems of trying to fit experimental findings into established but ill-defined constructs such as metacognitions, executive processors, and attributions. The model also clarifies how these variables can serve either as antecedent or consequent conditions to influence learning. Indeed, the beliefs that are held by the learner after task engagement can be very similar to those that are brought to the task the next time it is encountered.

Antecedents to Task Engagement

People enter learning contexts with a variety of characteristics. Some attributes, such as age or intelligence, are relatively stable; others, such as mood, interest, and effort, can fluctuate. All of these characteristics are resources that the learner brings to the task, but only some of them (e.g., effort) can be controlled easily by the self or others. We shall focus on available skills and motivation that can be controlled because they are the independent variables of ordinary learning. Considerable research has illustrated the importance for learning of activating relevant information (e.g., consideration of task difficulty and one's goals), but there has been notice-ably less research on how learners choose and plan their courses of action once this knowledge has been activated. In the following sections we discuss how considera-tion of task goals and personal abilities influences the individual's approach to learning. We review studies that illustrate the role of beliefs and attitudes in chil-dren's strategic allocation of effort.

Activating Relevant Resources for Learning

Activated knowledge orients the learner to the task and sets the stage for subse-quent learning. The principal sources of stimulation for activation come from other people's behavior (e.g., directions, expectations, standards) and the learner's fore-thoughts about the task (e.g., purposes, attitudes, beliefs). Research on metacogni-tion has been focused on many of these cognitive components and others have been delineated in social-motivational theories (Brookover & Erickson, 1969, 1975). Prompts about relevant strategies and response options can be provided by reflec-tion or by other people in order to alert the learner to relevant information prior to task engagement. We shall discuss only a few important variables to indicate how antecedent conditions influence subsequent learning. We shall examine the learner's evaluations of person, task, and strategy variables (cf. Flavell, 1978; Paris & Lindauer, 1982) in terms of (a) goals within the task context, (b) evaluations of the roles of self and others, and (c) strategies for learning. Each has been identified through research as foreknowledge critically related to learning. Finally, we shall discuss how knowledge and effort become allocated to tasks.

Goals. People engage in tasks for many reasons. Maehr (1983) has distinguished four categories of goals—task, ego, social solidarity, and extrinsic rewards—and described how each goal category elicits different kinds of learning behavior. *Task goals* include self-absorption in the activity. This type of immersion is the end in itself and is similar to the notion of task involvement advocated by Nicholls (1983) as the goal of education. Task goals also include the notion of competence moti-vation (Harter, 1981; White, 1959) or the desire to demonstrate one's ability. Task goals satisfy intrinsic needs for achievement, standards for performance, and subjective success. Individuals who hold mastery goals for the task strive to chal-lenge their abilities and to maximize their sense of competence. For example, they usually choose tasks of moderate difficulty in which favorable performance can be attributed to their own skills (Atkinson & Raynor, 1977).

Ego goals, according to Maehr, include social competition and self-enhancement at someone else's expense. Performance goals that are activated as antecedent con-ditions thus depend on the competitors' levels of skills and mutual social inter-actions. Ego goals also interact with personality characteristics to elicit defensive strategies for preserving self-worth (Covington & Beery, 1976).

Maehr's third goal category is *social solidarity.* This category includes con-formity, social compliance, deference, and altruism. Social solidarity goals reflect good intentions and conventional behavior. They may compensate for lack of demonstrated ability (e.g., "At least I tried") or they may minimize risk taking. The goals are somewhat novel when considered with regard to learning and achievement, but they are clearly important candidates for activated antecedent resources. Social solidarity goals remind us that goals are not just egocentric or cognitive.

Finally, *extrinsic goals* are tangible rewards provided for successful performance. The utility of reinforcement, from praise to money to food, has been amply demonstrated as an effective goal for modifying behavior. However, goal activation for extrinsic rewards can influence performance differently than other types of goals. When one works to maximize rewards, the result often is that challenge, uncertainty, and experimentation during learning are minimized. Thus, extrinsic rewards may actually decrease motivation for performance and creativity, especially on tasks that are interesting and meaningful to individuals without contingent external rewards (Lepper, 1981).

Each of these goal categories influences task engagement and motivation in different ways according to Maehr (1983). The learner's personality characteristics interact with the task and social context to produce widely different allocations of resources. For example, individuals with high self-concepts of ability perform equally well under task goal or ego goal conditions (Brockner, 1979). However, individuals with low self-concepts do much more poorly on ego-involving rather than task-involving conditions (Nicholls, 1983). Low-self-concept individuals also choose tasks on which success (or failure) is highly probable, so that performance outcomes offer minimal risks for attributions to low ability. Thus, a person's assessments of self-concept and ability often interact with the nature of the goal to determine how different resources are applied to the task at hand. In spite of these individual differences, however, goals are highly effective in promoting improved task performance. Locke, Shaw, Saari, and Latham (1981) suggest that goals enhance performance by focusing attention, mobilizing effort, encouraging persistence, and motivating strategy development.

A fundamental problem for the novice, of course, is to generate and activate *any* goal prior to task engagement. For example, preschool children have only a rudimentary understanding of cognitive goals for attending, searching, communicating, remembering, or reading (Flavell, 1978; Brown, 1978; Schmidt & Paris, 1983). Part of development involves the acquisition of a repertoire of cognitive and social goals. Another major milestone in development is reached when children can control the selection of alternative goals. This type of reflective awareness and selectivity is not often observed in children's learning before 5 years of age (Paris & Lindauer, 1982).

Evaluation of Self and Others. The role of self-concept in learning is not easy to pinpoint because it may be both a cause and a consequence of achievement (Hansford & Hattie, 1982; Wylie, 1979). Shavelson and Bolus (1982), for example, argued for a model of differentiated self-concepts (e.g., academic, social, physical) that are distinct from actual achievement and are hierarchically arranged from very specific domains, such as self-concept about mathematics ability, to a general notion of self-concept. They also found statistically significant causal paths from self-concept measures to achievement but not vice versa. Seventh and eighth graders' achievements in science, math, and English courses were predicted well by their academic self-concepts and particular appraisals of their abilities in each subject. Thus, self-concept appears to be a causal antecedent to academic achievement.

The view of related yet separate self-appraisals of ability is compatible with our emphasis on discrete task domains and current conceptualizations of cognitive skills (e.g., Fischer, 1980). Other research suggests that some of the student's self-concepts may be derived from parental attitudes and expectations (Eccles-Parsons, Adler, & Kaczala, 1982) or from school-related experiences (Eccles-Parsons, Kaczala, & Meece, 1982). In our proposal, it is easy to incorporate self-concept as both an antecedent *and* consequence of learning. Indeed, since neither learning nor self-concept of ability is expected to remain unchanged over time and practice, it is the successive patterns of correlations throughout learning cycles that must be analyzed to determine progressive changes in each.

Young children (and perhaps novice learners at other ages) often fail to evaluate their own ability at all. For example, before 6 or 7 years of age, children are not adept at estimating their memory spans, their readiness for recall, or their own degree of comprehension (Brown, 1978). Naive approaches to tasks include unrealistic expectations of effort and success, partly due to the failure to consider one's own abilities or knowledge beforehand. But even when children consider relevant variables, they often do so erroneously. Young children are notoriously imprecise and inconsistent in their predictions about their own cognitive abilities (e.g., Flavell, Friedrichs, & Hoyt, 1970).

Young children are also poor at judging other people's abilities, perspectives, and intentions (Shantz, 1975). However, inaccuracies in social cognition and egocentric insensitivity are dependent on the task and context. Egocentrism is not evident when tasks are simplified to elicit socially directed responses (e.g, sharing a view of a picture; Lempers, Flavell & Flavell, 1977), when tasks and the context are familiar and ordinary (e.g., Maratsos, 1973; Menig-Peterson, 1975), or when the audience's abilities are discriminable and familiar (e.g., modifying speech according to the ages and abilities of listeners; Bloom & Lahey, 1978; Shatz & Gelman, 1973). Thus, the task and social context influence the likelihood that children will evaluate their abilities and those of other people prior to engagement.

Activating Knowledge and Strategies for Learning. Cognitive strategies are the primary resources described in cognitive accounts of learning and development. Strategies can be general orientations to tasks (such as finding a good light to read by) or they can be specific rules for processing information (such as skimming concluding sentences of paragraphs).

The important point for learning is that novices could fail to use relevant knowledge or strategies because they lack cognitive resources or they do not have the inclination or knowledge to apply them appropriately. During the past several years, many studies have demonstrated that young children and novices are often unaware of appropriate cognitive strategies for tasks of intentional learning and remembering. For instance, young children fail to monitor their own understanding adequately while listening or reading (Markman, 1977, 1979; Paris & Myers, 1981).

They rarely consider ways of disambiguating messages or clarifying communication without specific instruction (Flavell, Speer, Green, & August, 1981; Patterson & Kister, 1981; Schmidt & Paris, 1983) and are often oblivious to strategies for remembering (Kreutzer, Leonard, & Flavell, 1975). They do not engage in these activities nor sense the need to do so. Task involvement seems sufficient without consideration of additional information or learning strategies. When performance appears adequate by the child's standards without additional effort, then ignorance is bliss, or at least the path of least resistance.

Simple activation of cognitive resources, such as considering particular actions as aids for comprehension monitoring, is not terribly difficult. Most teachers and parents tell children important strategies for tasks, or they show them, prompt them, and remind them to practice. Often tasks are structured so that induced activation is likely or necessary. Many strategies become apparent to children in these fashions through training and instruction. The critical breakdown seems to occur when beginning learners or children are left to their own devices. Consider how most children perform on memory tasks. When 5- and 6-year olds are presented with lists of words or series of pictures from several discrete categories (e.g., toys, food, animals), they often do not organize their study or recall by the categories (Neimark, Slotnick, & Ulrich, 1971). If young children are instructed to use grouping to aid learning, they do so successfully; but on unprompted trials they do not generate the strategy that they just used. This phenomenon is referred to as a "production deficiency" for mnemonic strategies and is a familiar finding for young children, as well as elderly adults and retarded people (Borkowski, Reid, & Kurtz, in press; Hagen, Barclay, & Schwethelm, 1981; Reese, 1976). Clearly individuals could and did use the "strategies" like grouping to perform the task, but the available actions were never coordinated with the task goal of recall (cf. Paris, 1978) and were thus not applied to the task in an instrumental self-guided manner. Behavioral compliance is quite different from a cognitive strategy. This raises the important issue of translating activated knowledge into strategically allocated effort.

Allocating Effort: Plans and Strategies

Following activation of task-related information, goals, and expectations, a person has to make choices about a course of action. These decisions involve selecting among potential actions, assigning priorities to various goals, and planning sequences of behavior. This is not a dispassionate or automatic phase preceding task engagement. It represents *personal investment* in the task, a wager of effort and self-esteem against the importance of the task, expectations of success, and risks of failure. Allocation of resources is thus a synthesis of beliefs and abilities into a plan for action. For now, we want to focus on two processes for allocating effort— attaching values to activated knowledge, and establishing intentions.

Attaching Values to Activated Knowledge. People can view tasks with different attitudes depending on the situation. An exam, race, or concert could provide an opportunity to demonstrate one's competence that is seen as challenging and rewarding; or it could be viewed as trivial, insurmountable, or embarrassing. Attitudes confer values on task-oriented behavior that must be judged in relation to a larger context of personality, sociocultural context, and selfhood (Rokeach, 1979; Sherif, 1979). Indeed, attitudes vary in importance (as well as centrality, relevance, meaningfulness, salience, involvement, and intensity) because of their diverse influences and origins.

Consider, for instance, the socialization of children's attitudes toward school and learning. Children's attitudes are largely a function of the attitudes of their parents and teachers (McMillan, 1980). For example, Eccles-Parsons, Adler, and Kaczala (1982) found that junior high school students' attitudes toward mathematics were more closely related to their parents' beliefs about their children's mathematics abilities and about task difficulty than to the child's sex or previous mathematics performance. Parental modeling was not related to junior high school students' attitudes about mathematics. This study suggests that social influences are important in determining the personal significance of task outcomes.

Research on how beliefs and attitudes influence learning is just beginning but promises to be a fruitful area of study. For example, Champagne, Klopfer, and Anderson (1980) studied the effects that preconceptions (i.e., beliefs) have on learning classical physics. They were interested in assessing the relative contributions of mathematics skill, reasoning ability, and experience-based preconceptions about physics to learning classical physics. They found that physics preconceptions were related to achievement in physics class, although not as strongly related as mathematical skill. Furthermore, they found that each student usually had an elaborate and personal system of commonsense beliefs about motion. This commonsense belief system was qualitatively different from the formal system of classical physics and influenced how students solved problems. Here we see that beliefs play something more than an energizing role; they help to determine the actual *processing* of information.

Beliefs help the learner order and organize strategic allocation of effort. For example, some task goals might be dismissed as unimportant and others pursued vigorously. Or erroneous beliefs about the importance of goals and skills could lead children to pursue inappropriate objectives or select poor strategies. Incongruence between teachers' and students' attitudes toward learning and discrepancies between their respective beliefs in the utility of classroom activities can lead to wasted effort and little achievement. Academic achievement is thus related to student interests, attitudes, and self-concepts, especially for students at the extremes of attitude or achievement distributions (Bloom, 1974). Some studies suggest more than correlation; attitudes such as self-concept may be causally linked to achievement (Shavelson & Bolus, 1982). The issue is no longer *whether* attitudes influence behavior, but *when* and *how* they affect behavior (Cialdini, Petty, & Cacioppo, 1981).

Establishing Intentions. Personal values assigned to tasks help to determine learners' intentions. These judgments reflect a balance among the anticipated payoffs, risks of failure, expected task difficulty, and social prescriptions. The learner must decide if the goal and behavioral effort are reasonable and worthwhile. When these choices are entirely left to the learner, decisions about allocated effort are relatively easy. On the other hand, when parents or teachers provide imperatives that leave little room for personal judgment, orientations toward task mastery and learning may be superseded by compliance or obedience. Positive values attached to the effort and utility of strategies are therefore important ingredients in children's establishment of intentions to learn rather than to comply. In our view, the transition from activated knowledge to allocated strategic effort is crucial because it reveals self-controlled learning. The attitudes become *rationales for action* adopted by learners and applied to task goals.

We will illustrate the difference between compliance and understanding with a recent experimental study of children learning to use memory strategies (Paris, Newman & McVey, 1982). In this study 7- and 8-year-olds were given two memory trials with 24 pictures on each of 5 consecutive days. Days 1 and 2 were simply practice trials; Day 3 included strategy training; and Days 4 and 5 were tests of strategy maintenance. All children were instructed how to label, rehearse, and group the pictures into related categories as study strategies. They were also taught to test their own memories and to recall together the names of pictures in related groups. Half of the children were simply shown the mnemonic actions and told to do them. The other half received elaborated feedback on the usefulness and appropriateness of the techniques for remembering.

Children who received the elaborated instructions manifested significantly greater recall, clustering, and strategic study behavior. They also reported greater appreciation for the utility of the strategies than did children who simply mimicked the actions. The latter children were compliant and followed directions but did not regard the mnemonic techniques as strategies relevant to the goal of recall. Children who received the elaborated feedback actually used the techniques as cognitive *strategies* because they selected the behaviors spontaneously on subsequent trials as useful means by which to accomplish particular task goals. Compliance and recall goals were both achieved by using the same resources.

This "microgenetic" study of learning clearly reveals a relationship between understanding the utility of strategies and subsequent performance. Through successive trials children realized that the allocation of strategic study behavior was worth the effort. Whereas both groups of children used the actions successfully following instructions, only children who understood the instrumental value of the actions continued to use them in subsequent self-directed learning efforts. This 5-day experiment on children's learning can be viewed as a compressed learning spiral analogous to ordinary learning over prolonged time periods.

We believe that many views of learning, particularly those that portray learning as the cognitive accumulation of information, emphasize only the availability and activation phases of learning. Novices either do not have some critical knowledge or strategy available or they do not activate their relevant resources in appropriate circumstances. But in our view, novices can also be disinterested, misguided, naive, impulsive, or inept. Our framework calls attention to "wrong-headedness" in addition to "empty-headed" lack of knowledge as a reason for nonallocation of knowledge and effort. The trademark of poor learning is not so much bewilderment about what to do as it is pursuit of inappropriate goals and persistent application of inefficient strategies. In Piagetian terms, preoperational children are often quite sure about their judgments of nonconservation, nontransitivity, and so on. The incorrigibility of young learners is due partly to the tenacity with which they cling to their beliefs about how to engage tasks.

Stubbornness is an interesting notion to introduce to learning because it is willful, cognitive, and affective. It is a characteristic of beliefs and attitudes that affects any decision about how a person will engage a task. We view the decision-making phase before task engagement as crucial because it determines personal orientations to ordinary tasks. Learning will be incremented when more efficient decisions are made about allocation of appropriate skills and effort. But even more important, these repeated decisions can promote or deter *continued* motivation and learning for particular tasks (Maehr, 1983). Whereas cognitive psychologists have eschewed such self-gauged decisions, social psychologists such as Brookover and Erickson (1969, 1975) regard them as the premise of their learning theory.

Task Engagement

Performance on a task is the actualization of one's intentions. The behavior may occur smoothly, automatically, and with little effort if the responses are not difficult or complex. However, initial attempts at learning are often characterized by application of less fluid responses in a deliberate manner. This extra effort and attention may prohibit the learner from doing other things simultaneously. "Other things" include, most notably, the ability to reflect upon and monitor one's behavior during task engagement. Novices may not often activate the metacognitive knowledge to monitor (e.g., Markman, 1977) nor allocate effort toward self-monitoring (Brown, 1980; Meichenbaum & Asarnow, 1978). They may also have difficulty trying to monitor themselves concurrently with their attempts to respond appropriately to the task.

Self-regulation of behavior—including monitoring, checking, and correcting—has been considered a crucial component of task engagement and learning by many theorists (e.g., Brown, 1978; Flavell, 1979; Paris & Lindauer, 1982; Vygotsky, 1978). The importance of self-regulative learning processes for children's development is demonstrated by recent research in a variety of behavioral domains: comprehension of oral communication (Flavell et al., 1981); reading (Baker & Brown, in press; Paris & Myers, 1981); study skills (Owings, Peterson, Bransford, Morris, & Stein, 1980); memory strategies (Belmont & Butterfield, 1977); and writing skills (Scardamalia & Bereiter, 1983). These studies reveal how school-age children gradually learn to attend simultaneously to multiple goals and to monitor their own performance. Most cognitive developmental studies have emphasized young children's lack of knowledge rather than motivation as the main factor underlying self-regulation. We shall use research by Anderson (1979) to illustrate how attitudes and cognitive skills can interact during task engagement.

Prior to actually reading a text, skilled readers will often scan it in order to get some idea about its content and organization, an activity Anderson (1979) called *surveying*. Anderson found that nearly all of the college students in his study surveyed, and that they did so in order to assess their prior knowledge, interests (e.g., attitudes), and the amount of time and effort necessary to learn the material. Furthermore, while surveying, students attended to three levels of information in the text. One level included the easy-to-process aspects of the text, such as titles, subtitles, marked words, highlighted sections, pictures, charts, graphs, and reference lists. A second level included information-rich portions of the text in predictable locations, such as introductory and summary paragraphs and the first sentences of any paragraph. The third level of information was intact portions of the text, including larger subsections and consecutive paragraphs.

Students rarely, if ever, surveyed by using only one level of information. Instead, they frequently moved from one level to another, rapidly and flexibly. Moreover, movement among the levels was not random. Instead, the following patterns were seen: (a) Students initially engaged in Level 1 behavior to assess prior knowledge, interest, and time and effort required for learning; (b) they moved from Level 1 to Level 2 or 3 if the initial assessments were difficult to make, *or* if they were interested in the materials; (c) they moved from Level 2 or 3 to Level 1 if the above assessments were made easily, *or* if they were uninterested in the text. Surveying broke down altogether if the text was not formatted to facilitate the use of Level 1 and Level 2 information; in this case the students resorted to some other strategy, such as reading the text paragraph by paragraph.

In addition, Anderson found that the results of surveying predicted students' actual study behavior. Students would not study at all if they already knew the material, or if the judged time to learn the material exceeded the time available for study. They would not study for long if interest was low and the effort required was high.

There are two relevant themes in Anderson's observations of students' surveying activities. The first is the strategic nature of surveying. Students' behavior is strategically guided by their prior knowledge, attitudes, time, effort, and organizational properties of the text. The second theme is the important role that interest plays in the students' surveying. One of the goals of surveying was assessing interest, and interest in turn guided students' movement from one level of information to another. This is a good demonstration that interest is not only an important antecedent, but can also be important during task engagement.

Although some studies have focused extensively on the cognitive aspects of self-regulation, Anderson suggests that such a sterile cognitive view could be misleading. In particular, he found that students displayed several emotions (e.g., satisfaction, displeasure, anxiety) while studying and were emotionally fatigued following studying. These emotions are potentially important resources for the student, and should not be overlooked in a model of learning.

Consequent Activities

Acquired and Activated Knowledge Following Performance

Immediate consequences to performance are often provided by the task itself. Responses continue to be applied until a desired end is achieved in most instances of ordinary learning. This source of feedback—refinement of responses to a personally satisfying standard—is often overlooked, perhaps because it is so common and interlocked in the behavioral pattern of persistent task engagement. Two other sources of information—extrinsic and intrinsic reactions to performance—are denoted more often. We consider these briefly in order to set the stage for a more complicated interpretaton of consequences to performance.

Extrinsic stimuli following performance include well-known rewards and punishments such as food, money, praise, shock, and criticism. When these events are delivered immediately, consistently, and contingently after particular responses, they exert great control over children's performance in many domains (Bandura, 1977). Whether consequences to performance are managed by the self or by others, the stimuli typically provide (a) information about the appropriateness of the response and (b) incentive to continue to respond and acquire additional rewards or avoid punishments.

Intrinsic reactions represent the cognitive and affective consequences to performance. Learners often gauge the adequacy of their efforts and skills following task engagement. They may compare performance to their prior records or to someone else's behavior. They may attribute success or failure to a variety of causes, and may experience guilt, pride, satisfaction, dismay, or other feelings (Bar-Tal, 1978; Frieze, 1980; Weiner, 1979, 1983). Self-evaluations, social comparisons, attributions, and metacognitions are typical intrinsic reactions that can provide motivation for ordinary learning. Internal sources of performance evaluation may, however, divert learners' attention from tasks, and the actual frequency of such afterthoughts is difficult to measure. They may often be ephemeral and epiphenomenal.

Introspective reports of thoughts and feelings are the focus of research on metacognitions and attributions (e.g., Kreutzer, Leonard, & Flavell, 1975; Weiner, 1979). These kinds of data have been analyzed to uncover subjects' intended goals and the strategies recruited to accomplish those ends. The attributions are considered self-perceptions of the causes for performance; but verbal reports, whether spontaneous or elicited, can distort the information in many ways (Nisbett & Wilson, 1977) and the validity of data on metacognitions and attributions has been questioned. We agree with this criticism and suggest that researchers measure intrinsic reactions and learning concurrently in order to establish functional relationships between performance and attributions or metacognitions. Measuring the functional impact on behavior of learners' thoughts and feelings helps to circumvent the problem of nonveridical verbal reports. Subjects can indeed "tell more than they know" and that is exactly why we should analyze the patterns of their "telling" and "doing" in order to understand their "knowing."

Whether or not immediate extrinsic or intrinsic consequences occur, several types of outcomes are possible. Either knowledge or motivation or physical capability (or any combination) could be enhanced following task engagement. One outcome would be an *acknowledgment* of the appropriateness of applied effort. This would confirm the learner's original plan and signal that persistence is warranted. A second type would involve *activation* of available knowledge in new combinations or settings—for example, learning to hit a Bobo doll in a particular context. A third type of intrinsic reaction can involve *acquisition* of novel behavior, such as imitation of new words or motor responses. Thus, immediate outcomes include cognitive, physical, and affective reactions to performance provided by the self or others. However, like knowledge and attitudes activated before engagement, these outcomes may require interpretation before they can be applied. Values become attached to performance outcomes with reference to the learner's initial characteristics, goals, beliefs, and intentions. Thus, *derived* knowledge and attitudes do not necessarily follow automatically from task performance and immediate outcomes. Attitudes and abilities are synthesized into the skills and inclinations of future available resources. Next we consider some recent research that highlights the importance of investigating how children derive meaning from consequences to their performance.

Justification and Dissonance Reduction

Extrinsic consequences of performance do not always have anticipated reinforcing effects. As a consequence of ineffective learning, conceptualizations of reinforcement have been altered to include situational and subjective interpretations of reinforcing stimuli. Vicarious reward, self-reinforcement, and self-efficacy are standard behavioral constructs that attempt to incorporate affect and self-regulation into conditioning paradigms. Indeed, self-efficacy and intrinsic motivation are becoming powerful explanatory terms (Bandura, 1982; Harter, 1981).

The importance of self-perception of extrinsic controls is illustrated in the classic forbidden toy paradigm (Aronson & Carlsmith, 1963). In this study, preschool children rated the attractiveness of several toys. Subsequently they were left alone in the room with all the toys but were admonished not to play with one particularly attractive toy. Half of the children received mild threats of punishment if they played with the forbidden toy and the other half received severe threats. Later, the experimenters reassessed children's toy preferences and found striking differences between the two groups. Children who were mildly threatened devalued the forbidden toy that was previously attractive much more than did children threatened seriously. Preschoolers who resisted temptation with little external control apparently justified their restraint by depreciating the toy. Those with external controls did not need to readjust their attitudes about the toy's attractiveness, since they could attribute their restraint to the threatened consequences.

Attitudes can change to provide justifications for one's behavior. This is analogous to planful "rationales for action" discussed earlier. But self-justification of attitudes does not only follow aversive conditions. It can also occur as a derivation from positive extrinsic outcomes. In the same way that mild threats present *under-justifications* for children's behavior, superfluous extrinsic rewards provide *over-justification* for task engagement. Both discrepancies stimulate attitudinal changes.

The expectation, delivery, or salience of superfluous reward for enjoyable tasks *decreases* children's subsequent interest in the rewarded task (e.g., Lepper & Greene, 1975). We should note that Lepper and his colleagues typically assess task involvement through unobtrusive measurements of everyday behavior in children's classrooms. Their tasks and methods exemplify our temporal model of meaningful learning. Their research (and related work, e.g., Condry, 1977; Harter, 1978) reveals that superfluous extrinsic rewards can have negative effects on interests, attitudes, and choices of tasks. Problem-solving strategies and effort can also be inhibited. Devaluation of task interest and intrinsic motivation following unnecessary rewards for appealing tasks can have debilitating consequences on continuing motivation and learning. A variety of research supports Lepper's (1981) contention that behavior performed (or viewed) as instrumental for achieving only limited goals decreases in intrinsic value (Kruglanski, 1978; Nicholls, 1983). Thus, a fundamental requirement for understanding children's learning is the differentiation of task goals from other objectives, such as ego or social compliance goals.

Lepper, Sagotsky, and Greene (1980; cited by Lepper, 1981) indicate how children differentiate goals in various situations and interpret extrinsic rewards as relevant or not on the basis of this differentiation. In the experimental sessions, children were rewarded on a fixed-interval schedule over multiple trials on four alternative activities. They earned tokens that could be redeemed for attractive toys. Their task engagement was compared to that of various control groups who received noncontingent rewards. Following these standard procedures for delivering rewards, children's subsequent interests in the four activities were assessed in two situations. First, their interests were measured unobtrusively in classrooms where the expected detrimental effects of superfluous (but effective) reinforcement procedures were observed. Children played less with rewarded activities when given a free choice with no expectation of reward. However, when children's interests in the four tasks were observed in further experimental sessions, there were marked *increases* in task engagement. This may reflect children's discrimination of the value of work for tokens or their efforts to please the experimenter. More generally, the study reveals children's cleverness in adjusting their behavior to different goals and situations. This situational and attitudinal flexibility is precisely why our analyses of learning, particularly continuing learning with choice and interest and challenge, must focus on children's derived interpretations of task engagement. We must examine their attributions and rationalizations following success and failure experiences in order to understand patterns of task engagement and learning over time.

Coping and Defending

Covington (1983) has synthesized cognitive and personality variables in his views of academic achievement. His construct of "motivated cognitions" captures the self-serving relationship between one's thoughts and motives and reaffirms the fusion of skill and will. Motivated cognitions blend two historical approaches to achievement motivation: (a) the emotional balancing of hope for success and fear of failure that was part of Atkinson's (1957) original formulation of "need for achievement" and (b) the cognitive interpretations of one's success and failures that reflect attributions for effort, ability, and so forth (Heider, 1958; Kelley, 1967; Weiner, 1979). For Covington, the interesting aspect about students' attributions, excuses, and rationalizations is their psychodynamic function as ego defenses that preserve self-esteem.

One advantage of motivated cognitions over attributions is the emphasis on personal meaning and function in the former. Attributions as after-the-fact hypotheses about causes for performance are often variable, inaccurate, and irrational. Motivated cognitions, though, reflect beliefs and intentions that can preserve feelings of competence and self-worth (Covington & Beery, 1976). For example, following failure on a task, a student could attribute poor performance to low ability and could subsequently lower his or her self-esteem. If this attribution inhibits future effort or task engagement, then it is dysfunctional for learning as well. However, attributions of failure to lower effort, whether true or not, may be more functional for preserving a sense of one's competence and enhancing future learning efforts. Fortunately, young children do not readily attribute failures to low ability and hence feel little personal shame or disdain for the task following ordinary failures (Covington & Beery, 1976). With age and schooling, however, children decrease their expectations for learning (Dweck & Elliott, 1983; Eccles-Parsons & Ruble, 1977; Eccles-Parsons, Midgley, & Adler, in press), improve the accuracy of their attributions (Nicholls, 1978, 1979a), and experience shame, guilt, and task disdain following failure.

Cognitive accuracy requires an emotional tax. This is precisely why Covington's analysis helps us to understand learning and development. In a positive vein, motivated cognitions influence levels of aspiration by helping the learner to set challenging yet realistic goals. They also serve to defend against damaging attributions to inability and consequent derogations of self-concept. This psychodynamic function is discussed by Haan (1977) and elaborated by Covington (1983). Postdictive explanations for behavior, especially when they are elicited by someone else's query, are subject to distortion, defensiveness, and inaccuracy. One can interpret this as methodological error or as a rich source of data about motivation. In our framework, the derived interpretations of prior performance can shape future learning. It is easy to see how justifications for performance could be elaborate defenses constructed to deceive the self and others. Excuses provided before or after a task serve similar defensive justifications.

Effort and Ability: The Double-Edged Sword

Two of the primary causes of performance in most attributional analyses are effort and ability, reflecting Heider's (1958) original focus on "can" and "try." The presumption by many attribution theorists has been that poor learning often results from little effort, which in turn is due to incorrect attributions of poor performance to low ability. Instruction to correct these attributions should thus lead to greater effort and learning. The argument is only reasonable, however, if everyone has equal ability or if effort can overcome differences in ability. Otherwise, not everyone will learn equally, even with maximum effort. When school learning is measured by social comparison of relative achievement, educational inequality is inevitable (Nicholls, 1979b; Paris & Oka, 1982).

Expending great effort is risky, however, because failure after trying hard presumably indicates low ability (Covington & Omelich, 1979). Personal deprecation then leads to lower expectations and negative attitudes for future task involvement. Teachers cannot maintain that students are "really capable" in the face of their repeated failures with effort because they would lose credibility by obvious lies. Even if students believed the false compliments, they would probably devalue the task through overjustification. Although students feel the most shame following failure with great effort, they cannot choose the easy alternative of not trying. Although discounting task appeal and decreasing effort may be rational defensive coping strategies, they are rarely useful options with regard to ordinary learning, especially in school. Thus, students need to expend enough effort to avoid reprimands from teachers but not so much effort that failure leaves low ability as the only plausible cause. Of course, this is how excuses become functional as alternative attributions for failure. Covington (1983) stated the maxim as "Try, or at least appear to try, but not too energetically and with excuses always handy."

Recent research has examined the development of children's knowledge about causes for their own performance. These inquiries illustrate the convergence of metacognitions and attributions as functional self-guided learning resources. For example, Harari and Covington (1981) asked students from first grade through college to evaluate the performance of hypothetical pupils from both the teacher's perspective and their own. The performance of the hypothetical pupils was described in terms of outcome (success and failure), effort (high or low), and ability (high or low). Individuals at all ages perceived high effort and success as worthy of teachers' rewards and low effort and failure as displeasing. A student's ability was not viewed as central to teachers' delivery of rewards and punishments. In contrast, all students valued personal ability highly, but evaluations of effort were high for children but low for teenagers. Why? Harari and Covington (1981) concluded that young children equate effort and ability. Thus, great effort permits children to regard themselves as both able and virtuous. Nicholls (1978) and Diener and Dweck (1978) reached similar conclusions for children up to 10 or 12 years of age. Dweck and Bempechat (1983) suggest that young children create a theory of intelligence that is *incremental*, in which increases in effort lead directly to increases in ability. Older children modify this view and construct an *entity* theory of mind that is less influenced by effort.

Some children, however, believe that performance is totally unaffected by effort (e.g., Butkowsky & Willows, 1980). Dweck and Licht (1980) describe learned-helpless schoolchildren as those who suffer repeated failures and blame their own inabilities. No amount of effort seems to compensate for failure. Their expectations, self-esteem, and task interest plummet. Dejection and inactivity thus become defensive ways of coping with failure by devaluing the task and justifying lack of effort, a set of attitudes that invites future failure. Indeed, the gulf widens over time between learned-helpless and "mastery-oriented" children, those students who succeed in school and continue to set challenging goals, invest effort, and derive satisfaction from their accomplishments. This common example of individual differences in schooling illustrates the necessity of considering attitudes and recursive temporal loops in ordinary learning.

Continuing Learning and Development

The learner's subjective appraisal of consequences following performance is embedded in repeated exposures to ordinary tasks. Attributions made by the learner (or others) about success or failure signal the importance of different variables, such as effort or skill, for particular tasks. But attributions can be self-serving (Covington, 1983) and emotionally charged (Weiner, 1983). Thus, they engender attitudes toward future task involvement that are both derived consequences of performance and antecedents to later learning.

Attitudes toward task involvement can influence future learning through many paths. For example, expectancies for future success or failure are built from repeated task experiences (Covington & Omelich, 1981; Forsyth & McMillan, 1981). These expectancies lead to attributions of high or low ability and are accompanied by emotions such as apprehension or pride. Expectancies, attributions, and emotional reactions in turn influence people's willingness to engage tasks again, to invest effort, and even to recruit specific learning strategies (Covington, 1983). Fyans and Maehr (1979) observed that students selected tasks that matched their own attributions so that students who made ability, effort, or luck attributions in turn selected tasks seen as requiring ability, effort, or luck, respectively, for successful performance.

It is important to note the dual functions of attitudes in the recursive framework and the repeated opportunities to alter attitudes and task performance. Some of the debates concerning how attitudes, metacognitions, and attributions are related to behavior might be resolved by consideration of the embedded dual roles that they serve in recursive learning. There is a growing body of evidence that clearly indicates that attitudes do energize and direct behavior (Bentler & Speckart, 1981) and that metacognitions and attributions improve with practice and skill proficiency (Paris & Lindauer, 1982). Thus, the issue is not simply whether attitudes, attributions, and metacognitions cause behavior but rather how thoughts, feelings, and actions change in reactive and synchronous manners throughout learning. We believe that our framework provides a broad conceptualization of these relationships with useful implications for developmental theories and methods.

We would like to suggest two paths along which learning "pulls" development, to follow the metaphor of Vygotsky (1978). First, the dynamic process of learning cycles permits children to infer many general regularities about the acquisition of information. Repetition, modeling, practice, corrective feedback, and pleasing others, for example, are common attributes of ordinary learning. Children learn about the nature of learning itself—the social, pragmatic, enjoyable aspects of expending effort to acquire new behavior and understanding. Young children may not display or articulate such awareness well, but it is evident in their gradual control over their own behavior. Children's understanding of intentionality and responsibility emerge from repeated experiences with ordinary tasks. These concepts play a vital role in social cognition and self-regulation that develop during childhood (Harter, 1982; Shultz, 1980). The strategic allocation of effort to selected purposes is one of the hallmarks of children's learning between 4 and 10 years of age and it is evident in a wide range of social and cognitive skills (Paris & Lindauer, 1982).

A second way in which learning can influence development is through the specific knowledge acquired in isolated domains. Parents and teachers usually try to relate new information to existing knowledge. Indeed, children themselves often assimilate disparate bits of information into novel combinations. (Piaget referred to some of these erroneously assembled connections as transductive, syncretic, or juxtaposed reasoning.) The reconciliation of new and old information is referred to as equilibration by Piaget, and we would like to reaffirm rationality as part of that process. Children "make sense," in a very constructive way, of what they know. Young children are not very cautious or logical, though, and often devise sweeping concepts or rules from limited evidence. With repeated confirmation of the rule, whether right or not, children establish beliefs about the phenomena with stronger convictions. These beliefs can become reinforced and applied to new situations if the learned rule leads to pragmatic payoffs (i.e., has utility or adaptive value). Reasonableness and functional value are therefore important attributes of equilibration that are derived from specific learning experiences and promote general development.

The issue of the relationship between learning and development has a converse problem also, namely, what are the developmental constraints on learning? Besides the obvious limitations due to physical immaturity and cognitive naiveté, we believe that children often fail to learn new skills because they do not understand the goals and strategies required for learning nor the necessity for perseverance. Half-hearted effort or compliance with superficial task goals rarely leads to learning or persistence. Changes in personal and social motivation are required for the activity to increase in significance and for the strategies to assume utilitarian value. This does not guarantee learning, but it maximizes the opportunities by providing appropriate and continued goal-directed efforts. The pragmatic value of effort and strategies is derived from an interaction of the learner's abilities with other people in particular contexts. Cognitive competence alone does not bestow value and significance on the pursuit of some task goals, nor does it trigger learning automatically.

Our speculations on learning and development plainly emphasize pragmatics of learning activities and the functional value of learning processes and outcomes. The framework is compatible with behavioral accounts of learning, structuralist characterizations of cognitive development, and information-processing analyses of tasks, but it is clearly an eclectic alternative to current conceptualizations. Because the proposal is constructive, contextual, and motivational in ways that other views are not, new kinds of research are implied. "One-shot" studies that compare groups of children on simple nonordinary tasks are discouraged. Instead, repeated measurements over longer periods of time and practice reveal continuous changes in performance efficiency. These measures must include many variables, including self-reported goals, strategies, interests, and attitudes. Estimates of children's willingness to engage tasks and their beliefs about their own abilities are crucial for learning. Certainly elicited reports of children's plans and attributions constitute related knowledge. What we advocate is combining assessments of affective and cognitive dimensions of children's task-relevant knowledge. The *patterns* of beliefs, intentions, knowledge, and performance over time are the keys to understanding children's learning.

As an example of the suggested research paradigm, we shall describe briefly a study on children's reading comprehension that we conducted (Paris, Lipson, Cross, Jacobs, DeBritto, & Oka, Note 2). In this study we tested reading skills of 8- and 10-year-olds three times during a $1\frac{1}{2}$-year period. Each child received standardized reading tests, individual interviews, and a battery of tasks designed to measure reading performance, metacognitive knowledge about reading, attributions for success and failure, attitudes toward school, and use of particular reading strategies. The study was also experimental by design. Half of the children at each age (two third-grade and two fifth-grade classes) received 4 months of classroom instruction about the importance and usefulness of various strategies for reading comprehension. The remaining children (two classes at each grade level) received tutorial help unrelated to the intervention.

Tests administered at the end of the intervention and again 6 months later revealed that children who received informed instruction regarding comprehension skills performed significantly better than children in control classrooms. In interviews, they reported greater awareness about strategies for evaluating, planning, and regulating their own reading. On reading comprehension tests they showed significant advantages over the control groups on the posttest and long-term follow-up test. Path analyses revealed that the gains in reading skill were mediated through their acquisition of knowledge about reading provided by the treatment. Thus, children's understanding about goals, plans, and the usefulness of reading strategies enhanced their actual reading abilities. Furthermore, the data revealed significant correlations between reading ability and children's enjoyment, effort, and self-evaluation of reading skill.

The relationship between achievement and personal evaluation revealed several developmental trends. In both the third and fifth grades there was a positive relationship between achievement and self-evaluation of ability. However, the strength of the relationship was stronger for the fifth-grade children. The same pattern of results was evident for the relationship between achievement and enjoyment of reading: There was a positive correlation in both grades, but the correlation was higher in the fifth grade. In the third grade there was a positive relationship between an effort appraisal (i.e., "When I try hard, I always understand what I read better") and achievement, whereas in the fifth grade there was a positive relationship between achievement and a noneffort appraisal (i.e., "Reading does not take much effort for me"). Evidently third graders equated effort with ability, whereas fifth graders distinguished between these two constructs. These developmental trends coincide exactly with the hypotheses of Covington, Dweck, and Nicholls referred to earlier.

This study illustrates the kinds of rich information afforded by repeated measurements of children's learning and the usefulness of collecting data on achievement, attitudes, and metacognitions concurrently. There are two major findings. First, the study is an experimental demonstration of the importance of planning, regulation, and evaluation—in short, self-management—for successful reading. Second, the study provides correlational evidence for the relationship between children's reading achievement and self-evaluations. Besides illustrating the benefits of a repeated-measures design with multiple assessments, this study indicates that part of good teaching is persuading children about the importance of cognitive strategies and the necessity of expended effort. Conversely, children's learning involves understanding the significance of using strategies to enhance reading comprehension. If we can equip children with enthusiasm and knowledge for ordinary activities like reading, then they can manage and enjoy the tasks and enrich their own reading.

Summary

In this chapter we have outlined a broad conceptual framework for studying children's learning. We have tried to organize diverse empirical findings into a framework of social and cognitive variables that affect learning. We emphasize repeated task engagements by motivated learners and try to explain how children's attitudes influence their distribution of effort and knowledge toward particular goals. Our approach emphasizes the learner's subjective construction of goals and plans as well as active interpretation of the consequences of performance. We believe that expert or idealistic characterizations of cognitive plans and strategies emphasize uniformity rather than individuality, in much the same manner that traditional learning theories presumed standard effects of response consequences. Our pragmatic framework calls attention to constructive changes in pre- and post-task orientations due to age, intelligence, self-concept, social context, degree of experience, and personal beliefs and attitudes.

We are enthusiastic about generating a comprehensive approach to children's learning because such an approach organizes many empirical results in a temporal and causal framework. The cyclical model also helps to dissolve artificially enlarged dichotomies between encoding and decoding, planning and reflection, and behavioral versus cognitive learning. Our focus is on the functions served by thoughts and feelings throughout learning. We believe that the recursive model, which integrates work from cognitive, social, and educational psychology, encourages syntheses rather than divisions among psychological approaches to children's learning and provides a cohesive view of cognitive development.

Acknowledgments. Many of our ideas in this chapter were stimulated by discussions during the Summer Institute on Learning and Motivation held in Ann Arbor. We hope that some of the optimism and excitement about new syntheses that was shared among participants is captured in the chapter. We would like to acknowledge especially the impact on our thinking of Marty Covington, John Nicholls, and Marty Maehr, as well as the constructive editorial advice of Connie Schmidt, Richard Newman, Jacquelynne Eccles, Jim Stigler, Karen Wixson, and the editors of this volume.

Reference Notes

1. Beilin, H. *Piaget and the new functionalism.* Invited address to the 11th symposium of the Jean Piaget Society, Philadelphia, May 1981.
2. Paris, S. G., Lipson, M. Y., Cross, D. R., Jacobs, J. E., DeBritto, A. M., & Oka, E. R. *Metacognition and reading comprehension.* A research colloquium presented at the annual meeting of the International Reading Association, Chicago, April 28, 1982.

References

Anderson, T. H. Study skills and learning strategies. In H. F. O'Neil, Jr., & C. D. Spielberger (Eds.), *Cognitive and affective learning strategies.* New York: Academic Press, 1979.

Aronson, E., & Carlsmith, J. M. The effect of the severity of threat on the devaluation of forbidden behavior. *Journal of Abnormal and Social Psychology,* 1963, *66,* 584–588.

Atkinson, J. W. Motivational determinants of risk-taking behavior. *Psychological Review,* 1957, *64,* 359–372.

Atkinson, J. W., & Raynor, J. D. *Personality, motivation, and achievement.* New York: Hemisphere, 1977.

Baker, L., & Brown, A. L. Metacognitive skills of reading. In D. Pearson (Ed.), *Handbook of reading research.* New York: Longman, in press.

Bandura, A. *Social learning theory.* Englewood Cliffs, NJ: Prentice-Hall, 1977.

Bandura, A. Self-efficacy mechanisms in human agency. *American Psychologist,* 1982, *37,* 122–147.

Bar-Tal, D. Attributional analysis of achievement-related behavior. *Review of Educational Research,* 1978, *48,* 259–271.

Belmont, J. M., & Butterfield, E. C. The instructional approach to developmental cognitive research. In R. V. Kail & J. W. Hagen (Eds.), *Perspectives on the development of memory and cognition.* Hillsdale, NJ: Erlbaum, 1977.

Bentler, P. M., & Speckart, G. Attitudes "cause" behavior: A structural equation analysis. *Journal of Personality and Social Psychology,* 1981, *40,* 226–238.

Bloom, B. S. Affective consequences of school achievement. In M. K. Pringle & V. P. Varma (Eds.), *Advances in educational psychology* (Vol. 2). New York: Barnes & Noble, 1974.

Bloom, L., & Lahey, M. *Language development and language disorders.* New York: Wiley, 1978.

Borkowski, J. G., Reid, M. K., & Kurtz, B. E. Metacognition and retardation: Paradigmatic, theoretical, and applied perspectives. In R. Sperber, C. McCauley, & P. Brooks (Eds.), *Learning and cognition in the mentally retarded.* Baltimore: University Park Press, in press.

Brockner, J. Self-esteem, self-consciousness, and task performance: Replications, extensions, and possible explanations. *Journal of Personality and Social Psychology,* 1979, *37,* 447–461.

Brookover, W. B., & Erickson, E. L. *Society, schools, and learning.* Boston: Allyn & Bacon, 1969.

Brookover, W. B., & Erickson, E. L. *Sociology of education.* Homewood, IL: Dorsey Press, 1975.

Brown, A. L. The development of memory: Knowing, knowing about knowing, and knowing how to know. In H. W. Reese (Ed.), *Advances in child development and behavior* (Vol. 10). New York: Academic Press, 1975.

Brown, A. L. Knowing when, where, and how to remember: A problem of metacognition. In R. Glaser (Ed.), *Advances in instructional psychology* (Vol. 1). Hillsdale, NJ: Erlbaum, 1978.

Brown, A. L. Metacognitive development and reading. In R. Spiro, B. Bruce, & Brewer (Eds.), *Theoretical issues in reading comprehension.* Hillsdale, NJ: Erlbaum, 1980.

Butkowsky, I. S., & Willows, D. M. Cognitive-motivational characteristics of children varying in reading ability: Evidence for learned helplessness in poor readers. *Journal of Educational Psychology,* 1980, *72,* 408–422.

Case, R. Intellectual development from birth to adulthood: A neo-Piagetian perspective. In R. S. Siegler (Ed.), *Children's thinking: What develops?* Hillsdale, NJ; Erlbaum, 1978.

Champagne, A. B., Klopfer, L. E., & Anderson, J. H. Factors influencing the learning of classical mechanics. *American Journal of Physics,* 1980, *48,* 1074–1079.

Cialdini, R. B., Petty, R. E., & Cacioppo, J. T. Attitudes and attitude changes. *Annual Review of Psychology,* 1981, *32,* 357–404.

Condry, J. C. Enemies of exploration: Self-initiated versus other initiated learning. *Journal of Personality and Social Psychology,* 1977, *35,* 459–477.

Covington, M. V. Motivated cognitions. In S. Paris, G. Olson, & H. Stevenson (Eds.), *Learning and motivation in the classroom.* Hillsdale, NJ: Erlbaum, 1983.

Covington, M. V., & Beery, R. *Self-worth and school learning.* New York: Holt, Rinehart & Winston, 1976.

Covington, M. V., & Omelich, C. L. Effort: The double-edged sword in school achievement. *Journal of Educational Psychology,* 1979, *71,* 169–182.

Covington, M. V., & Omelich, C. L. As failures mount: Affective and cognitive consequences of ability demotion in the classroom. *Journal of Educational Psychology*, 1981, *73*, 796–808.

Diener, C. I., & Dweck, C. S. An analysis of learned helplessness: Continuous changes in performance, strategy, and achievement cognitions following failure. *Journal of Personality and Social Psychology*, 1978, *36*, 451–462.

Dweck, C. S., & Bempechat, J. Children's theories of intelligence: Consequences for learning. In S. Paris, G. Olson, & H. Stevenson (Eds.), *Learning and motivation in the classroom*. Hillsdale, NJ: Erlbaum, 1983.

Dweck, C. S., & Elliott, E. S. Achievement motivation. In P. Mussen (General Ed.) & E. M. Hetherington (Volume Ed.), *Carmichael's manual of child psychology: Social and personality development*. New York: Wiley, 1983.

Dweck, C. S., & Licht, B. G. Learned helplessness and intellectual achievement. In J. Garber & M. E. P. Seligman (Eds.), *Human helplessness: Theory and applications*. New York: Academic Press, 1980.

Eccles-Parsons, J. E., Midgley, C., & Adler, T. F. Age-related changes in the school environment: Effects on age-related changes in achievement motivation. In J. H. Nicholls (Ed.), *The development of achievement motivation*. New York: JAI Press, in press.

Eccles-Parsons, J. E., & Ruble, D. The development of achievement related expectancies. *Child Development*, 1977, *48*, 1075–1079.

Eccles-Parsons, J. E., Adler, T. F., & Kaczala, C. M. Socialization of achievement attitudes and beliefs: Parental influences. *Child Development*, 1982, *53*, 310–321.

Eccles-Parsons, J. E., Kaczala, C. M., & Meece, J. Socialization of achievement attitudes and beliefs: Classroom influences. *Child Development*, 1982, *53*, 322–339.

Fischer, K. W. A theory of cognitive development: The control and construction of hierarchies of skills. *Psychological Review*, 1980, *87*, 477–531.

Fishbein, M. A theory of reasoned action: Some applications and implications. In H. J. Howe, Jr., & M. M. Page (Eds.), *Nebraska Symposium on Motivation* (Vol. 27). Lincoln: University of Nebraska Press, 1979.

Flavell, J. H. Metacognitive development. In J. M. Scandura, & C. J. Brainerd (Eds.), *Structural/process theories of complex human behavior*. The Netherlands: Sijthoff & Noordoff, 1978.

Flavell, J. H. Metacognition and cognitive monitoring: A new area of cognitive developmental inquiry. *American Psychologist*, 1979, *34*, 906–911.

Flavell, J. H., Friedrichs, A. G., & Hoyt, J. D. Developmental changes in memorization processes. *Cognitive Psychology*, 1970, *1*, 324–340.

Flavell, J. H., Speer, J. R., Green, F. L., & August, D. L. The development of comprehension monitoring and knowledge about communication. *Monographs of the Society for Research in Child Development*, 1981, *46*(5, Serial No. 192).

Forsyth, D. R., & McMillan, J. H. The attribution cube and reactions to educational outcomes. *Journal of Educational Psychology*, 1981, *73*, 632–641.

Frieze, I. H. Beliefs about success and failure in the classroom. In J. H. McMillan (Ed.), *The social psychology of school learning*. New York: Academic Press, 1980.

Fyans, L. J., & Maehr, M. L. Attributional style, task selection, and achievement. *Journal of Educational Psychology*, 1979, *71*, 499–507.

Glaser, R. Instructional psychology: Past, present and future. *American Psychologist*, 1982, *37*, 292–305.

Haan, N. *Coping and defending: Processes of self-environment organization*. New York: Academic Press, 1977.

Hagen, J. W., Barclay, C. R., & Schwethelm, B. Cognitive development of the learning disabled child. In N. R. Ellis (Ed.), *International review of research in mental retardation*. New York: Academic Press, 1981.

Hansford, B. C., & Hattie, J. A. The relationship between self and achievement/performance measures. *Review of Educational Research*, 1982, *52*, 123–142.

Harari, O., & Covington, M. V. Reactions to achievement behavior from a teacher and student perspective: A developmental analysis. *American Educational Research Journal*, 1981, *18*, 15–28.

Harter, S. Pleasure derived from optimal challenge and the effects of intrinsic rewards on children's difficulty level choices. *Child Development*, 1978, *49*, 788–799.

Harter, S. A model of mastery motivation in children: Individual differences and developmental change. In W. A. Collins (Ed.), *Minnesota symposium on child psychology* (Vol. 14). Hillsdale, NJ: Erlbaum, 1981.

Harter, S. A developmental perspective on some parameters of self-regulation in children. In P. Karoly & F. Kanfer (Eds.), *Self-management and behavior change: From theory to practice*. Elmsford, NY: Pergamon Press, 1982.

Heider, F. *The psychology of interpersonal relations*. New York: Wiley, 1958.

Jenkins, J. J. Four points to remember: A tetrahedral model and memory experiments. In L. S. Cermak & F. I. M. Craik (Eds.), *Levels of processing in human memory*. Hillsdale, NJ: Erlbaum, 1979.

Kail, R., & Bisanz, J. Information processing and cognitive development. In H. Reese (Ed.), *Advances in child development and behavior* (Vol. 17). New York: Academic Press, 1982.

Kelley, H. H. Attribution theory in social psychology. In D. Levine (Ed.), *Nebraska Symposium on Motivation* (Vol. 15). Lincoln: University of Nebraska Press, 1967.

Kreutzer, M. A., Leonard, C., & Flavell, J. H. An interview study of children's knowledge about memory. *Monographs of the Society for Research in Child Development*, 1975, *40*(1, Serial No. 159).

Kruglanski, A. W. Endogenous attribution and intrinsic motivation. In M. R. Lepper & D. Greene (Eds.), *The hidden costs of reward: New perspectives on the psychology of human motivation*. Hillsdale, NJ: Erlbaum, 1978.

LaBerge, D., & Samuels, S. J. Toward a theory of automatic information processing in reading. *Cognitive Psychology*, 1974, *6*, 293–323.

Lempers, J. O., Flavell, E. H., & Flavell, J. H. The development in very young children of tacit knowledge concerning visual perception. *Genetic Psychology Monographs*, 1977, *95*, 3–53.

Lepper, M. R. Intrinsic and extrinsic motivation in children: Detrimental effects of superfluous social controls. In W. A. Collins (Ed.), *Minnesota symposium on child psychology* (Vol. 14). Hillsdale, NJ: Erlbaum, 1981.

Lepper, M. R., & Greene, D. Turning play into work: Effect of adult surveillance and extrinsic rewards on children's intrinsic motivation. *Journal of Personality and Social Psychology*, 1975, *31*, 479–486.

Locke, E. A., Shaw, K. N., Saari, L. M., & Latham, G. P. Goal setting and task performance: 1969–1980. *Psychological Bulletin,* 1981, *90,* 125–152.

Maehr, M. On doing well in science: Why Johnny no longer excels: Why Sarah never did. In S. Paris, G. Olson, & H. Stevenson (Eds.), *Learning and motivation in the classroom.* Hillsdale, NJ: Erlbaum, 1983.

Maehr, M. L., & Nicholls, J. G. Culture and achievement motivation: A second look. In N. Warren (Ed.), *Studies in cross-cultural psychology* (Vol. 3). New York: Academic Press, 1980.

Maratsos, M. Nonegocentric communication abilities in preschool children. *Child Development,* 1973, *44,* 697–700.

Markman, E. M. Realizing that you don't understand: A preliminary investigation. *Child Development,* 1977, *48,* 986–992.

Markman, E. M. Realizing that you don't understand: Elementary school children's awareness of inconsistencies. *Child Development,* 1979, *50,* 643–655.

Masur, E. G., McIntyre, C. W., & Flavell, J. H. Developmental changes in apportionment of study time among items in a multitrial free recall task. *Journal of Experimental Child Psychology,* 1973, *15,* 237–246.

McMillan, J. H. Attitude development and measurement. In J. H. McMillan (Ed.), *The social psychology of school learning.* New York: Academic Press, 1980.

Meichenbaum, D., & Asarnow, J. Cognitive behavior modification and metacognitive development: Implications for the classroom. In P. Kendall & S. Hollon (Eds.), *Cognitive-behavioral interventions: Theory, research, and procedures.* New York: Academic Press, 1978.

Menig-Peterson, C. L. The modification of communicative behavior in preschool aged children as a function of the listener's perspective. *Child Development,* 1975, *46,* 1015–1018.

Neimark, E., Slotnick, N. S., & Ulrich, T. Development of memorization strategies. *Developmental Psychology,* 1971, *5,* 427–432.

Nicholls, J. G. The development of the concepts of effort and ability, perception of academic attainment, and the understanding that difficult tasks require more ability. *Child Development,* 1978, *49,* 800–814.

Nicholls, J. G. Development of perception of own attainment and causal attributions for success and failure in reading. *Journal of Educational Psychology,* 1979, *71,* 94–99. (a)

Nicholls, J. G. Quality and equality in intellectual development. *American Psychologist,* 1979, *34,* 1071–1084. (b)

Nicholls, J. G. Conceptions of ability and achievement motivation: A theory and its implications for education. In S. Paris, G. Olson, & H. Stevenson (Eds.), *Learning and motivation in the classroom.* Hillsdale, NJ: Erlbaum, 1983.

Nisbett, R. E., & Wilson, T. D. Telling more than we know: Verbal reports on mental processes. *Psychological Review,* 1977, *84,* 231–279.

Owings, R. A., Peterson, G. A., Bransford, J. D., Morris, C. D., & Stein, B. S. Spontaneous monitoring and regulation of learning: A comparison of successful and less successful fifth graders. *Journal of Educational Psychology,* 1980, *72,* 250–256.

Paris, S. G. Coordination of means and goals in the development of mnemonic skills. In P. A. Ornstein (Ed.), *Memory development in children.* Hillsdale, NJ: Erlbaum, 1978.

Paris, S. G., & Lindauer, B. K. The development of cognitive skills during child-hood. In B. Wolman (Ed.), *Handbook of developmental psychology*. Englewood-Cliffs, NJ; Prentice-Hall, 1982.

Paris, S. G., & Myers, M. Comprehension monitoring in good and poor readers. *Journal of Reading Behavior*, 1981, *13*, 5-22.

Paris, S. G., Newman, R. S., & McVey, K. A. Learning the functional significance of mnemonic actions: A microgenetic study of strategy acquisition. *Journal of Experimental Child Psychology*, 1982, *34*, 490-509.

Paris, S. G., & Oka, E. R. Schoolcraft. *Academic Psychology Bulletin*, 1982, *4*, 291-300.

Patterson, C. J., & Kister, M. C. The development of listener skills for referential communication. In W. P. Dickson (Ed.), *Children's oral communication skills*. New York: Academic Press, 1981.

Reese, H. W. The development of memory: Lifespan perspectives. In H. W. Reese (Ed.), *Advances in child development and behavior* (Vol. 11). New York: Academic Press, 1976.

Resnick, L. Instructional psychology. *Annual Review of Psychology*, 1981, *32*, 659-704.

Rogoff, B. Integrating context and cognitive development. In M. Lamb, & A. Brown (Eds.), *Advances in developmental psychology* (Vol. 2). Hillsdale, NJ: Erlbaum, 1982.

Rokeach, M. Some unresolved issues in theories of beliefs, attitudes, and values. In H. J. Howe, Jr., & M. M. Page (Eds.), *Nebraska Symposium on Motivation* (Vol. 27). Lincoln: University of Nebraska Press, 1979.

Scardamalia, M., & Bereiter, C. Child as co-investigator: Helping children gain insight into their own mental processes. In S. Paris, G. Olson, & H. Stevenson (Eds.), *Learning and motivation in the classroom*. Hillsdale, NJ: Erlbaum, 1983.

Schmidt, C. R., & Paris, S. G. The development of children's verbal communication skills. In H. Reese (Ed.), *Advances in child development and behavior* (Vol. 18). New York: Academic Press, 1983.

Shantz, C. U. The development of social cognition. In E. M. Hetherington (Ed.), *Review of child development research* (Vol. 5). Chicago: University of Chicago Press, 1975.

Shatz, M. The relationship between cognitive processes and the development of communication skills. In C. B. Keasey (Ed.), *Nebraska Symposium on Motivation* (Vol. 26). Lincoln: University of Nebraska Press, 1978.

Shatz, M., & Gelman, R. The development of communication skills: Modifications in the speech of young children as a function of the listener. *Monographs of the Society for Research in Child Development*, 1973, *38*(5, Serial No. 152).

Shavelson, R. J., & Bolus, R. Self-concept: The interplay of theory and methods. *Journal of Educational Psychology*, 1982, *74*, 3-17.

Sherif, C. W. Social values, attitudes, and the involvement of the self. In H. J. Howe, Jr., & M. M. Page (Eds.), *Nebraska Symposium on Motivation* (Vol. 27). Lincoln: University of Nebraska Press, 1979.

Shultz, T. R. Development of the concept of intention. In W. A. Collins (Ed.), *Minnesota symposium on child psychology* (Vol. 13). Hillsdale, NJ; Erlbaum, 1980.

Vygotsky, L. S. *Mind in society*. Cambridge, MA: Harvard University Press, 1978.

Weiner, B. A theory of motivation for some classroom experiences. *Journal of Educational Psychology,* 1979, *71,* 3–25.

Weiner, B. Some thoughts about feelings. In S. Paris, G. Olson, & H. Stevenson (Eds.), *Learning and motivation in the classroom.* Hillsdale, NJ: Erlbaum, 1983.

Wertsch, J. V. *The concept of activity in Soviet psychology.* Armonk, NY: M. E. Sharpe, 1981.

White, R. W. Motivation reconsidered: The concept of competence. *Psychological Review,* 1959, *66,* 297–333.

Wylie, R. C. *The self-concept* (Vol. 2). Lincoln: University of Nebraska Press, 1979.

7. Learning from Children Learning

John D. Bransford and Karen Heldmeyer

The purpose of this chapter is to explore the general issue of children's learning. We begin by comparing two views about children as learners that appear to be widely accepted both by lay persons and by professionals in the field. According to the first view, children are universal novices who only gradually develop the ability to perform at levels that are characteristic of adults. For example, over time children improve their ability to remember information (e.g., Kail & Siegel, 1977), to comprehend and communicate effectively (e.g., Chapman, 1978; Chomsky, 1969; Glucksberg, Krauss, & Higgins, 1975), to solve problems (e.g., Inhelder & Piaget, 1958), to accurately predict their own abilities to perform various tasks (e.g., Flavell & Wellman, 1977), and so forth. The vast majority of developmental studies reveal the familiar "developmental trend" of older learners performing better on a number of dimensions than younger learners.

Theorists have suggested several general reasons why younger or less mature learners may perform less efficiently than more mature learners. First, the former have acquired less knowledge than older learners (e.g., Chi, 1978; Gelman, 1978). Second, younger learners are less likely to employ sophisticated strategies (e.g., Brown, 1979; Flavell, Beach, & Chinsky, 1966; Ornstein & Naus, 1978). Some theorists also argue that younger children's working memory is more limited, although whether this is a limitation of "actual" versus "functional" capacity is still a matter for debate (e.g., Case, 1974; Chi, 1976). For present purposes, the im-

Preparation of this chapter was supported in part by Grants NIE G-79-0117 and NIE G-80-0028 and a grant from the Spencer Foundation. We are grateful to Nancy Vye, as well as to the editors of this volume, for helpful comments and criticisms.

portant point is that, when compared to older learners, younger learners seem to have a number of disadvantages that hamper their performance in a wide variety of domains.

In sharp contrast to the preceding view is the popular view that children are exceptionally effective learners. For example, Vaughan (1977) found that well over half of the introductory psychology students she studied believed that children memorize more easily than do adults. It is easy to see how ideas such as this arise. As adults, we marvel at the ease with which young children acquire concepts, language, motor skills, spatial skills, social skills, and the like, often without the benefit of explicit instruction. We often wish that we could learn as effectively, enthusiastically, and seemingly effortlessly as we did when we were young. Note that if we hold this view of "children as exceptional learners" in conjunction with the "child as universal novice" view that was discussed above, we are forced to acknowledge that children are amazingly effective learners *despite* their lack of knowledge, *despite* their lack of sophisticated strategies, *despite* possible limitations on their working memory. How can children be such successful learners in the face of such disadvantages? Our goal is to explore this paradox.

This chapter is based on the assumption that young children do indeed seem to be extraordinarily enthusiastic and effective learners. We do not wish to dwell on what children do poorly; there are innumerable papers on that topic already. Rather, we shall view children as *exceptional learners* and ask how we as adults can learn from their approach to learning. We believe that a great deal can be learned by viewing children from this perspective. Since few studies have focused on children's strengths as learners, however, most of our arguments will be speculative. The major goal of our discussion is to generate questions for future research.

Before proceeding with our main discussion, it seems useful to consider some possible advantages of focusing one's attention on young children's remarkable learning abilities. Our assumption is that analyses of children's success in learning may help us increase the success rate of learning for people of all ages. We are especially concerned with the fact that many children seem to learn successfully in their home environments, yet experience considerable difficulty when they later attempt to learn in the formal educational environments of schools. There are a number of differences between formal and informal environments; many people argue that the structure of formal educational environments can hamper children's learning (e.g., Donaldson, 1978; Holt, 1964; Illich, 1972). We agree to some extent with the latter argument but shall not argue in favor of "deschooling society" (as does Illich, 1972, for example). Instead, our goal is to attempt to understand the successful learning of young children in the hopes of better specifying how knowledge is acquired and of finding ways in which formal education might incorporate some of the advantages that are available to the young learner in the home environment. In order to do so, we will look at both the cognitive and motivational advantages of the young learner.

Our discussion of cognitive advantages will focus on factors such as the relationship between to-be-learned information and the current knowledge and skills available to the learner, and the presence of tutors. Our discussion of motivational advantages will emphasize factors such as the freedom to choose tasks and to define one's own criteria for success. However, we want to emphasize that our decisions to label advantages as either cognitive or motivational were frequently arbitrary. It seems clear that cognitive and motivational processes are interrelated. For example, the learning literature illustrates quite clearly that the motivation or intent to learn is not sufficient to ensure learning; one must also possess relevant background knowledge (e.g., Bransford & Johnson, 1972, 1973) and utilize appropriate cognitive strategies (e.g., Postman, Adams, & Bohm, 1956). Conversely, individuals who have already acquired the prerequisite knowledge and skills necessary to learn about a new domain will undoubtedly be much more likely to maintain their motivation to learn than will those who lack important prerequisites. Paris and Cross (Chapter 6, this volume) provide an excellent discussion of cognition, motivation, and their relationships.

Cognitive Advantages of the Child's World

As mentioned earlier, the cognitive handicaps that afflict young learners seem both numerous and apparent. Young children lack relevant knowledge structures (or frames, scripts, schemata; e.g., see Minsky, 1975; Rumelhart & Ortony, 1977; Schank & Abelson, 1977), have not yet developed a repertoire of sophisticated strategies (e.g., Flavell & Wellman, 1977), and may have limited working memories (Case, 1974; Chi, 1976). Given liabilities such as these, are there any possible cognitive advantages that young children might have?

Some Advantages of Naiveté

One possible advantage available to children is that their *lack* of knowledge may reduce the probability that they apply incorrect information or inappropriate strategies to a task. In short, there are times when ignorance may be bliss. As teachers of psychology, the present authors are often struck by how much of our jobs consists of getting college students to "unlearn" the naive psychology they have developed (Vaughan, 1977), or of preventing them from using inappropriate skills (e.g., footnotes instead of APA style, flowery language instead of scientific precision) that they have learned in other contexts. Teachers of other topics such as physics and mathematics report similar problems (e.g., DiSessa, 1982; Tobias, 1978). Many special programs and techniques (e.g., "conceptual blockbusting," Adams, 1979) have been developed to free adults from the negative effects of past experience. Children are much less likely to suffer from such negative transfer because they do not have the disadvantage of having already learned the wrong ways to approach various problems. Furthermore, many of the interesting and creative behaviors that young children display may often be the direct result of their lack of preconceived strategies and ideas.

Young children's naiveté may also contribute to their seeming lack of a fear of failure (e.g., Caplan, 1973). Parents and psychologists alike marvel at young children's ability to keep coming back to tasks at which they have repeatedly been unsuccessful (Brazelton, 1969). Children may be more willing to tackle new learning situations because they have less idea of what it means to be wrong and to make a fool of oneself.

It is interesting to note that research on second language learning by college students suggests that the successful students are those who are more willing to take risks by attempting to interpret, speak, and so forth (e.g., Rubin, 1975). Similarly, many college students and adults with whom we have worked who have had no computer experience become quite apprehensive when asked to learn to perform tasks on computers (see also Sieber, O'Neil, & Tobias, 1977). In contrast, young children show no fear of computers, presumably because they have no knowledge that there is anything to fear (Papert, 1980).

Parents as Successful Tutors

Even though ignorance may sometimes be bliss, it seems doubtful that the only advantage available to young children is that they lack knowledge. Young learners must have additional advantages as well. One obvious and important advantage enjoyed by preschool children is that they frequently are guided by individual tutors or "mediators" (e.g., Feuerstein, Rand, Hoffman, & Miller, 1980; Vygotsky, 1978). In contrast, school-age children are much more likely to have to learn from group instruction. There are a number of possible cognitive advantages that are associated with the type of tutorial instruction that young children receive.

Parent-child relationships differ from teacher-child relationships in a number of ways, many of which can affect learning and even affect whether the children use their natural abilities to their fullest extent. Parents are in a unique position to be effective tutors. To begin with, parents usually deal with a very small "class size." This allows them to provide an individualized program of analysis and instruction that is often an impossibility in large classroom situations.

Additionally, most parents usually have a strong attachment to their children. Because of this, they usually find observing and playing with their children interesting and rewarding experiences. This involvement leads parents to exemplify several hallmarks of good teaching. They are interested in the learner; they have detailed knowledge of the learner's abilities, deficits, and learning environment; they embed learning in the context of the evolving interaction of the teacher and the learner; and they are in a position to continually monitor and assess the progress of their "pupil." We would like to examine each of these factors in greater detail.

Consider first the fact that most parents are fascinated by their young children. Parents spend a great deal of time studying their children's behavior in minute detail and hence learn a considerable amount about them. As a result, parents are frequently able to predict their children's level of performance on everyday tasks (e.g., Wells, 1980). They therefore have the opportunity to supply the child's environment with materials that are interesting and appropriate for their child's developmental level. Furthermore, parents can use this knowledge to modify the input they give the child. For example, parents seem to modify the complexity of their expressions according to their knowledge of the linguistic competence of their child (e.g., Sachs, 1977); this type of modification is directly related to the child's linguistic progress. We suspect that parents' knowledge of their children also allows them to suggest appropriate instructional analogies (e.g., "See, this is like your game [book, toy] at home") that facilitate their children's ability to learn..Studies have shown that learners do better on tasks that are related to their preexisting knowledge base and to topics that are of personal significance to them (e.g., Asher, 1980; Bransford & Johnson, 1972; Chiesi, Spilich, & Voss, 1979).

In comparison to parents, schoolteachers undoubtedly know much less about the preexisting knowledge and skills of their students. Furthermore, teachers must usually use instructional materials that were selected by their school board from the range of materials generated by publishers. Publishers can make only very general assumptions about the types of materials that are appropriate for each child.

As an illustration, consider the task of helping elementary school students learn how to read (which includes helping them understand what they read). In a volume edited by Anderson, Osborn, and Tierney (in press), several examples are provided of the difficulties that publishers experience when they attempt to create materials that are appropriate for each child. Several authors in the Anderson et al. volume provide evidence to show that teaching behavior is strongly affected by the nature of published material (e.g., the stories to be read, the nature of workbook exercises). Some argue that the vocabulary, sentence structure, and paragraph structure of many published stories and exercises are not optimal for helping many students learn how to comprehend what they read. For example, in some cases students undoubtedly lack the knowledge (schemata) necessary to understand various stories (see Anderson, et al., in press; Beck, in press; Bransford, in press; Pearson, in press). This is disheartening in light of clear evidence that people at all ages can learn much more readily if the material is congruent with what they already know (e.g., see Ausubel, 1977; Bransford, 1979; Novak, 1977; Siegler, 1978).

We suspect that teachers could be more effective if they had a "parents'-eye view" of the knowledge and skills of their pupils. For example, teachers who realize that individual students do not have the knowledge necessary to understand particular topics could undoubtedly be more effective if they could draw analogies to other knowledge domains that the students already know (e.g., see Hayes & Tierney, Note 1). Teachers could also be more effective if they were aware that certain styles of interaction are more or less appropriate for students from different cultures. Freedle (1981) discusses a number of instances where particular culturally specific modes of speaking and questioning can cause problems for students who come from cultures or subcultures that are based on different sets of individual and social norms. For instance, Native American children often have a difficult time adjusting to the idea of "volunteering in class" because in their culture it is considered impolite for children to spontaneously address their elders and it is considered boastful for anyone to publicly demonstrate knowledge in the presence of those who do not share that knowledge. Since parents and their children usually share the same culture, problems such as these rarely arise.

Since parents are interacting with their child and modifying the instructional environment so that it best benefits the child, they are also in a position to "dynamically assess" (see Feuerstein et al., 1979, 1980; Vygotsky, 1978) the child's performance—to monitor the learning and understanding that is taking place. Teachers, because of the pressures of time and class size, may be able to assess learning only in infrequent "testing" situations that are divorced from the original learning context. Compared to teachers, parents therefore have more of a chance to respond in ways that are contingent upon the child's response. Gleason (1977) describes some ways in which this monitoring takes place. Parents may watch the child's expression, request repetition of information, ask questions, spot-check later performance, and so forth. They are therefore able to gauge when and how to intervene and, perhaps just as importantly, when intervention is unnecessary.

Studies by Wood and his colleagues illustrate the importance of monitoring children's activities in order to respond in ways that are conditional on their performance. In one study, Wood and Middleton (1975) asked mothers to teach their 3- to 4-year-old children how to assemble a construction toy. Mothers who simply demonstrated (e.g., lectured) how to perform the task (an instructional technique frequently found in schools) were quite ineffective; their children rarely learned to construct the toy. In contrast, those mothers who carefully monitored their child's activities and responded in ways that were tailored to these activities experienced excellent success in teaching their child. For present purposes, the most important results were that "successful" mothers were also able to teach children whom they did not know (e.g., Wood, 1980). Furthermore, mothers who were helped to learn how to monitor children's attempts and to intervene appropriately were able to help other children learn effectively. The ability to "dynamically assess" children's current levels of skill and knowledge therefore seems to be important for helping them learn. Indeed, several investigators have argued that one of the difficulties faced by learners of all ages is that they frequently think they have adequately understood and mastered new information when, in fact, they have failed to do so (e.g., see Bransford, 1979; Brown, Bransford, Ferrara, & Campione, in press; Nitsch, 1977). The availability of tutors who can help students assess their current levels of comprehension and mastery can therefore have very positive effects.

Flexibility of Curriculum: Cognitive Advantages

An additional advantage that the parent-child relationship has over the teacher-student relationship is that there is no set curriculum to follow. For the most part, parents take great pride and pleasure in all of their young children's accomplishments. Thus, if progress in one area is temporarily stalled, the emphasis of teaching and learning can be shifted to another area; this shift of emphasis is also an important device for maintaining attention and motivation. Additionally, since young children are learning so many things all the time, there are many small victories to celebrate, thus keeping up the morale of both teacher and learner.

This flexibility of the "curriculum" allows the parent to accept a variety of contributions from the child to the learning process. Snow (1977), for example, describes how parents of very young infants model conversational behavior for their children by making appropriate pauses where the child's response should be. She also observed that parents of young infants accepted almost anything (e.g., a burp or a hand movement) as a correct conversational response. As the infants became older (and presumably more competent conversationalists), parents narrowed the criteria regarding what constitutes a valid response. Thus, the child can be included in the learning process at any level of competence. This is difficult to do in a classroom situation, especially when a teacher must deal with several different competence levels within one classroom while following the curriculum recommended by the school.

There appear to be several cognitive advantages that stem from the fact that parents do not follow a set curriculum with their children and that they encourage children to contribute to interactions. Studies by Bloom, Hood, and Lightbown (1974) and by Slobin and Welsh (1973) represent cases in point. Their research suggests that children's abilities to deal with information that is imposed on them may lag behind their abilities to perform when they have the intent to communicate about contextually relevant events. For example, Bloom asked Peter (aged 32 months) to imitate sentences such as "I'm trying to get this cow in there" or "You make him stand up there." Peter's responses were "Cow in here" and "Stand up there," respectively. One might conclude from these data that Peter's language skills were still quite immature, but there was another aspect of the experiment that raises questions about this assumption. In particular, each of these statements had been *produced* by him on earlier occasions. For example, Peter had said "I'm trying to get the cow in there" while playing with a toy cow and talking to an observer. He therefore had contextual support for his own utterance, but this support was absent during the subsequent imitation test. Slobin and Welsh (1973) would undoubtedly argue that Peter also had an intent to say something and that the "intent to say X" provides support for more complex utterances. Factors such as "contextual support" and "intent to say X" may therefore have important effects on children's performance. The act of performing—of utilizing potentially available skills and knowledge to achieve particular goals—is undoubtedly important for learning. For example, people need to automatize various processes in order to achieve efficiency (e.g., Chase & Simon, 1973; LaBerge & Samuels, 1974). Students who are asked to respond only when tasks are imposed upon them may therefore have less of a chance to practice utilizing potentially available knowledge and skills. In addition, teachers may underestimate what these students know and can do.

Research by Bloom, Lightbown, and Hood (1975) illustrates an additional advantage in learning that young children may have as a result of their relative flexibility to select tasks and goals. Young children have the opportunity to "choose" the domains within which they can develop new knowledge and skills. For example, Bloom et al. (1975) studied the development of children's linguistic abilities. At many stages of language acquisition, children seem to be experimenting with new means of linguistic expression; for example, they may begin to use more complicated forms of syntax. A similar process has been observed for lexical development (Brown, 1973). For present purposes, the important question is whether there is any relationship between children's experimentation and what they already know. The data from Bloom et al. suggest that the answer is yes. They found that new syntactic forms of expression appeared mainly when children talked about events with which they were already very familiar. If children are forced to talk about relatively unfamiliar events (events that require the use of relatively unfamiliar verbs, for example), it may well be too taxing to experiment with new syntactic constructions at the same time. Similarly, if one wants to learn how to write effectively, it is probably better to begin with a topic that is well understood than to begin with one that is relatively unfamiliar (e.g., Chiesi et al., 1979). Children's greater flexibility to choose tasks and topics may therefore facilitate the development of new skills.

Motivational Advantages of the Child's World

In the preceding discussion we emphasized some of the cognitive advantages available to most young children and argued that these are less likely to be available to older children in formal academic settings. It is instructive to note, however, that most of our examples involved advantages that derive from the structure of the child's instructional environment. We said little about the contributions of the child to the learning process.

From our perspective, the most obvious strength of preschool learners involves motivation. It is this self-directedness of young learners that has fascinated many researchers (e.g., Bruner, 1968; Piaget, 1952). Young learners may spend hours "practicing" activities such as stacking objects (e.g., blocks, pans), looking at picture books, and walking up and down inclines. Furthermore, they often approach adults with questions (e.g., "What's that?") or tasks (e.g., "Read this book") and, in effect, "demand" that the adults participate. In contrast, older children often approach formal learning tasks with a marked lack of enthusiasm and sometimes with strong resistance (e.g., Holt, 1964; Lipman, in press; McDermott, 1974). We could learn a great deal from young children if we could begin to understand what accounts for their enthusiasm for learning, and if we could understand why some individuals seem to maintain such enthusiasm whereas many others do not.

Some authors argue that a decrease in the motivation to learn is due to a biologically timed attenuation of a natural predisposition for learning. This attenuation is beneficial, they argue, because the adaptive significance of curiosity declines with age. For example, one writer maintains that curiosity becomes a less affordable biological luxury when the young organism loses the protection of its parents and must fend for itself (Lorenz, 1972). Theories such as these are interesting, but they offer little hope to those of us who would like to incorporate some aspects of the young child's style of learning into the repertoire of older learners. If curiosity and love of learning have strict biological time limits placed on them, the motivation to learn must decline with age. Since there are many individuals who stand as strong counterarguments to this assumption, we shall assume that the biological theories are not entirely correct and shall concentrate on those aspects of motivation that appear to be modifiable at all ages.

Children's apparent "motivation to learn" is probably not a unitary phenomenon. Much of their motivation to learn seems to arise from their attempts to maintain social contact with significant others. The acquisition of particular motor skills, of language, and so forth may be means to this general end. Many times, however, children seem oblivious to others; they become fascinated with what they are doing, whether it is looking at a picture book or stacking blocks. These solitary activities do not seem to be motivated by social goals. White (1975) uses the term *competence motivation* to describe such situations. He sees the child's desire to continue to improve as being the impetus for much of the self-directed learning activity in which children engage. In many situations, however, there is more than one motivating factor at work. For example, Ashley, the almost 2-year-old daughter of one of the authors, has suddenly begun to imitate everything she sees or hears. This is a very social (and highly rewarded) activity, but it is one that seems to involve "competence motivation" as well.

The Importance of Attachment

Children's motivation to learn may be strongly affected by attachments that they form with significant others. Intuitively, it seems very important to have someone who cares about one's progress in various domains. Many children who experience difficulty in school may lack this type of support. Many of the available written accounts of how poor or indifferent learners were made into successful learners are in fact accounts of how a highly motivated (and often idealistic) tutor provided interested learners with sufficient motivation to learn (e.g., Holt, 1967). Note that a child presumably could be strongly motivated by a significant other even if the latter did not possess the knowledge and skills necessary to serve as an expert tutor. What would seem to be important is whether the significant other values and rewards learning. Although this is mentioned anecdotally by many educators and theorists (e.g., Piaget, 1981), it is not a question that has received much attention from researchers.

Flexibility of Curricula: Motivational Advantages

The child's initial motivation to learn coupled with the parents' interest in the child undoubtedly creates a learning environment that maintains the child's motivation. For example, as was mentioned earlier, young children are generally able to learn *what* they want *when* they want. They have considerable freedom to set their own curriculum based on their own needs and interests. In contrast, older children in formal educational settings are usually expected to learn a set curriculum, the content and timing of which are determined by adults. A flexible curriculum has the cognitive advantages mentioned earlier; it also has the primary motivational advantage of allowing the individual to learn when interest is at its optimal level.

Imagine attempting to implement a learning curriculum for an 18-month-old child. The first hour of the child's day might be devoted to motor skills (e.g., walking, balancing), the second hour to oral language, the third to affective activities such as cuddling and laughing, the fourth to block building, the fifth to looking at books, and so forth.

At first glance, this schedule might seem like a reasonable way to structure information so that each task received the child's full attention, without distraction or negative transfer from other areas. There are several problems with this approach, however. One is that the content and timing of the lessons are imposed on the child rather than selected by the child. This decreases the possibility that the information will be presented to the child at the time when the child is optimally ready, both cognitively and emotionally, to receive it. Problems of motivation are also less likely to arise when tasks are chosen by children rather than imposed by someone else. Additionally, this scheme does not allow the child the opportunity to learn about how various skills can interact and complement each other. Finally, this curriculum assigns a value to skills that is dependent not on their overall usefulness to the child but on their correct place in the curriculum. Thus, a child who succeeded in stacking three blocks for the first time during the oral language period might find herself chastized for doing the "wrong" thing at the wrong time.

Note further that young children are able not only to select one particular activity from among several choices, but also to move from one activity to another according to their momentary interests and needs. This freedom would seem to increase the likelihood that they will become involved in each activity. In contrast, children in school may often fail to become involved in a lesson because they prefer to be doing something else.

One reason for preferring to do something else is that one has encountered a problem in a particular area that is gripping (and one wants to keep working at it) or frustrating (and one must do something else for awhile). Young children are usually free to choose their own "strategies" for dealing with situations such as these. As an illustration, imagine a child who is stuck on a particular problem (e.g., learning to walk or to stack blocks). One of the child's options is to stick with the task until the problem is solved. An infant may sit for a half hour trying to fit a peg into a hole or may refuse to eat or sleep in order to practice the newly acquired skill of walking (cf. Brazelton, 1969).

Brazelton (1969) states that he knows when children are getting close to major developmental milestones because at such times everything else in their life "goes to pot." We suspect that almost everyone will remember situations where they needed to let everything else go to pot. In such instances, people generally sense that they are on the verge of a breakthrough in their work and want to devote all their time to that area, yet they are supposed to attend a class on an unrelated topic. It can be very frustrating to have to stop what one is doing in these circumstances. Indeed, most adults would probably prefer to skip the class. Young children not only have the advantage of "skipping classes," they have the opportunity to make them up later, at a more convenient time.

Young children also have the advantage of "skipping classes" in other circumstances, namely, when they are unable to master a particular problem and need to get away from it for a while. The child who may at one point spend a half hour on a peg task at another time may play with five different toys in 5 minutes. In short, young children have the luxury of flexibility. They can move from the extremes of dropping almost everything else in order to work on a problem to that of working on anything *but* the problem that is causing frustration. These luxuries are generally unavailable to students in formal educational settings because such students are subject to external pressures to learn particular types of information at particular times. This experience can be valuable, of course; the ability to acquire information on demand is an important skill in our culture. Nevertheless, schoolchildren who are not prepared or motivated to learn the material at the designated time may frequently fail to receive another opportunity and hence may fall hopelessly behind, particularly when later learning is dependent on the earlier acquisition of knowledge.

Flexible Criteria for Success

Young children are not only afforded the luxury of deciding what tasks to perform and when to do them, they are also frequently permitted to define their own criteria for success. Given a set of blocks, for example, children may hit them together to make sounds, place them in some sort of container, organize them by shape, use them to build, and so forth; these may all be worthwhile and educational activities. Parents may sometimes attempt to get children to achieve particular goals (e.g., stacking the blocks), but we suspect that the child who is not developmentally ready for this activity, or who is momentarily disinterested, will usually be allowed to select his or her own goal (e.g., clapping the blocks together rather than building with them). Similarly, a young child trying to fit a square peg into a round hole may seem doomed to fail, but this is the case only if success is defined in terms of matching the peg and the hole. If success can be thought of as learning what *won't* work or merely as having a good time in the face of an impossible task, the child may indeed be successful. Children in formal educational environments rarely have the luxury of defining their own goals; the criteria for success are imposed by someone else (e.g., teachers and testmakers). Imagine setting a rigid criterion for a 13-month-old child who is playing with blocks; the criterion might be that the child stack at least three of them on top of one another. If the child cannot achieve this goal—and the parents make their displeasure clear—it seems doubtful that the child will continue to love playing with blocks.

Attitudes Toward Achievement

Note that the preceding discussion of children's motivation to explore and learn presupposes that most adults value children's accomplishments and communicate these feelings to the child. Consider a child who is just beginning to walk, for example. All the adults we know express delight at this achievement. It does not matter that millions of other humans have already mastered this skill; we as adults are genuinely delighted for the child. Similarly, a child may learn to hit two blocks together to make a noise or may stack one on top of another, and so forth. It does not matter that the task is "nonacademic" or that the child is far from the first human being to have made such a breakthrough. Most adults genuinely appreciate these achievements and the child must perceive (at some level) that he or she is making some contribution to the adult's life. This perception may contribute to the attachment between parent and child, an attachment that facilitates the teacher-learner relationship (Ainsworth & Bell, 1970; Hoffman & Saltzstein, 1967).

Older, school-aged children may not always receive credit for their accomplishments. Many of their everyday areas of expertise are frequently not valued in school because they seem "nonacademic" (see Donaldson, 1978). It would be interesting to see if older children's motivation for learning would seem much higher if we valued their nonacademic as well as academic activities and helped them integrate the two. Consider a child who knows a lot about baseball, for example. Expertise in baseball involves a large technical vocabulary, knowledge of sophisticated strategies, knowledge of facts that involve descriptive statistics (e.g., why we compute *earned* run averages for pitchers rather than just the average number of runs they allow per game), and so forth. There is a great deal that a young baseball expert could contribute to discussions about the value of technical vocabulary, strategies, reasons for changing various rules, and so forth. However, many children are not allowed to utilize their everyday expertise in academic settings, nor are they helped to appreciate its relationship to those facts and skills that the educational establishment finds valuable (often because many teachers do not realize this potential value). In contrast, almost anything that the young child learns is a source of delight and pride.

In general, young children are likely to be viewed as achievers whenever they improve relative to their own past performance. In school, success is often defined in terms of norms, which means that a large number of the students are of necessity termed "below average." They therefore may receive more feedback about their inadequacies than about their successes. Parents of young children seem determined to help their children realize their strengths; they attempt to *develop* talent. In contrast, the structure of the school system often forces teachers to *select* talent along prespecified dimensions. People who fail to do well in these areas may face several problems. They may be perceived by their instructors as being less likely to learn, and for this reason may receive less than their share of the teacher's interest and attention. What is even worse is that they may perceive themselves as unsuccessful learners, and this may diminish their motivation to learn.

It is interesting in this context to note that some educators have attempted to make educational tasks more motivating for older children by relating them to children's outside interests. For example, some educators (cf., Potter, 1981; Wright, 1979) have designed reading programs that involve reading scripts of familiar television shows or comic books. Results from these studies have been encouraging, but this approach has also been subject to the criticism that students should be taught to read what they "ought" to read and what would be "good" for them to read, regardless of what interests them. In some ways, this comes down to a matter of taste. We do not want to enter into this debate; rather, we are using this example to illustrate how community values often influence the content of educational programs. This is not unintentional; our schools are designed to serve the social function of enculturating our children. The important question that we wish to emphasize, however, is: When the educational goals of the schools clash with cultural goals, which will take precedence?

Summary and Implications for Research

We began this chapter by considering two views about children as learners. The first is that children are "universal novices" who have a number of disadvantages relative to more mature learners. The second is that children are exceptionally enthusiastic and effective learners despite their lack of knowledge, lack of sophisticated strategies, and possible limitations on their working memory. Most researchers have focused on the first characteristic of children as learners; the vast majority of all developmental studies indicate that younger children perform less well than older children. We have emphasized the strengths of young children's learning. By addressing the question of how young children learn so effectively despite their cognitive limitations, it may be possible to develop a deeper understanding of the processes by which meaningful learning occurs.

It is possible, of course, that the effectiveness of children's learning is only an illusion. Perhaps they appear to be effective learners simply because they know so little that any improvement seems dramatic. Alternatively, young children may indeed be effective learners, but only in those areas for which they are biologically "prepared" as a species (e.g., see the discussion of canalization by Fishbein, 1976). From this perspective, our attempts to focus on children's strengths in the hope of discovering principles of learning that apply across age groups and content areas may seem naive.

We have argued that a great deal *can* be learned by focusing on young children's success as learners. Much of our discussion has centered on aspects of the child's world that, in comparison with the structure of formal education, appear to provide cognitive and motivational advantages. It seems highly plausible that many individuals would be much less likely to experience academic difficulties in school—and be less likely to receive labels such as *slow* or *retarded*—if they had instructional advantages similar to those enjoyed during childhood (e.g., see Brown & French, 1979; Feuerstein et al., 1979, 1980). Furthermore, many successful educational innovations (e.g., individualized instruction geared to the preexisting knowledge and skills of the learner; see Glaser, 1977) can be viewed as attempts to recapture some of the instructional advantages of youth.

Our argument is not that all instruction should be identical to that available during childhood (although it is interesting to note that graduate education generally involves a tutorial mode of instruction). Individuals must obviously learn to learn on their own (e.g., Bransford, 1979; Brown, 1979). Nevertheless, people may need tutorial help in order to develop the skills necessary to learn in formal educational contexts. An important question for further research involves the degree to which many children who appear to be "poor learners" once they enter school are not poor learners in general, but only in the context of the formal educational system. Holt (1964) argues that many students seem to "disconnect their intelligence from their schooling"; they do poorly in school yet seem to learn effectively in informal settings. Studies involving the dynamic assessment of learning potential (assessments based on students' abilities to learn from carefully crafted tutorial instruction) suggest strongly that people's inability to learn in school is far from indicative of a general inability to learn (e.g., see Brown & Ferrara, Note 2; Feuerstein et al., 1979; Vye, Note 3).

A related direction for future research involves the possibility of creating learning environments that greatly alter the ease of acquiring particular types of skills and knowledge. For example, most children readily learn their native language, whereas it takes a great deal of time and effort for them to learn mathematics. One might attempt to account for this fact by arguing that human canalizations (cf. Fishbein, 1976) are organized in a way that favors language over mathematics. Note, however, that the domains of language and mathematics differ not only in terms of content, but also in terms of the manner in which they are taught and learned.

Papert (1980) provides a provocative account of differences in learning language and mathematics:

> The belief that only a few people are mathematically minded is a truism in our culture and a cornerstone of our educational system. It is therefore sobering to reflect on the flimsiness of our reasons for believing it. In fact, the only evidence is crass empiricism: Look around you and you will see that most people are very poor at mathematics. But look around and see how poor most Americans are at speaking French. Does anyone draw the conclusion that most Americans are not French-minded?—that they are not capable of learning French? Of course not! We all know that these same people would have learned to speak French perfectly well had they grown up in France. If there is any question of lack of aptitude, the aptitude they lack is not for French as such but for learning French in schools. (in Becker, Note 4, pp. 48–49.)

Papert proceeds to ask whether there might be a "mathland" that is to mathematics as France is to French. He believes it is possible to create learning environments where people can learn to "speak" mathematics as easily and successfully as they learn to speak their native language. In agreement with Papert, we believe that modern computer technology makes it possible to create interactive learning environments that heretofore have been unavailable to the human species. For example, children can learn to teach (program) computers, they can be exposed to simulated worlds (e.g., gravity-free environments) whose properties were heretofore "knowable" only through abstract formalisms, and so forth (e.g., DiSessa, 1982; Papert, 1980). Experiences such as these could have important effects on cognitive development. For example, children who are allowed to play with computer programming in a manner analogous to playing with blocks may develop competencies that previously seemed inaccessible to many individuals (e.g., see Papert, 1980). More detailed analyses of the advantages of young children's learning environments should play an important role in guiding the design of interactive computer environments that could have important developmental effects.

In addition to our discussion of the advantages of children's learning *environments*, we have also argued that young children have some definite strengths as *learners*, and that these should be taken seriously and studied more thoroughly. Many types of research designs fail to assess young children's strengths. For example, several authors have asked children of different ages to learn new games and have reported that the older children developed more sophisticated strategies than did younger children (e.g., DiSessa, 1982; Rayner, 1958). Similarly, Becker (Note 4) notes that older children are able to produce more sophisticated computer programs than are younger children. Results such as these are not surprising; they support the familiar "developmental trend." Nevertheless, they fail to address issues such as the reactions of students to their experiences (especially their failures), the degree to which students who have experienced only partial success would return to the situation to try again, the degree to which participants learned something valuable even if it was not the intended goal of the instructor, and so on. Criteria such as these are not easy to measure, but we believe that they are extremely important. These criteria may alert us to the fact that some of our potential as human beings is frequently *lost* with development; they may alert us to "reverse developmental trends."

Imagine, for example, that researchers focused on dimensions such as "positive attitudes toward a new learning task" (e.g., learning to program computers) or "perseverance in the face of ego-threatening difficulty." We suspect that research on factors such as these would reveal a number of "reverse" developmental trends. One place to look for such trends might be the literature on computers and education. In a recent review article, for example, Becker (Note 4) estimates that the ratio of males to females who show an interest in learning to program computers would be about 1:1 in the first grade but 4:1 by the ninth grade. Presumably the first-grade girls have not yet learned that computer programming is not for them. Becker also cites an informal pilot study which suggests that older students (ninth graders) were more resistive to learning computer programming (treating it as just another course) than were seventh and fifth graders. On an "enthusiasm for learning about a new area" dimension, these data suggest a reverse developmental trend.

There are a number of reasons why research on reverse developmental trends could be valuable. One is that adults might become more adventuresome learners if they were helped to understand how—in their youth—they were able to learn effectively despite the large number of cognitive disadvantages that they possessed. As noted earlier, for example, we know a large number of college students and adults who are quite fearful of computers and hence avoid learning about them. The availability of sophisticated learning strategies does no good given avoidance behaviors such as these.

An emphasis on reverse developmental trends should also raise questions about how to prevent changes that are negative. For example, does early exposure to an area (e.g., computers, school) decrease the probability that people will avoid it later on? Gray, Ramsey, and Klaus's (1981) analyses of the effects of preschool education suggest that the development of positive attitudes toward school may be one of the most important effects of early education. Intuitively, early positive experiences with new inventions such as computers should have similar effects. Evidence for any unique benefits of early experience may be less likely to be found if researchers focus *only* on cognitive or intellectual variables (e.g., see Clarke & Clarke, 1977). Children's attitudes toward learning may be their greatest strength; hence, it is in the general affective-motivational domain that early exposure may have its most significant and pervasive effects. Children's attitudes toward learning may also serve as important models for adults.

Reference Notes

1. Hayes, D. A., & Tierney, R. J. *Increasing background knowledge through analogy: Its effects upon comprehension and learning.* (Tech. Rep.). Urbana: University of Illinois, Center for the Study of Reading, 1980.
2. Brown, A. L., & Ferrara, R. A. Diagnosing zones of proximal development: An alternative to standardized testing? Paper presented at Conference on Culture, Communication and Cognition: Vygotskian Perspectives, Center for Psychological Studies, Chicago, 1980.
3. Vye, N. J. Procedures for the dynamic assessment of learning potential: A review. Paper submitted for publication, Vanderbilt University, 1982.
4. Becker, N. J. *Microcomputers in the classroom—dreams and realities.* (Tech. Rep. 319). Baltimore: Johns Hopkins Center for Social Organization of the Schools, 1982.

References

Adams, J. L. *Conceptual blockbusting.* New York: Norton, 1979.

Ainsworth, M. D. S., & Bell, S. M. Attention, exploration, and separation: Illustrated by the behavior of one-year-olds in strange situations. *Child Development,* 1970, *41,* 49-67.

Anderson, R., Osborn, J., & Tierney, R. (Eds.). *Learning to read in American schools.* Hillsdale, NJ: Erlbaum, in press.

Asher, S. R. Topic interest and children's reading comprehension. In R. Spiro, B. Bruce, & W. Brewer (Eds.), *Theoretical issues in reading comprehension.* Hillsdale, NJ; Erlbaum, 1980.

Ausubel, D. P. The facilitation of meaningful verbal learning in the classroom. *Educational Psychologist,* 1977, *12,* 162-178.

Beck, I. L. Developing comprehension: The impact of the directed reading lesson.

In R. Anderson, J. Osborn, & R. Tierney (Eds.), *Learning to read in American schools*. Hillsdale, NJ: Erlbaum, in press.

Bloom, L., Hood, L., & Lightbown, P. Imitation in language development: If, when, and why. *Cognitive Psychology*, 1974, *6*, 380–420.

Bloom, L., Lightbown, P., & Hood, L. Structure and variation in child language. *Monographs of the Society for Research in Child Development*, 1975, *40*(2, Serial No. 160).

Bransford, J. D. *Human cognition: Learning, understanding, and remembering*. Belmont, CA: Wadsworth, 1979.

Bransford, J. D. Schema activation versus schema acquisition. In R. C. Anderson, J. Osborn, & R. Tierney (Eds.), *Learning to read in American schools*. Hillsdale, NJ: Erlbaum, in press.

Bransford, J. D., & Johnson, M. K. Contextual prerequisites for understanding: Some investigations of comprehension and recall. *Journal of Verbal Learning and Verbal Behavior*, 1972, *111*, 717–726.

Bransford, J. D., & Johnson, M. K. Considerations of some problems of comprehension. In W. G. Chase (Ed.), *Visual information processing*. New York: Academic Press, 1973.

Brazelton, T. B. *Infants and mothers: Differences in development*. New York: Dell, 1969.

Brown, A. L. Theories of memory and the problems of development: Activity, growth and knowledge. In L. S. Cermak & F. I. M. Craik (Eds.), *Levels of processing and human memory*. Hillsdale, NJ: Erlbaum, 1979.

Brown, A. L., Bransford, J. D., Ferrara, R., & Campione, J. C. Learning, understanding and remembering. In J. Flavell & E. Markman (Eds.), *Mussen handbook of child psychology* (2nd ed., Vol. 1). New York: Wiley, in press.

Brown, A. L., & French, L. A. The zone of potential development: Implications for intelligence testing in the year 2000. *Intelligence*, 1979, *3*, 255–273.

Brown, R. W. *A first language: The early stages*. Cambridge, MA: Harvard University Press, 1973.

Bruner, J. S. *Processes of cognitive growth: Infancy*. Worcester, MA: Clark University Press, 1968.

Caplan, F. *The first twelve months of life*. New York: Grossett & Dunlap, 1973.

Case, R. Structures and strictures: Some functional limitations on the course of cognitive growth. *Cognitive Psychology*, 1974, *6*, 544–573.

Chapman, R. S. Comprehension strategies in children. In J. Kavanagh & W. Strange (Eds.), *Speech and language in the laboratory, school, and clinic*. Cambridge, MA: MIT Press, 1978.

Chase, W. G., & Simon, H. A. The mind's eye in chess. In W. G. Chase (Ed.), *Visual information processing*. New York: Academic Press, 1973.

Chi, M. T. H. Short-term memory limitations in children: Capacity or processing deficits? *Memory & Cognition*, 1976, *4*, 559–572.

Chi, M. T. H. Knowledge structures and memory development. In R. S. Siegler (Ed.), *Children's thinking: What develops?* Hillsdale, NJ: Erlbaum, 1978.

Chiesi, H. L., Spilich, G. J., & Voss, J. F. Acquisition of domain-related information in relation to high and low domain knowledge. *Journal of Verbal Learning and Verbal Behavior*, 1979, *18*, 257–273.

Chomsky, C. *The acquisition of syntax in children from 5 to 10*. Cambridge, MA: MIT Press, 1969.

Clarke, A. M., & Clarke, A. D. B. *Early experience: Myth and evidence.* New York: Free Press, 1977.

DiSessa, A. A. Unlearning Aristotelian physics: A study of knowledge-based learning. *Cognitive Science,* 1982, *6,* 37–75.

Donaldson, M. E. *Children's minds.* New York: Norton, 1978.

Feuerstein, R., Rand, Y., & Hoffman, M. B. *The dynamic assessment of retarded performers.* Baltimore: University Park Press, 1979.

Feuerstein, R., Rand, Y., Hoffman, M. B., & Miller, R. *Instrumental enrichment.* Baltimore: University Park Press, 1980.

Fishbein, H. D. *Evolution, development and children's learning.* Pacific Palisades, CA: Goodyear Publishing Co., 1976.

Flavell, J. H., Beach, D. R., & Chinsky, J. M. Spontaneous verbal rehearsal in a memory task as a function of age. *Child Development,* 1966, *37,* 283–299.

Flavell, J. H., & Wellman, H. M. Metamemory. In R. V. Kail & J. W. Hagen (Eds.), *Perspectives on the development of memory and cognition.* Hillsdale, NJ: Erlbaum, 1977.

Freedle, R. Interaction of language with ethnography and cognition. In J. H. Harvey (Ed.), *Cognition, social behavior, and the environment.* Hillsdale, NJ: Erlbaum, 1981.

Gelman, R. Counting in the preschooler: What does and does not develop. In R. S. Siegler (Ed.), *Children's thinking: What develops?* Hillsdale, NJ: Erlbaum, 1978.

Glaser, R. *Adaptive education: Individual diversity and learning.* New York: Holt, Rinehart & Winston, 1977.

Gleason, J. B. Talking to children: Some notes on feedback. In C. E. Snow & C. A. Ferguson (Eds.), *Talking to children.* New York: Cambridge University Press, 1977.

Glucksberg, S., Krauss, R., & Higgins, E. T. The development of referential communication skills. In F. D. Horowitz (Ed.), *Review of child development research* (Vol. 4). Chicago: University of Chicago Press, 1975.

Gray, S. W., Ramsey, B. K., & Klaus, R. A. *From 3 to 20: The early training project.* Baltimore, MD: University Park Press, 1981.

Hoffman, M. L., & Saltzstein, H. D. Parent discipline and the child's moral development. *Journal of Personality and Social Psychology,* 1967, *5,* 45–57.

Holt, J. *How children fail.* New York: Dell, 1964.

Holt, J. *How children learn.* New York: Pitman, 1967.

Illich, I. *Deschooling society.* New York: Harper & Row, 1972.

Inhelder, B., & Piaget, J. *The growth of logical thinking from childhood to adolescence.* New York: Basic Books, 1958.

Kail, R. V., & Siegel, A. W. The development of mnemonic encoding in children: From perception to abstraction. In R. V. Kail & J. W. Hagen (Eds.), *Perspectives on the development of memory and cognition.* Hillsdale, NJ: Erlbaum, 1977.

LaBerge, D., & Samuels, S. J. Toward a theory of automatic information processing in reading. *Cognitive Psychology,* 1974, *6,* 293–323.

Lipman, M. Thinking skills fostered by the middle-school philosophy for children's programs. In J. Segal, S. Chipman, & R. Glaser (Eds.), *Thinking and learning skills: Relating instruction to basic research* (Vol. 1). Hillsdale, NJ: Erlbaum, in press.

Lorenz, K. The enmity between generations and its probable ethological causes. In M. W. Piers (Ed.), *Play and development.* New York: Norton, 1972.

McDermott, R. P. Achieving school failure: An anthropological approach to illiteracy and social stratification. In G. Spindler (Ed.), *Education and cultural processes: Toward an anthropology of education.* New York: Holt, Rinehart & Winston, 1974.

Minsky, M. A framework for representing knowledge. In P. H. Winston (Ed.), *The psychology of computer vision.* New York: McGraw-Hill, 1975.

Nitsch, K. E. *Structuring decontextualized forms of knowledge.* Unpublished doctoral dissertation, Vanderbilt University, 1977.

Novak, J. N. *A theory of education.* New York: Cornell University Press, 1977.

Ornstein, P. A., & Naus, M. J. Rehearsal processes in children's memory. In P. A. Ornstein (Ed.), *Memory development in children.* Hillsdale, NJ: Erlbaum, 1978.

Papert, S. *Mindstorms: Children, computers, and powerful ideas.* New York: Basic Books, 1980.

Pearson, D. P. Guided reading. In R. C. Anderson, J. Osborn, & R. Tierney (Eds.), *Learning to read in American schools.* Hillsdale, NJ: Erlbaum, in press.

Piaget, J. *The origins of intelligence in children.* New York: International University Press, 1952.

Piaget, J. *Intelligence and affectivity: Their relationship during child development.* Palo Alto, CA: Annual Reviews, 1981.

Postman, L., Adams, P. A., & Bohm, A. M. Studies in incidental learning: V. Recall for order and associative clustering. *Journal of Experimental Psychology,* 1956, *51,* 334–342.

Potter, R. L. The link between reading instruction and commercial TV: Is this a bandwagon? *Journal of Reading,* 1981, *24,* 377–382.

Rayner, E. H. A study of evaluative problem solving: Developmental observations. *Quarterly Journal of Experimental Psychology,* 1958, *10,* 193–205.

Rubin, J. What the "good language learner" can teach us. *TESOL Quarterly,* 1975, *9*(1), 41–51.

Rumelhart, D. E., & Ortony, A. The representation of knowledge in memory. In R. C. Anderson, R. J. Spiro, & W. E. Montague (Eds.), *Schooling and the acquisition of knowledge.* Hillsdale, NJ: Erlbaum, 1977.

Sachs, J. The adaptive significance of linguistic input to prelinguistic infants. In C. E. Snow & C. A. Ferguson (Eds.), *Talking to children.* New York: Cambridge University Press, 1977.

Schank, R. C., & Abelson, R. P. *Scripts, plans, goals, and understanding: An inquiry into human knowledge structures.* Hillsdale, NJ: Erlbaum, 1977.

Sieber, J. E., O'Neil, H. F., & Tobias, S. *Anxiety, learning, and instruction.* Hillsdale, NJ: Erlbaum, 1977.

Siegler, R. S. The origins of scientific reasoning. In R. S. Siegler (Ed.), *Children's thinking: What develops?* Hillsdale, NJ: Erlbaum, 1978.

Slobin, D. I., & Welsh, C. Elicited imitation as a research tool in developmental psycholinguistics. In C. A. Ferguson & D. I. Slobin (Eds.), *Studies of child language development.* New York: Holt, Rinehart & Winston, 1973.

Snow, C. E. The development of conversation between mothers and babies. *Journal of Child Language,* 1977, *4,* 1–22.

Tobias, S. *Overcoming math anxiety.* New York: Norton, 1978.

Vaughan, E. D. Misconceptions about psychology among introductory psychology students. *Teaching of Psychology,* 1977, *4,* 138–141.

Vygotsky, L. S. *Mind in society.* Cambridge, MA: Harvard University Press, 1978.

Wells, G. Apprenticeship in meaning. In K. Nelson (Ed.), *Children's language* (Vol. 2). New York: Gardner Press, 1980.

White, B. L. Critical influences in the origins of competence. *Merrill-Palmer Quarterly*, 1975, *21*, 243–266.

Wood, D. Teaching the young child: Some relationships between social interaction, language, and thought. In D. Olson (Ed.), *The social foundations of language and thought*. New York: Norton, 1980.

Wood, D., & Middleton, D. A study of assisted problem solving. *British Journal of Psychology*, 1975, *2*, 181–191.

Wright, G. The comic book—a forgotten medium in the classroom. *Reading Teacher*, 1979, *33*, 158–161.

Author Index

Subject Index